THE QUEST FOR NATIONAL EFFICIENCY

THE QUEST FOR NATIONAL EFFICIENCY

A Study in British Politics and
Political Thought, 1899-1914

G. R. SEARLE

UNIVERSITY OF CALIFORNIA PRESS

Berkeley and Los Angeles 1971

University of California Press
Berkeley and Los Angeles, California

ISBN 0-520-01794-3

Library of Congress Catalog Card Number: 75-126758

Printed in Great Britain

CONTENTS

TO MY PARENTS

ACKNOWLEDGEMENTS

I began my work on National Efficiency while a research student at Cambridge, where I was fortunate enough to have as my supervisor Dr Kitson Clark; my debt to him is a deep one. Since taking up my present appointment at the University of East Anglia, I have also enjoyed the assistance and encouragement of many colleagues and students, which I gratefully acknowledge. I must particularly thank Christopher Wrigley and Joan Marr for the work they have done on my behalf. Finally, I am grateful to the University of East Anglia for granting me a study leave term in which to complete this book.

I have received much helpful assistance from the staff of the many libraries in which I have worked, including the British Museum Reading Room, Department of Manuscripts, and Newspaper Library; Cambridge University Library; the Bodleian Library; Birmingham University Library; the British Library of Political and Economic Science; the India Office Library; the National Library of Scotland; the Beaverbrook Library; the Library of New College, Oxford. I must thank all these libraries for giving me access to manuscript collections; I have given the exact location of particular collections of papers in my Bibliography. I am also obliged to Lieutenant-Colonel Gell, who kindly gave me access to the papers of Philip Lyttelton Gell; also to Miss May Wallas for permission to use material in the Graham Wallas Papers.

I must thank Dr Roy Macleod for giving me his permission to make a short extract from his Cambridge doctoral dissertation. Finally, I must make the following acknowledgements to owners of copyright for permission to quote from hitherto unpublished letters and documents: Birmingham University Library (Austen and Joseph Chamberlain); Beaverbrook Newspapers (Lloyd George);

the Passfield Trustees (Sidney and Beatrice Webb); the National Library of Scotland (Haldane's letters deposited in that Library); Dr A. R. Haldane (other letters of Lord Haldane); the Warden and Fellows of New College (Lord Milner); Mr Mark Bonham Carter (Asquith); the Society of Authors for the Bernard Shaw Estate; the Estate of H. G. Wells.

I have made every effort to clear all copyright material. In the event of any inadvertent infringement I express my regret and would welcome information which would remedy such oversight in any future edition.

CHAPTER I

THE REACTION AGAINST
GLADSTONIANISM

MOST MODERN PERIODS in British history have been dominated
by a political catchcry: some phrase or slogan which sums up the
hopes and fears of the hour, though in a maddeningly imprecise
way. Thus, in the early 1960s politicians of all parties, newspaper
columnists and other public figures were vying with one another
to proclaim their commitment to 'Modernization'. More recently,
the virtues of 'Participation' have been dinned into our ears. At
the start of the twentieth century the equivalent expression was
'National Efficiency' or, simply, 'Efficiency'. 'At the present time,
and perhaps it is the most notable social fact of this age,' wrote the
Spectator in 1902, 'there is a universal outcry for efficiency in all the
departments of society, in all the aspects of life. We hear the outcry on all hands and from the most unexpected of persons. From
the pulpit, the newspaper, the hustings, in the drawing-room, the
smoking-room, the street, the same cry is heard: Give us Efficiency,
or we die.' This journalist went on to remark that there was 'a
great deal of cant' in this glorification of Efficiency: a goal of which
everyone approved, but no-one knew how to attain.[1] H. W.
Massingham of the *Speaker* was still more sceptical on this score;
besides, as he sardonically observed, one could hardly expect
champions to enter the lists under the banner of 'Inefficiency'.[2]

But, as Massingham himself well knew, the phrase 'Efficiency'
had a quite definite meaning and significance in the political debate
of the day. Public opinion had been dismayed by the revelation

[1] The *Spectator*, 16.8.02.   [2] The *Speaker*, 21.12.01 p. 324.

of Britain's military incompetence during the Boer War, and
many people were naturally anxious to re-structure the 'national
life' and overhaul the machinery of government, to fit Britain more
adequately for the Great Power rivalries of the twentieth century.
'National Efficiency' was their diagnosis of what had gone wrong
with Britain, but also a skeletal plan of campaign, a rough
description of the direction reform would have to take, if the country were to escape future disaster. The present book has as its
theme the story of this political slogan: its origins, its meanings and
implications, and its impact on the course of Edwardian politics.

But why, it might be asked, has such a central theme not previously been the subject of a full-length study? The answer possibly lies in the kind of restriction which political historians have
imposed upon themselves when dealing with the early twentieth
century. Much of the writing on this period is concerned with
party, and the familiar account of Edwardian politics is one that
has been shaped by the conflict and rivalries of Liberals and
Unionists.[1] The story of 'National Efficiency', however, does not
really suit this method of approach, since, from the party point of
view, it is a complication, if not an irrelevance. For the quest for
'National Efficiency' cut completely across the conventional dis-
tinctions between 'left' and 'right', 'liberals' and 'conservatives',
and even 'socialists' and 'capitalists'. Lord Rosebery, R. B. Haldane, Alfred Milner, L. S. Amery, Robert Morant, Professor
Hewins, Sidney and Beatrice Webb, H. G. Wells:[2] the names of
these famous people, all of whom played a leading part in articu-
lating or attempting to implement a programme of 'Efficiency',
bear witness to the catholic appeal of a political ideal which was
strong enough on occasions to transcend the barriers offered by
party organization and tradition.

If the history of party politics, narrowly conceived, fails to
provide an appropriate framework for an examination of 'National
Efficiency', neither can this theme be accomodated within studies

[1] The word 'Unionists' is used in its contemporary sense to denote both
Conservatives and Liberal Unionists, the latter being one-time Liberals, who
had left the official Liberal Party over Gladstone's commitment to Irish Home
Rule in 1886.
[2] For a brief sketch of the careers of these men and others who figure prominently in this book, see Glossary of Names.

of particular institutions or of particular areas of policy. For here was an attempt to find a set of governing principles that could control 'national policy' in *all* its aspects. Thus the breaking-down of historical writing into well-worn categories like 'Imperialism,' 'Social Reform', 'National Defence' and 'Education' simply fragments a subject that has a unity and significance of its own for those who set out to describe it.[1]

This analysis of the 'National Efficiency Movement' is not, however, an attempt to rearrange the events of the past into a pattern dictated by the preoccupations of the present—except in the sophisticated sense that all historical reconstruction partakes of this character. People *at the time* thought and argued in these terms; Efficiency, so A. G. Gardiner claimed, was 'the hardest worked vocable in politics'.[2] More to the point, those who persistently brought up the phrase had a fairly well developed sense of their *corporate identity*. This is all the more remarkable in view of the varied political backgrounds possessed by the men and women who together formed the 'efficiency group' (to coin a convenient phrase). Included in the group were Liberals, mainly from the Imperialist wing of the party, of whom the most heavily committed was Haldane, the politician thought by one observer to have *invented* the word Efficiency, so often was it on his lips.[3] But there were also Conservatives and Liberal Unionists, invariably youngish men, impatient with the passive mood of the Party's leadership. Between these party political opponents there was, nevertheless, an undeniable ideological affinity, and this self-same affinity enabled them all to co-operate easily with bureaucratic socialists of the Fabian school, notably the Webbs. Journalists, civil servants and academics, with no fixed party allegiance, also became caught up in the activities of this informal group of like-minded men.

In this way the strangest alignments and associations came into being. Lord Esher, the éminence grise of the Edwardian Court, wrote to a popular journal, hailing H. G. Wells as a modern

---

[1] The best and the fullest account of the 'National Efficiency Movement' so far published is probably in Professor Bernard Semmel's stimulating book: *Imperialism and Social Reform* (1960).

[2] A. G. Gardiner: *Prophets, Priests and Kings* (1908), p. 211.

[3] ibid.

Luther, whose influence on the practical thought of the English people had been equalled in modern times only by Seeley and the naval historian, Admiral Mahan. There is a certain symbolic appropriateness in the fact that the periodical which printed Esher's article was called *The World's Work: An Illustrated Magazine of National Efficiency and Social Progress*.[1]

Of course, the 'efficiency group' did not see eye to eye on all issues. But there were strong ties of sympathy and common concern, even a sense of camaraderie, to counter-balance the disagreements and the occasional political friction. In 1895 the Webbs chose Professor Hewins, the economic historian, as the first Director of the London School of Economics. In 1903 Hewins abandoned this post to become Secretary of Joseph Chamberlain's Tariff Commission. He ended up as a Conservative M.P. But although Hewins would seem to have drifted right out of the Webbs' orbit, he still felt that they were his fellow workers in a common endeavour. In a letter to Beatrice Webb, of August 1906, Hewins struck a note of affectionate nostalgia, before concluding:

If we are no longer directly associated, it is I believe because the field of operations is wide and many movements are necessary against the enemy we both oppose. When the end comes we shall find that we have both been trying to make a new England possible, with the same faith in the future, and I don't believe posterity, if it knows or cares about the individuals who have done the work, will find our methods or our policy dissimilar.[2]

Hewins was referring to what can be called 'the quest for National Efficiency'.

The context within which people like Hewins and the Webbs were thinking and acting is unintelligible, however, without some understanding of those Victorian values, principles and institutions against which they were in revolt. We must therefore start with a brief glance at three distinct, though related, issues: Britain's decline as a Great Power in the last quarter of the nineteenth century; the loss of confidence in Liberalism and British

[1] *The World's Work*, June 1909, Vol. 14, pp. 19–23: Lord Esher: 'The New Imperial Life'.
[2] *Passfield Papers*, II 4 c: Hewins to B. Webb, 28.9.06: f. 191.

constitutional practice which this entailed; and the first, faltering steps to define an alternative theory and practice of government which would promote greater 'National Efficiency'.

Writing in 1905, the journalist, J. L. Garvin asked his readers: 'Will the Empire which is celebrating one centenary of Trafalgar survive for the next?'—to which he gave his own reply: 'national instinct recognizes that the answer is no foregone affirmative. In the opinion of nearly all foreign observers, and of some sincere thinkers of our own, the British political system represents an extent and magnificence of dominion beyond the natural, and unlikely to be permanent'.[1] As pessimism about Britain's political and commercial future settled upon many intelligent students of the international scene at the end of the nineteenth and the start of the twentieth centuries, longing eyes were cast back on to the happier mid-Victorian period, when British naval and industrial supremacy was still unchallenged, and a self-satisfied pride in the institutions of the country could be professed without absurdity.

In the year of the Great Exhibition these sentiments had been much in evidence. The *Manchester Guardian* articulated the mood of the hour in its Christmas editorial of 1851: 'It would be unseasonably invidious to institute a minute comparison between our own and our neighbour's pudding; but we cannot refrain from saying that there are few Christmas parties in Europe to which we can turn a momentary glance, without greatly heightening the satisfaction with which we turn again towards home.'[2] This complacency was soon to be shattered by the revelation of the appalling military and administrative blunders of the Crimean campaign, and in the winter of 1854–5, under the shock of these revelations, there took place an introspective and self-critical debate about the proper ordering of the national life that anticipates certain features of the later Boer War outcry about the need for greater 'National Efficiency'.[3]

---

[1] J. L. Garvin: 'The Maintenance of Empire' in C. S. Goldman (ed.): *The Empire and the Century* (1905), p. 69.

[2] Cited in Asa Briggs: *Victorian People* (1954, Pelican ed., 1965), p. 58.

[3] See Olive Anderson: *A Liberal State at War* (1967), *passim*.

Yet the smugness of tone which imbued the *Manchester Guardian*'s editorial of December 1851 was likely to predominate until a change in the balance of power had deprived Britain of the somewhat artificial pre-eminence which she had enjoyed since the collapse of Napoleonic France. Therefore, it is not surprising to detect a new mood of doubt appearing during the 1865–75 period, when Bismarck's unification of Germany finally and irrevocably destroyed the assumptions about Britain's natural leadership in Europe that had shaped Palmerston's foreign policy. Already in the Schleswig-Holstein affair, Bismarck had exposed the gap between British power and British pretensions. In the following decade, as first one, then another of the European States adopted military conscription, British Foreign Secretaries found their options narrowing and their influence in the Concert of Europe greatly diminished, though it proved difficult to educate public opinion at home in the realities of the new situation. One of these realities was that Britain depended on a small volunteer Army which never at any time before 1914, except in the middle of the Boer War, exceeded 300,000 men, of which about a quarter were tied down in the defence of India; and this meant that, unaided, she lacked the capacity to take on even a second-rate European Power. In 1887 Charles Dilke believed that the British 'could place in the field in Europe a force about equal to that of Servia or Belgium, that is, a force far inferior in numbers to the Roumanian army, and while certainly superior to the Servians in efficiency, not certainly superior to the Roumanians . . .'[1]

Sea-power, Britain's traditional support, by no means fully compensated for this military weakness, since, as Salisbury for one was acutely aware, the Navy could not be used to bring pressure on areas remote from the sea; it was impossible, as he noted in 1897, for the British Fleet to sail up the Seine.[2] The main role of the British Navy was to provide global protection for the overseas trade which was the life-blood of the British economy. This became absolutely crucial in the last quarter of the nineteenth century, when the influx of cheap grain from the New World began to face

[1] Charles Dilke: *The Present Position of European Politics* (1887), p. 306.
[2] C. J. Lowe, *The Reluctant Imperialists: Vol. I: British Foreign Policy, 1878–1902* (1967), p. 7.

the British farmer with ruinous competition. By 1900 the country was importing approximately four-fifths of its total grain consumption.[1] Had the British command of the seas ever been lost in time of war, an enemy power could have sat back and starved her people and government into submission, without going to the bother of landing a single soldier on British soil. By comparison with this danger, the prospect of foreign troops trampling over the English countryside, killing and looting, was remote. Nevertheless, a succession of invasion scare stories, beginning with George Chesney's *Battle of Dorking* (1871), kept such fears very much alive throughout the late Victorian and Edwardian periods, however unfounded these fears might have been.[2] Spasmodic panics about national security, whipped up by certain popular newspapers, made politicians of both parties even more determined than they would otherwise have been to place British naval supremacy beyond any reasonable possibility of doubt. When Gladstone tried to stand out against this resolve in 1893, his ministerial colleagues drove him into retirement.

The yardstick of national security, first spelt out in the Naval Defence Act of 1889, was the so-called 'two power standard': that is to say, the British Fleet was at all times to match the next two most powerful navies in the world in both numbers and efficiency. However, the difficulties in maintaining this margin of superiority proved to be formidable, and they did not diminish with time. Between 1865 and 1885 expenditure on the Navy had remained virtually static; in 1870 Gladstone had brought down the Estimates to the low point of £9½ million.[3] But from the mid-1880s onwards, the annual expenditure on naval construction moved sharply upwards again. In part, this was due to the rapid technological developments, which had been initiated by the French Government's launching of the first 'iron clad' warship, *La Gloire*, in 1858. There followed over the next 50 years dramatic changes in marine design and construction which were a cause, not only of

---

[1] A. J. Marder, *The Anatomy of British Sea Power* (Connecticut, 1940), p. 85.
[2] On this literary genre, see I. F. Clarke, 'The Battle of Dorking, 1871–1914' (*Victorian Studies*, June 1965, Vol. 8, pp. 309–27).
[3] D. M. Schurman, *The Education of a Navy: The Development of British Naval Strategic Thought, 1867–1914* (1965), p. 2. A. J. Marder, op. cit., p. 119.

B

great expense but also of tension and insecurity, since an efficient capital ship now had a limited life, before becoming obsolescent.[1]

Even more important was Britain's occupation of Egypt in 1882 which led to a rapprochement between France and Russia, culminating in the Dual Alliance of 1894; in this way Britain's two most formidable naval rivals were brought together, an outcome which alarmingly increased the vulnerability of her scattered Empire. In the 1890s certain well-informed people were arguing that, as the Mediterranean Fleet could not fend off a combined Franco-Russian assault, the British should withdraw from these waters altogether.[2] Yet 16 per cent of British imports and 21 per cent of British exports passed through the Suez Canal and another 10 per cent and 8.5 per cent respectively was carried on with Mediterranean Europe,[3] and so any such withdrawal would have been fraught with most serious consequences. In the event, nothing of the sort occurred. And throughout the 1890s the 'two power standard' was narrowly maintained, on paper. But the cost of this achievement was a heavy one, and successive governments found that the strain on the nation's existing fiscal resources was becoming acute: a consideration which did more than anything else to make the prospect of a full alliance with one of the Great Powers of Europe an attractive proposition in the final years of the nineteenth century.[4]

The relative decline of the British Navy was one of many indications that Britain had lost her old monopolistic position as an industrial state; for by the end of the nineteenth century naval warfare had become highly mechanized, and the efficiency and strength of a fleet reflected, up to a point, a nation's industrial efficiency in a wider sense. Britain's earlier advantage had been that her industrial capacity and technological skills were so much greater than those of other European states that she could afford to wait upon new developments in marine design sponsored by foreign admiralties, confident of being able to catch up, before rival Powers had stolen a decisive lead. This advantage was probably retained until the 'Germania' shipyards at Kiel and Krupps' armaments works

[1] ibid., Ch. I.   [2] ibid., pp. 210–11.   [3] ibid., p. 144.
[4] See G. W. Monger, *The End of Isolation: British Foreign Policy, 1900–1907* (1963), pp. 8–14.

at Essen were extended in 1908–09, to allow for an acceleration in German naval construction—or so the British Admiralty feared.[1] Yet although Britain's capacity to outbuild her rivals may have survived intact until as late as 1909 or so, it had been threatened at a much earlier date. In this way the rapid industrialization of Germany and other Continental countries contributed towards that marked shift in the European Balance of Power, which operated so decisively to Britain's disadvantage from about 1870 onwards.

In manpower resources, too, Britain suffered a relative decline during this period. In each decade between 1870 and 1914 the British population increased more slowly than that of almost any other European state. When Germany was first unified, its population already numbered 41 million, about 10 million more than the United Kingdom's. By 1914 this gap had approximately doubled. This was because whereas in western and central Europe the growth in the birth-rate had experienced a check after 1875 or so, in Britain the process was more marked than in any other major nation—except France.[2] All this while, the United States of America was developing into a country of a quite different scale; by 1914 the American population was approaching 100 million and still expanding dramatically.

The significance of these factors was realized from as early as 1870. The success with which the northern states had preserved the American Union and the absorption of the various German states into a Federal Empire seemed to show that the future lay with large units of power, capable of mobilising correspondingly large manpower resources. The insuperable barriers which had once prevented territory of scattered geographical extent from owning common allegiance to a central government had been removed by improved methods of communication.

Moreover, given the belief that size and numbers were important determinants of national power, it followed that those countries which failed to exploit the new technological possibilities would soon find themselves reduced to insignificance. Britain

---

[1] E. L. Woodward, *Great Britain and the German Navy* (1935), pp. 160–4, 206.
[2] See National Birth-Rate Commission, *The Declining Birth-Rate: Its Causes and Effects* (1916), esp. pp. 28–9.

herself might go the way of Holland. This warning was most persuasively delivered by J. R. Seeley, who argued in his *Expansion of England* (1883) that the British must create a federal Empire, if they were not to be eclipsed in the future by the new 'giant states', such as America and Russia.[1]

Despite the fame of Seeley's book, the substance of this argument had actually been elaborated by J. A. Froude over ten years previously:

When we consider the increasing populousness of other nations, their imperial energy, and their vast political development, when we contrast the enormous area of territory which belongs to Russia, to the United States, or to Germany, with the puny dimensions of our own island home, prejudice itself cannot hide from us that our place as a nation is gone among such rivals unless we can identify the Colonies with ourselves, and multiply the English soil by spreading the English race over them.[2]

Froude's organized Empire, like Seeley's, was to be primarily a racial union of the 'English folk' scattered throughout the globe. When he referred to the colonies, he meant the lands that had been colonized by settlers of English stock. It was only in the 1880s and later that India and the dependencies inhabited by 'native peoples' were given an important place in the imperialist's scheme of things. However, all the English 'imperialists from Froude onwards, were preoccupied with Britain's relative decline as a Great Power, and believed that the only way she could keep in the front rank was to construct an intelligently co-ordinated imperial unit, capable of taking on any foreign power bloc that might try to attack her.

British imperialism was thus, in many respects, a defensive response to contemporary events: a novel method of underpinning traditional and well-established national interests in a changing international world where they were increasingly threatened. In the words of Robinson and Gallagher, 'whereas the early Victorians could afford to concentrate on the extension of free trade,

---

[1] J. R. Seeley, *The Expansion of England* (1883), pp. 18–19, 344–6.
[2] J. A. Froude, 'England's War' (1871), printed in his *Short Studies on Great Subjects*, Vol. II (1894 ed.), p. 500.

their successors were compelled to look above all to the preservation of what they held, since they were coming to suspect that
Britain's power was not what it had once been'.[1] The change from
informal to formal Empire and the rapid expansion of British rule
in Africa and Asia proceeded quite as much from a recognition
of waning power, as it did from a superfluity of aggressive
energy.

The insecurity and defensiveness of mind underlying so much of
the rhetoric about Britain's 'imperial mission' manifested itself
even more obviously in the public debate about the state of the
economy, which accompanied the Great Depression of 1873–96.
'In all our industries you find a steady slowing-down,' wrote Eric
Williams in 1896; 'it is Germany who is in for the "marvellous
progress" now. England made hers when and because she had
command of the world's markets': a position from which, as
Williams demonstrated, Britain had slipped back.[2] The black
pessimism with which so many people viewed the mounting
economic competition from Germans, Americans and others was
all the more intense during the years of the Great Depression,
since, at a time when world trade was increasing very slowly, it
was tempting to suppose that the industrial progress of one country
could only take place at the expense of another. If this were so,
then British business men stood to lose more than their foreign
rivals did. The popularity of Darwinian modes of argument
strengthened the prevailing view of the Great Powers as competitive trading units engaged in a desperate struggle for economic,
and thus for national, survival.

As early as 1870 plaintive cries were being heard in the Press
that Britain's industrial supremacy was a thing of the past and that
the 'singularity of her position' had gone.[3] There had certainly
been a falling-back since the middle of the nineteenth century,
when, according to Professor Hobsbawm's estimate, Britain had
'produced perhaps two thirds of the world's coal, perhaps half its
iron, five sevenths of its small supply of steel, about half of such
cotton cloth as was produced on a commercial scale, and 40 per

[1] R. Robinson and J. Gallagher, *Africa and the Victorians* (1961), p. 472.
[2] E. Williams, *Made in Germany* (1896), p. 5.
[3] See J. E. Tyler, *The Struggle for Imperial Unity, 1868–95* (1938), p. 12.

cent (in value) of its hardware'.[1] But in 1870 Britain's overseas trade still exceeded that of France, Germany and Italy combined.[2] It was over the next thirty years that Britain was demoted to the position of being merely one great industrial state among many. In the course of the 1890s her output of steel was surpassed by both America and Germany. And between 1883 and 1913 the share of world trade in manufactured goods in British hands dropped from 37·1 per cent to 25·4 per cent, while Germany's proportion rose from 17·3 per cent to 23 per cent, and America's from 3·4 per cent to 11 per cent.[3] In terms of industrial output, Britain's relative decline was even more striking.

So far the discussion has been concentrated upon the quantitative elements in Britain's loss of power, relative to Germany and America. The difficulty arises when one tries to interpret these rough and ready statistics. For example, Britain, as the first country to go through an industrial revolution, enjoyed in the mid-Victorian years a superior position that was bound to diminish in time, when other countries followed in her wake. Germany, with a large, well educated population and abundant natural resources, was bound, sooner or later, to break into fields of economic activity which the British had once monopolized. The crucial problem, however, is the efficiency with which Britain deployed what manpower and material resources she possessed; was she more efficient in this respect than, say, Germany? Here caution must be exercised. It is dangerous, on the available evidence, to attempt sweeping international comparisons of standards of entrepreneurial competence and inventiveness. In any case, a close industry by industry examination reveals glaring discrepancies in the standards *within* the different sectors of major British industries, like iron and steel, cotton, chemicals and so on. This is not the place for a discussion of such intricate and technical issues.[4]

[1] E. J. Hobsbawm, *Industry and Empire* (1968), p. 110.
[2] J. E. Tyler, op. cit., p. 28.
[3] D. H. Aldcroft, 'The Entrepreneur and the British Economy, 1870–1914' (*Economic History Review*, Aug. 1964, 2d Series, Vol. XVII, no. 1, p. 124).
[4] See D. H. Aldcroft (ed.), *The Development of British Industry and Foreign Competition, 1875–1914*, (1968).

One can, however, say that, with certain notable exceptions, Britain's performance in the new science-based industries compared very poorly with Germany and America. By the early twentieth century the British were importing over 80 per cent of their synthetic dye-stuffs from Germany and had fallen into a similar state of dependence on that country in respect of chemical and optical glass, the more sophisticated electrical goods and other objects which called for precision and a high level of expertise. This was a startling reversal of fortune for a community where the level of technological skill had a few decades earlier been the highest in the world.

As contemporaries realized, this poor showing in the new science-based manufactures owed something to Britain's defective system of technical education and scientific research. Prince Albert saw very clearly the problems which British industry would soon be facing when he composed a memorandum for the Commissioners of the Great Exhibition in August 1851: 'The improvement in locomotion, the increased means offered by science for the extraction, preparation, or culture of the raw material, have lessened the peculiar local advantages of certain nations, and have thus depressed the relative value of the raw material as an element in manufacture; while they have immensely increased the value of skill and intelligence as the other great element of production.' France and Germany, he pointed out, were 'continually economizing and perfecting production by the applications of science', and Britain would have to pay more attention to technical education herself, if she hoped to 'keep foremost in the struggle with nations'.[1]

Prince Albert's warnings and his encouragement of prominent scientists were little heeded at the time, and it required the shock administered by the poor showing of British exhibits at the Paris International Fair of 1867, coupled with the onset of a trade depression, to gain the advocates of State-sponsored technical instruction a sympathetic hearing for perhaps the first time. In 1868 a Select Committee was set up to inquire into the whole

[1] Wemyss Reid, *Memoirs and Correspondence of Lyon Playfair* (1899, popular ed., 1900), p. 132.

subject.[1] A year later the Government appointed the Royal Commission on Scientific Instruction and the Advancement of Science. Also in 1869 came the founding of *Nature* which, under the editorship of Sir Norman Lockyer, the astronomist, acted as the mouthpiece of a small, but highly articulate, group of scientists who were convinced of the social utility of science and felt that the state should do far more to develop it.[2] Most of these men had close connections with Germany; in fact, a high proportion of British scientists in these years had been trained in German laboratories, because suitable facilities were almost non-existent at home; and so, understandably, the Prussian model was the one to which they most constantly appealed.

Matthew Arnold's report on the *Higher Schools and Universities in Germany*, published in 1868, must have deepened the public's sense of unease. In this report Arnold calculated that England had barely half the proportion of her population coming under higher instruction that France and Prussia had; Arnold thought that this figure even flattered England since Oxford and Cambridge Universities were, in his opinion, no more than 'hauts lycées' and London University a mere Board of Examiners. The industrial significance of this was that when the English met the Germans and Swiss on equal terms as to capital, the latter often came out on top because of their educational advantages. 'Our rule of thumb has cost us dear already', observed Arnold, 'and is probably destined to cost us dearer still'.[3] These words were prophetic of much that was to be said at the end of the century on the subject of British amateurishness and slip-shodness, compared with the thoroughness and scientific method of the Germans.

Why should Britain's educational system have lagged so far behind Germany's? One reason was that the facilities offered were not only inadequate in themselves, they also suffered from not fitting into any overall design. When the Bryce Commission into

[1] D. S. L. Cardwell, *The Organisation of Science in England* (1957), pp. 84–98. G. Haines IV: 'German Influence Upon Scientific Instruction in England, 1867–1887' (*Victorian Studies*, March 1959, Vol. I, no. 3, pp. 215–17).

[2] ibid., p. 219. W. H. G. Armytage, *Sir Richard Gregory* (1957), p. 25. T. M. Lockyer and W. L. Lockyer, *Life and Work of Sir Norman Lockyer* (1928), Ch. VI.

[3] M. Arnold, *Higher Schools and Universities in Germany* (1868, ed. of 1874), pp. 233, 211, 215.

Secondary Education drew up its Report in 1895, some of the worst deficiencies of the past had already been remedied. Nevertheless, as the Commissioners noted, the growth that had taken place in recent years had not been 'either continuous or coherent', that is to say, it did not 'represent a series of logical or even connected sequences'. 'Each one of the agencies whose origin has been described,' wrote the Bryce Commission,

. . . was called into being, not merely independently of the others, but with little or no regard to their existence. Each has remained in its working isolated and unconnected with the rest. . . This isolation and this independence, if they may seem to witness to the rich variety of our educational life, and to the active spirit which pervades it, will nevertheless prepare the observer to expect the usual results of dispersed and unconnected forces, needless competition between the different agencies, and a frequent overlapping of effort, with much consequent waste of money, of time, and of labour.[1]

The situation in education had parallels in nearly every other branch of the national life.

But to follow through the implications of this was to question some of the most deep-seated assumptions about British politics and administration; for the weaknesses of organization and method, of which complaint was being made, seemed to be bound up intimately with those liberal values in which Englishmen had once taken such a complacent pride.

To generalize somewhat crudely, mid-Victorian constitutional government involved three central principles, which lay at the heart of the ideology of liberalism. The first of these principles was that government should be responsive to movements of popular opinion, and that this could best be guaranteed by making the executive responsible through Parliament to a wider political community. Secondly, there was the commitment to cheap, efficient and 'disinterested' administration, which meant in practice a 'neutral' civil service appointed by open competitive examinations. Finally, great store was set by a vigorous system of local government which, enjoying a considerable measure of

[1] *Report of Royal Commission on Secondary Education* (1895); C. 7862, pp. 17–18.

independence, could check any tendency in the central executive to behave in an arbitrary manner.

The reliance on 'checks and balances' was part of the old Whig tradition that good government was limited government, a tradition in some ways fortified by the 'individualism' of mid-Victorian political and economic thought. In the 1840s and 1850s the Utilitarian reformer, Edwin Chadwick, had pressed for a simplification and rationalization of the areas of local government, in the interests of a more efficient public health system; but his bureaucratic and centralizing approach, modelled in part upon French practice, had seemed too 'un-English', too much of a threat to popular liberties. The reaction against Chadwick's ideas that set in during the late 1850s held back much needed measures of local government reform for a whole generation and thus per-petuated administrative arrangements that made no pretence to functional efficiency. 'If anyone were to attempt to say what the internal government of England is, how it is carried on or how it is superintended', wrote James Fitzjames Stephen, 'he would be smothered in the attempt under a chaos of acts, charters, com-missioners, boards, benches, courts, and vestries of all sorts and conditions, which have no unity, are subject to no central control in most instances, and are suffered to atone for all their other defects by what Frenchmen praise as "le self-government", which not infrequently means the right to misgovern your immediate neighbours without being accountable for it to anyone wiser than yourself.'[1] This description was scarcely an exaggeration of the confused state of affairs that prevailed in the 1870s.

Later, some order was superimposed upon the chaos when elec-ted county councils were created in 1888, and urban and rural district councils in 1894. Yet many of the old *ad hoc* bodies, charged with performing some specific local service (notably School Boards and Boards of Guardians) continued to exist along-side these new authorities, each retaining its own administrative area and rating powers, its own composition and constitution. Confusion and over-lapping were therefore charges commonly

[1] J. F. Stephen, *Liberty, Equality, Fraternity* (1873: edited by R. J. White, Cambridge, 1967), p. 218.

raised against English local government throughout the Victorian period and into the early years of the twentieth century. Here, however, was perhaps one of the inconveniences necessarily suffered by a society in which concern for civic freedom and local autonomy so completely outweighed all considerations of administrative efficiency.

The idea of a 'neutral' civil service filled by open competitive examination was of more recent origin. It had, of course, been popularized by the Northcote-Trevelyan Report of 1854, which provided a blue-print for the important Civil Service reforms put into practice over the following twenty years. However, the opinions of Northcote and Trevelyan by no means passed without contradiction at the time. While the public raged against the aristocratic jobbery and mismanagement which they believed to be responsible for the sufferings of the British troops before Sebastopol in the black winter of 1854–5, alternative proposals were being put forward for staffing the higher posts in the government departments. And though the Northcote-Trevelyan recommendations were finally acted upon, at least in broad outline, these rival schemes were intermittently revived in periods of stress and anxiety during the course of the next half century; for this reason, they are worth a brief investigation.

One of these alternatives was that advanced by the Administrative Reform Association of 1855. The slogan of this organization was 'the right man in the right place' and its professed aim was 'to bring up the public management to the level of private management in this country'. Its sponsors believed that there was an essential similarity between commercial enterprise and public administration; and, of course, they took it for granted that the middle class business man enjoyed an enormous superiority in all the 'practical matters of life' over aristocratic officials and Army officers.[1] Layard, a spokesman for this aggressive middle class pressure group, told the Commons that he had often heard it asked, why does the Government not allow some firm to contract

---

[1] Olive Anderson, 'The Administrative Reform Association of 1855' (*Victorian Studies*, March 1965, Vol. VIII, no. 3, pp. 231–42); O. Anderson, *A Liberal State at War* (1967), pp. 104–18.

for carrying on the War?; he added that this suggestion contained good common sense.[1]

Such a crude identification between commercial enterprise and public administration was never accepted, of course, by either Northcote or Trevelyan. These men and their supporters, notably Gladstone, wanted to replace the patronage system by a new mode of recruitment and promotion, but one which, far from reflecting the values of the business community, would be decidedly aristocratic in its tendency. They recommended the division of the public service into two grades, a 'mechanical' and an 'intellectual' branch, entry into the latter being by open competitive examination run by a Board of Commissioners. This Board would have the task of testing, not technical aptitude or administrative ability narrowly defined, but the qualities derived from the sort of 'liberal education' supplied by the reformed public schools and the older universities. In fact, the Civil Service reformers were deliberately working to strengthen the ties between the established educational institutions of the country and the public service, in the confident expectation that, as Gladstone put it, 'those that may be called gentlemen by birth or training' would then monopolize the important posts.[2] Objectively tested proficiency in certain disciplines, acquired in the atmosphere of one of the older seats of learning, produced, or so these men believed, a well-developed character and an all-round judgment: qualities that could be applied with profit to any administrative task that came to hand.

Naturally, the Northcote-Trevelyan proposals were disliked by the Administrative Reform Association, on the 'democratic' ground that they would have the effect of erecting barriers between the public service and the commercial middle classes. Although the A.R.A., too, favoured open examinations, members of this organization had a different sort of examination in mind— one that would have a more 'practical' bias. Successful candidates, they suggested, could be awarded a certificate which would both serve as a preliminary qualification for entry into the civil service and also be of use to private business employers when recruiting new personnel. This was obviously a far cry from the

[1] ibid., p. 116.   [2] J. Morley, *Life of Gladstone* (1903), Vol. I, p. 649.

'irrelevant' academic tests that Northcote and Trevelyan wanted the Civil Service Commissioners to organize.[1]

On this issue, the A.R.A. won the support of Edwin Chadwick. Having been pushed into an attorney's office at the age of fourteen or fifteen, Chadwick had little reverence for the education of the older universities. 'An academic examination,' he contended, 'would have let in to the Poor Law service a candidate who could give the names of Actaeon's hounds, but who knew nothing of the chief statutes relating to the work in hand, and had no grounding in administrative principles, law or political economy. . .'[2]

Yet Chadwick really represented a viewpoint equally distinct from both the A.R.A. and the Northcote-Trevelyan coterie. Thus, he had no patience with the notion that private business management should set the criteria by which the public service was to be judged; still less did he agree with the A.R.A.'s chairman, Samuel Morley, a self-confident hosiery manufacturer, that there should be 'less rather than more government'. Chadwick looked to foreign experience, when he argued that administration and government depended for their efficiency on the maintenance of a staff of full-time, salaried experts, trained for their specific duties. Through the application of science and expertise, he held, admitted social evils could be steadily and systematically eradicated.[3]

This vision of a trained bureaucracy using all the resources of science and the coercive powers of the state for a more efficient and humane ordering of the life of the community made little appeal to the men who actually carried through the reorganization of the Civil Service in the latter half of the 19th century. As for the A.R.A.'s belief that the public service was simply 'private business writ large', this had become discredited even before the end of the Crimean War,[4] though it was to make a reappearance nearly

[1] O. Anderson, *A Liberal State at War*, p. 115; O. Anderson, 'The Administrative Reform Association of 1855' (*Victorian Studies*, March 1965, Vol. VIII, no. 3, p. 235).

[2] R. A. Lewis, 'Edwin Chadwick and the Administrative Reform Movement, 1854–1856' (*University of Birmingham Historical Journal, 1949–1950*, Vol. II, p. 186).

[3] ibid., pp. 183, 197.

[4] O. Anderson, *A Liberal State at War*, pp. 118–24.

fifty years later during the course of the Boer War.[1] In the end, it was Northcote and Trevelyan who emerged triumphant.

One aspect of the Northcote-Trevelyan reforms needs to be strongly emphasized. The intention was to recruit a new administrative élite from gentlemen whose minds had been fertilized by contact with a 'liberal education'. This meant in practice that most senior administrators would have to pass through a public school and one of the older universities. Yet the curriculum in these institutions was still dominated to a surprising degree by classics, much less attention being devoted to 'modern' subjects, like science and modern languages. This kind of education, obviously, was singularly detached from the circumstances and requirements of commercial and industrial life.[2] Indeed, as early as the 1850s there was some criticism of the relatively low status accorded to science and technology in a society which depended for its strength and prosperity on the application of science to industry. Such criticisms mounted as the century drew to its close.

What the public schools *did* provide their pupils with was an education based on a belief in the civilizing influence of classical studies and in the 'formation of character' through the prefectorial system and organized games. The public schools were not primarily concerned with encouraging academic zeal, still less with imparting useful or specialized courses of study, but rather with bringing out the moral qualities of earnestness, probity and 'leadership'.[3]

At Oxford and Cambridge, too, the emphasis was on the training of a new kind of national leadership, which could take the place of the old aristocracy of landed wealth. This preoccupation with the role of élites was characteristic of the thinking of Victorian intellectuals, not least of reforming 'liberals' in the university world. These men were determined to place the direction of national affairs in the hands of the 'educated classes'. Thus, Seeley looked on Cambridge University as 'a great seminary of politicians'.[4] And Jowett himself, it is well known, took an intense interest in the

[1] See below, Ch. III, pp. 87–9 and Ch. IV, p. 113.
[2] G. Kitson Clark, *The Making of Victorian England* (1962), pp. 270–1.
[3] ibid.
[4] Cited in S. Rothblatt, *The Revolution of the Dons* (1968), p. 169.

worldly success of the young men who had passed through his hands at Balliol.[1]

However, despite a half-hearted commitment to 'German' ideals of scholarship, these dons were not themselves profound scholars, and they tended to dislike specialized academic courses which encouraged scholarly tastes and aptitudes in others. A product of Jowett's Balliol, Asquith, proclaimed in his rectorial address to Aberdeen University in October 1910: 'a University which is content to perform the office of a factory of specialists is losing sight of some of its highest functions . . . there is much to be said for the old University ideal of the "all round" man. . .'[2] It goes without saying that Asquith was as averse to a utilitarian, as he was to a narrowly academic, conception of University education. Such liberal intellectuals were disposed to disparage the 'profit motive' by which business men conducted their lives and to hold the world of commerce at a distance by preaching a lofty 'ideal of service'.[3]

And this was precisely the ideal which set the norms of the higher civil servants who entered Whitehall through the medium of the open competitive examination. Thus, the most important administrative appointments soon became the preserve of 'gentlemen' who had benefited from a 'liberal' university education, but who possessed neither practical experience nor knowledge relevant to their work. Yet, partly because of the assumption that 'specialists' were spendthrifts who needed tight curbing, public officials with technical qualifications and attainments usually found themselves subordinated at all points to these 'general administrators'. The intention of the civil service reforms was to root out the abuses of the old aristocratic methods of administration, when jobbery and extravagance had been rife. Yet the effect was to exclude not only the grossly incompetent, the extravagant and the corrupt, but also powerful administrators of the Chadwick stamp.

Even as early as the 1850s, so Dr. Roy Macleod has informed us, 'divisions had begun to appear between the "generalists" or

[1] See M. Richter, *The Politics of Conscience: T. H. Green and His Age* (1964), Ch. 3.

[2] *The Times*, 26.10.10.

[3] See S. Rothblatt, op. cit., pp. 90–3.

"administrators" in public service, and those other individuals who were beginning to offer formally acquired, specialized knowledge to the work of Government.' 'Their separation,' he notes, 'was accentuated by the Northcote-Trevelyan Reforms and by the subsequent introduction of the established civil servant'. By the 1860s the specialists, though few in number, formed in aggregate ' "invisible colleges" of authoritative opinion on questions of science, law and policy'. But as the reforms of the Civil Service began, under Gladstone's influence, to take effect, these specialists, engineers, doctors and so on, lost the semi-autonomous position they had occupied in the 1870s and 1880s, and became 'wedged into an increasingly rigid and departmentalised structure of administration'. In the late 1880s and 1890s there developed what Dr. Macleod has called 'the reign of law'. 'The calculation of legal and administrative precedent, and the presence of a second or third generation of Oxbridge-educated, classically-trained, senior civil servants, placed a premium on the application of formal rules to domestic policy.' The result of this was that the Permanent Secretary now had less to do with his 'experts', as these officials lost their initiating powers and were confined to a consultative role.[1] The resignation in 1873 of Sir John Simon, a trained doctor, from his post in the Local Government Board, is often taken to symbolize this supersession of skilled expertise by 'secretarial common sense'.[2]

Dr. Macleod's researches have shown, however, that 'secretarial common sense' did less to prevent the establishment of a State Medical Service in the late nineteenth century than the growing stringency of budgetary control, as the Treasury emerged as the dominant department of state, co-ordinating and directing the activities of the other spending ministries. Indeed, it would seem that the senior Treasury officials, together with most late Victorian Chancellors of the Exchequer, had an ingrained dislike of all specialists in administration. The specialist was seen as a monomaniac, whose enthusiasms made him incapable of judging a situation from a general, all-round point of view; if given too much

---

[1] Roy Macleod, 'Specialist Policy in Government Growth' (Cambridge doctoral dissertation, 1967), pp. 19, 370–83.

[2] Royston Lambert, *Sir John Simon* (1963), pp. 570–7.

scope, the specialist would therefore involve the community in unwarrantable expenditure and encourage governments to meddle in matters best left alone to private enterprise. Therefore, successive medical officers at the Local Government Board were obstructed and sometimes reprimanded by senior Treasury officials, who apparently suspected them of multiplying their tasks and expanding their staff in a mood of wanton extravagance.[1]

One possible reason for so violent a response was the fact that the specialist, by his very existence, threatened the rationale and nature of the civil service structure—and even, less directly, threatened the purpose of the liberal state itself. One senior Treasury official voiced the doubts that almost all 'general administrators' and politicians must sometimes have felt, when he minuted: 'I do not know who is to check the assertion of experts when the government has once undertaken a class of duties which none but such persons understand.'[2] Once the state's functions had grown to this point, it became difficult to draw any neat dividing line between policy-making and administration, a situation which made ministerial responsibility a pretence and parliamentary control a sham.

This difficulty can be illustrated by looking at the problem of War Office administration. In 1890 a Royal Commission Report appeared on the Administration of the Military and Naval Departments. Within the War Office the Commissioners found a confusion between the executive branches concerned with detail and routine administration, and the consultative branches concerned with collating information, proffering advice to the Secretary of State and preparing contingency plans. These latter duties, they suggested, should be separated from the other business of the department and entrusted to a Chief of the General Staff, as had happened in continental countries.[3]

However, one of the Commissioners, Sir Henry Campbell-Bannerman, a Liberal politician who had already held the post of

---

[1] R. Macleod, 'The Frustration of State Medicine, 1880–1899' (*Medical History*, Jan. 1967, pp. 15–40); R. Macleod, 'Treasury Control and Social Administration': *Occasional Papers on Social Administration*, no. 23, 1968.

[2] Ralph Lingen's minute of 1.6.71, cited by R. Lambert: op, cit., p. 452.

[3] *Report of Royal Commission into Civil and Professional Administration of the Naval and Military Departments and the Relation of Those Departments to Each Other and to the Treasury* (1890), C. 5979, pars. 70–2.

C

War Secretary, disagreed in a strongly-worded dissenting memorandum. Britain had no need of a ' "general military policy" in this larger and more ambitious sense of the phrase,' he argued; Campbell-Bannerman went on to hint that a Chief of the General Staff might be tempted to justify his own existence by embroiling governments in avoidable wars. If 'general military policy' meant preparing war plans, it was pernicious; if it merely meant military administration, this could best be left to those executive officers who possessed first-hand experience of the subject. Campbell-Bannerman also disliked the idea that, in the interest of continuity, a Chief of the General Staff might serve for a five year period; he felt that in practice this arrangement would prove quite unworkable; 'is it conceivable that if (to put an extreme, but quite a possible, case) Ministers were defeated in Parliament on some military question, their successors, coming into power upon this very issue, should have to accept as their confidential adviser the actual author of the condemned policy?'[1] Like most orthodox Liberals, Campbell-Bannerman was determined that responsibility should be vested in Ministers of the Crown accountable to Parliament. The meddling of departmental 'experts' in questions of *policy* seemed to represent an infringement of the principles of constitutional government. Add to this factor, the general distrust of 'militarism' which was part of the liberal ideology, and it is reasonably clear why there should have been such strong political opposition in Britain to the creation of a General Staff—not until 1905 was one established, some two or three decades later than in the major continental states.

Of all the professional groups, the Military may have had the most sinister reputation in liberal eyes. Yet in a way the scientist posed an even greater threat to the theory and practice of Parliamentary government. For the scientist possessed knowledge and techniques that escaped the comprehension, and thus the control, of the most intelligent 'layman'. When the Royal Commission on Scientific Instruction and the Advancement of Science examined the proper relationship that should exist between the State and the scientists, it was impressed by how little British governments did, in comparison with many continental countries, to

[1] ibid., pp. xxix–xxxi.

subsidize scientific research. To remedy this deficiency, the Commission advocated the formation of a Ministry of Science and Education, aided by 'a Council representing the Scientific Knowledge of the Nation'. Thus equipped, the government would be in a position to discharge its three main responsibilities with regard to science: which were, firstly, 'the treatment of the Scientific Questions incident to the Business of the Public Departments'; secondly, 'the direction of scientific instruction when given under the Superintendence or Control of the State'; and thirdly, 'the consideration of all questions involving State Aid towards the Advancement of Science, and of Administrative Questions arising out of such Aid'.[1]

Needless to say, the major recommendations of this Royal Commission were ignored. And the testimony of the three politicians who gave evidence before it helps explain why its labours proved so fruitless. The three politicians in question, Lord Salisbury, the 15th Earl of Derby and Sir Stafford Northcote, all had an interest in the promotion of science that was far in advance of most of their Parliamentary contemporaries. Lord Salisbury was himself an amateur scientist; he conducted some quite important physical investigations at his Hatfield laboratories, and held strong views about the obligations which the state owed to scientific research workers. But even Salisbury jibbed at the proposal that there should be a council of science to which the various government departments could go for expert advice. 'I am afraid,' said Salisbury, 'that those who [make this suggestion] are not practically acquainted with the working of the House of Commons. My impression is, that the House of Commons would never feel itself prevented from reversing the decision of a council of science of that kind.'[2]

Lord Derby and Sir Stafford Northcote felt similarly. 'One objection to it,' said Derby, 'is that if matters for which the head of a department is responsible are to be referred to the council, and if upon those matters the council is to pronounce an authoritative

[1] *8th Report of Royal Commission on Scientific Instruction and the Advancement of Science* (1875), C. 1298, pp. 24, 27.

[2] *Royal Commission on Scientific Instruction* . . . (Minutes of Evidence), 1874, C. 958, p. 345, q. 13, 564).

opinion, you will very materially lessen the responsibility of the one person who ought to be responsible to Parliament.' The scientific council would take no account of the question of expense: Parliament, on the other hand, would think of nothing else. So a Minister would find himself accountable to two authorities, each working to entirely different criteria. Derby clearly believed that, in cases of such conflict, Parliament would usually win, and that in consequence no competent scientist would care to sit on a council whose advice carried such little weight.[1]

The argument is an interesting one. Salisbury and Derby had a clear enough appreciation of the difficulties involved in any 'scientific policy', but they turned away from these difficulties in baffled helplessness. Nothing, they felt, could be done. And, indeed, nothing along the lines of the Devonshire Commission Report *was* done, despite the vociferous agitation of those articulate scientists organized around the periodical, *Nature* (which was actually founded in 1869, while the Commission was still in session). It goes without saying that though the contributors to *Nature* had a boundless optimism about the potentialities of State-aided science, they largely skirted round those *political* difficulties, which Derby and Salisbury found so insuperable.

How could the scientific equipment of government be improved without its representative and responsible character being destroyed? It must first of all be admitted that this was not an issue that very deeply engaged the interests of late nineteenth-century politicians. Neither of the two major parties seriously *tried* to devise a constructive solution of the difficulty. So long as Gladstone was their leader, the Liberals could not be expected to pursue the matter with any vigour: to have done so would have been tantamount to admitting the inadequacies of their own ideology. Nor in this field did the Conservatives offer any real alternative. It would be a waste of time and energy to scrutinize Disraeli's speeches and writings for any coherent statement of his views on the role of the scientist in government and administration. Disraeli's only deep conviction was that the landed interest should predominate, politically, socially and economically. The Conservative Leader also believed in the rights and privileges derived

[1] C. 1298, p. 42.

from tradition and heredity, and saw civil liberty and national greatness as depending upon a system of local government sufficiently strong to resist the encroachments of the central executive. This 'squirearchical' approach to public affairs clearly made Disraeli as sharply opposed as was Gladstone to bureaucratic, 'scientifically-ordered' government, though for different reasons. However, one should not write as though the two political parties stood for radically different conceptions of the state. After all, by the late nineteenth century many liberal ideas had become taken for granted by Conservatives, and 'Gladstonian' tenets—the belief in Free Trade, balanced budgets, 'responsible' government, economy and so on—added up to a dogma that was equally endorsed by both Front Benches.

But, paradoxically enough, the acceptance of a great deal of the liberal ideology by the political opponents of the Liberal Party coincided with a more general movement of opinion against liberal values. Before he died, Gladstone had the depressing experience of seeing discredited nearly all the principles to which he had dedicated his political career and, in his own words, the 'nation betrayed into levity and recklessness'.[1]

To explain why this reaction against Liberalism set in during the final years of the nineteenth century, one must return to the issue of Britain's relative decline as a Great Power. Basically, the Gladstonian creed assumed that Britain would continue to enjoy a pre-eminence which, even in Gladstone's heyday, had begun to slip away. Mid-Victorian Liberalism had been persuasive for a time, because it seemed to explain how Britain had successfully industrialized herself ahead of all the continental states. Bagehot saw the nineteenth century as primarily 'an age of discussion';[2] and herein apparently lay Britain's advantage over nations which continued to operate an autocratic, monarchical system of government; such states were suited for military expansion, perhaps, but not for those triumphs of economic organization which were the hall-mark of 'modern civilization'.

[1] F. E. Hamer (ed.), *The Personal Papers of Lord Rendel* (1931), p. 156: 14.2.98.
[2] W. Bagehot, *Physics and Politics* (1869), Ch. 5.

Professor Asa Briggs, in an apt phrase, once called the Liberals of Victorian England 'middle class Marxists',[1] that is to say, this generation of Liberals believed that the middle classes embodied the virtues of the society of the future, and that in time all other social classes would become assimilated to middle class principles and values. In much the same way, the mid-Victorian generation tended to see Britain as 'the nation of the future', the carrier of values to which all other 'progressive' nations were slowly turning. To those with a linear view of social development, the British liberal state—or at least an 'idealized' British liberal state purged of certain of its grosser abuses and defects—marked the farthest point yet reached by mankind in its onward quest for perfection. 'Advanced' Liberals and Radicals would naturally have cast America in this pioneering role and have argued that the British were lagging some way behind their cousins across the sea; essentially, however, their contention was the same one.

Such convictions as these were especially comforting, since they neatly reconciled the requirements of morality and expediency. The furtherance of liberal causes was a moral imperative; but liberalism could also be relied upon to promote national greatness and commercial prosperity. Conversely, illiberal doctrines, like Protection, stood condemned on two separate counts: tariffs were thought to belong to a vanishing world of aggressive nationalism and pushing greed, which had been productive in the past of much unnecessary evil and suffering; yet tariffs were also believed to damage the material interests of communities which resorted to them. A proper understanding of political economy and of the workings of the British Constitution thus enabled the citizen to go about his affairs with a calm conscience, all the while hearing the reassuring chink of gold sovereigns in his trouser pockets. Once, however, this facile equation of liberalism and material success had come to be questioned, then liberalism itself was bound to assume an altogether different guise.

There is a *Punch* cartoon of 1848, characteristic of the optimism and insular arrogance of the age, entitled 'John Bull Showing the Foreign Powers How To Make A Constitutional Plum-Pudding', in which a prosperous and smiling John Bull produces what is

[1] Cited in S. Beer, *Modern British Politics* (1965), p. 37.

obviously a culinary masterpiece, to the baffled admiration of the onlooking foreigners. 'Ah! We made a nice mess of it! ! !', says one of them despondently.[1] By the end of the century this cartoon could scarcely have been drawn. It was not just that foreigners no longer seemed quite so comically inept. Intelligent British people were also beginning to wonder whether repeated helpings of plum pudding were doing their digestive systems any good.

True, before the 1880s doubts about the efficacy of British liberalism had been frequently raised. One thinks of the trenchant attacks made by Carlyle and Ruskin on the British worship of the twin gods of industrialism and laissez-faire. On the other hand, these critics of the established order of values were, first and foremost, protesting about the social costs which industrialization and liberalism had entailed: the human suffering, the ugliness and the impoverishment of spiritual and cultural values. It was one thing, however, to criticize the maldistribution of the wealth which industrialization had produced or the social uses to which this wealth was being put. It was much more difficult to deny that, on its own materialistic and utilitarian terms, Victorian civilization had been a success; the social critics, on the whole, were simply concerned to reject and discredit the criteria by which success and failure were customarily assessed.

This was where Matthew Arnold saw further than, say, Ruskin. Almost alone of the mid-Victorian critics who arraigned the British liberal state on cultural grounds, Arnold also directed a few well-delivered shafts against it from a utilitarian vantage-point—as when he pointed out the commercial advantages conferred on the Prussians by their extensive system of public education, which was in turn the product of a bureaucratic and tightly ordered community.[2]

By the end of the nineteenth century this line of argument had become much more common. Since the Germans had emerged as Britain's most formidable commercial competitors, respectful attention was increasingly paid to that country's machinery of government and political traditions. Yet Germany, with its centralized

---

[1] Reproduced in D. Southgate, *The Passing of the Whigs, 1832–1886* (1962), p. 273.

[2] M. Arnold, op. cit., *passim*.

bureaucracy, its conscription, its tariffs and subsidies and its authoritarian regime, stood very far apart from the state-of-the-future, the laissez-faire state of traditional liberal aspiration.

Without abandoning their essential ideals, many staunch Liberals came in time to admit the existence of these disturbing trends. Their strategy henceforward was to go on to the defensive and to present their creed, not so much as the key to material success, but for its intrinsic ethical truth. Liberalism, they almost implied, was a luxury commodity, to be purchased out of Britain's accumulated reserves of wealth and strength.

But this raised the further question of whether, in view of the fierce commercial and diplomatic rivalries that had sprung up in Europe since 1870, Britain could *afford* to make such material sacrifices. Britain's relative loss of power thus necessitated a re-appraisal of methods and principles of government that had previously been taken for granted. In the field of foreign affairs, Liberals were forced to face up to the problem of *power* as a factor in the ordering of international life—though many of them, it is true, continued to evade this challenge. Meanwhile, a searching criticism was being made of the liberal state and its central features: parliamentary control, local self-government, and a neutral civil service with close ties with the public schools and the older universities. And this questioning of liberal principle and practice generated ideas and arguments to which later advocates of 'national efficiency' in the early twentieth century were to be powerfully indebted.

The ideology of Efficiency brought together at least three important strands of thinking that had been elaborated in the late nineteenth century, in reaction against orthodox liberalism. The first of these was 'imperialism'. India and the other overseas dependencies became the object of growing enthusiasm and interest in the 1880s and 1890s, and these were territories which faced Englishmen with the necessity of providing forceful, autocratic and centralized administration, for which no comparable opportunity existed at home. It is scarcely surprising that many people with experience of imperial administration began to wonder whether similar methods, modified, of course, to meet the different circumstances, might not also have beneficial consequences if applied within Britain itself. James Fitzjames Stephen, who had spent a period of office in India as legal member of the Viceroy's Council, believed that India was 'the best corrective in existence to the fundamental fallacies of Liberalism'.[1] The fruits of his reflections on his Indian experiences are contained in his *Liberty, Equality, Fraternity* (1873). Stephen's writing is prophetic of much that was to appear in the following half-century in the opposition it sets up between administration and government (people doing things) and parliamentary politics (people merely talking). Like many others after him, Stephen believed that Parliament and the party system paralysed the executive government and prevented much needed reforms from taking place.[2] This stress on the creative nature of administration was to carry over into the Edwardian cult of 'national efficiency'.

Another source of 'national efficiency' ideas can be located in the Broad Church tradition of social thought. Writers and theologians of this persuasion were concerned to attack the atomistic and mechanistic modes of thought characteristic of Utilitarianism and to commend an ordered and hierarchical society held together by 'natural' relationships and a set of common values. These values, they argued, could best be represented and expressed by a National Church, a liberal and comprehensive institution, under the auspices of which new developments in secular thought could be synthesized with Christian dogma. Such a body would act as the repository of national traditions and aspirations and also hold in check the disintegrating social and intellectual tendencies of modern life.

Broad Church writers could point to an actual contemporary society which largely exemplified their ideal: Germany. Matthew Arnold and Seeley, in particular, believed that the recent history of Germany held out lessons to the world which the British people would do well to note. They attempted to show that Germany's sudden rise to Great Power status would not have taken place, but for the educational and cultural renaissance which followed

[1] J. F. Stephen, op. cit., p. 11.
[2] Ibid., pp. 215–16.

upon Prussia's defeat by Napoleonic France. But, they added, this renaissance had been fostered by a State which had been prepared to take on 'spiritual' as well as the ordinary administrative functions.[1]

This was where liberal Britain apparently fell so far short of Germany. True, the possibility existed of adapting the Church of England, so that it could play a similar role. In its existing form, however, the Anglican Church failed to meet the requirements of the case. Moreover, as Matthew Arnold wrote, his countrymen had 'not the notion, so familiar on the Continent and to antiquity, of *the State*—the nation in its collective and corporate character, entrusted with stringent powers for the general advantage, and controlling individual wills in the name of an interest wider than that of individuals'. The result was 'anarchy', 'the worship of freedom in and for itself'.[2]

But Arnold then went on to show the logical interconnection between the Englishman's 'dislike of authority' and his 'disbelief in science'.[3] Science was a principle of reason and order, which denied any individual's right to 'do as he pleased', by suggesting standards and ideals to which the community should aspire. Germany, of course, provided an example to Arnold of a state based upon the idea of science and responsible for its dissemination through a centralized and well-articulated educational system: and as such worthy of emulation by the British.

Clearly, at this point the admiration of the Broad Church writers for an idealized state representing the 'best selves' of its citizens joins hands with the admiration of scientists like Sir Norman Lockyer, the editor of *Nature*, for the German state which recognized the *utility* of science. Admittedly, Arnold himself, writing in the 1860s, did not really associate 'science' with industrial growth, one or two isolated phrases notwithstanding; the Germany about which he wrote so fulsomely was certainly not the Germany of Krupps and the Allgemeine Elektrizitäts Gesellschaft

[1] R. T. Shannon, 'John Robert Seeley and the Idea of a National Church' in R. Robson (ed.), *Ideas and Institutions of Victorian England* (1967), pp. 236–67.

[2] M. Arnold, *Culture and Anarchy* (1869, edited by J. Dover Wilson, Cambridge, 1960), p. 75.

[3] M. Arnold, *Higher Schools and Universities in Germany* (1868, ed. of 1874), p. 217.

that emerged in the last quarter of the nineteenth century. To a later generation, however, his writings could be construed in a rather more utilitarian sense. The foremost apostle of 'national efficiency' in the Edwardian period, Haldane, drew heavily upon Arnold's educational reports, even appropriated some of their rhetoric.[1] Yet Haldane was also the ally of Lockyer and an effective campaigner for state-aided science and better technological instruction. Nor did he see anything incongruous in invoking Arnold's name when praising Germany's material achievements.

The ideology of 'national efficiency' thus has a somewhat complex intellectual ancestry. But though the ideas out of which it was formed were varied and disparate, they were fused into a common substance by the alarm felt about Britain's Great Power status; and this alarm had been slowly but steadily mounting throughout the late nineteenth century.

[1] e.g. his address at Liverpool in Oct. 1901, in R. B. Haldane, *Education and Empire* (1902), pp. 1–38.

CHAPTER II

THE LESSONS OF THE BOER WAR

IT REQUIRED SOME great crisis to bring these latent doubts and feelings of insecurity to the surface. The reverses suffered by the British Army during the Second Boer War fulfilled this role,[1] and national complacency received a severe jolt from which it never fully recovered. In the opening days of the war a quite irrational mood of confidence held sway in the army, the War Office, in the Cabinet and among the Fleet Street pundits,[2] and this made the ensuing disillusionment all the more bitter.

A private letter, written on 3 November, soon after the surrender at Nicholson's Nek, captures the atmosphere of stunned shock and dismay:

In my lifetime, this state of tension is unique. The War affects all, rich and poor alike. All have friends and relations in it and it is no exaggeration to say that we are all plunged in gloom . . . I shall never forget last Tuesday in London, when the news of the missing battalions arrived about midday. Picture the newsboys at the corners . . . shouting

---

[1] In my references to the Boer War, I have drawn upon the following accounts: Major-General Sir F. Maurice and M. H. Grant, *History of the War in South Africa* (1906); L. S. Amery (ed.), *The Times History of the War in South Africa*, 6 Volumes (1900–1909); D. James, *Lord Roberts* (1954); E. Holt, *The Boer War* (1958); R. Kruger, *Goodbye Dolly Gray* (1959); J. Symons *Buller's Campaign* (1963).

[2] For a war correspondent's viewpoint: Spenser Wilkinson, *Lessons of the War* (1900), pp. 2–3. For the views of the Under-Secretary at the War Office, see J. W. Mackail and G. Wyndham, *Life and Letters of George Wyndham*, Vol. I (1934?), p. 361; Wyndham to his Mother, 6.10.99: '. . . I believe the Army is more efficient than at any time since Waterloo.' This represents more than a kindly attempt to reassure an anxious mother who had a son serving in South Africa.

'Terrible Reverse of British Troops—Loss of 2,000'. Imagine the rush for papers as we all stood about the streets—regardless of all appearances, reading the telegrams with breathless anxiety. Carriages stopped at the corners for papers to be bought—bus conductors rushed with handfuls of pennies as deputation for their passengers. There was a perfect sea of newspapers and anxious faces behind—intense gravity prevailed. . . People walked along speaking in whispers and muttering, while ever echoed round the shrill and awful cry of 'Terrible Reverse of British Troops' . . .[1]

But worse was to come when the Army Corps, under the command of General Buller, arrived in South Africa, and 'Mournful Monday' was all but obliterated from the public mind by the much greater humiliations of 'Black Week'. On 9 December, 1899, General Gatacre, operating on the Centre Front, set off on a risky night march through territory that had not been properly reconnoitred, in the direction of Stormberg Junction; the guides lost their way in the dark, and on the following morning the weary troops launched their offensive from entirely the wrong position; Gatacre, seeing the impossibility of success, ordered a retreat; only on his return to base was it realized that 600 of his men, a fifth of his total force, had been unwittingly left behind, to be captured by the Boers. This was the Battle of Stormberg. Next day General Methuen, pushing on towards the relief of Kimberley, committed himself to a similarly reckless night march through unknown country; before the troops could deploy, dawn broke, leaving them exposed to the withering fire of Boer riflemen who had stealthily taken up positions in concealed slit trenches at only a few hundred yards' distance. This was the Battle of Magorsfontein, in which 1,000 casualties were sustained. It was left to Buller, who had taken charge of the Natal Front, with the aim of rescuing Sir George White's beleaguered troops in Ladysmith, to crown a week of disaster for British arms by an incredibly inept offensive over the River Tugela near Colenso; in this engagement the British lost 1,100 men, killed, wounded or missing, and nearly two batteries of guns were left in the hands of the enemy, when Buller sounded the retreat.

[1] C. Headlam (ed.), *The Milner Papers: South Africa, 1899–1905*, Vol. II (1933), pp. 43–4; Miss Bertha Synge to Milner, 3.11.99.

So ended what soon became known as 'Black Week'. The total number of casualties in all three battles amounted to a mere 3,000 or so: a small enough figure set beside the fighting of the First World War, when 'normal wastage' on the Western Front was 7,000 a day and a major offensive like Passchendaele could cost a quarter of a million. Nevertheless, in relation to the size of the forces taking part and by the standards of the day, these losses were heavy. Even harder for a proud people to bear was the galling thought that some of the finest units of the British Army had been out-manoeuvred and out-fought by the irregular troops of two tiny pastoral republics.

Popular despondency would have been more acute still, had it been generally realized at the time that Buller, his nerve broken by Colenso, had sent off a panicky telegram to White in Lady-smith, advising surrender. It was this act which persuaded the Government to replace Buller as Commander-in-Chief in South Africa by Lord Roberts and to send out heavy reinforcements. But barely had Roberts landed in Cape Town than news came through that Buller's second attempt to cross the Tugela River had produced another reversal. This was the fiasco of Spion Kop (24 January, 1900), when by a misunderstanding the command of the assault force was entrusted to two different officers, each believing himself in sole charge; a day of blunders had culminated in the British withdrawing from the kop with heavy casualties, unaware that the Boers were simultaneously beating a tactical retreat.

The squabble which then took place between the Generals, none of whom wished to assume responsibility, was laid bare for all the world to see when in April the War Secretary, Lord Lansdowne, published the compromising dispatches in only slightly edited form. Some Ministers were surprised when this happened, being of the distinct opinion that the Cabinet had decided *against* publication. Since the Cabinet kept no formal record of its decisions, it is difficult to say whether or not Lansdowne had correctly interpreted his colleagues' wishes on this matter.[1] The episode does at least show that the military had no monopoly of incompetence. In retrospect, Spion Kop assumes something of the character of a

[1] Lord Newton, *Lord Lansdowne* (1929), pp. 182–4. Balfour Papers, Add. Mss. 49, 691, Salisbury to Balfour, 19.4.00, and Balfour to Salisbury, 22.4.00.

farce, but, of course, it was not so regarded by contemporaries. 'Very bad news from Buller, my dear child,' wrote Lord Wolseley to his wife. 'I am in despair at all our misfortunes. God seems to be with the Boers and against us.'[1]

The blackest gloom lifted when Roberts and Kitchener, leaving Buller to blunder along by himself in Natal, struck due north into the Orange River State, cornering Cronje's Army and defeating it at Paardeberg in mid-February. But the failure to round up the Boer leaders at Poplar Grove on 7 March, robbed the British of the quick and decisive victory they needed.[2] Then, during their occupation at Bloemfontein in April, Roberts's troops suffered an appalling tragedy. An epidemic of enteric fever swept through the camp, and at its height was killing fifty men a day and incapacitating thousands. The Army Medical Corps was not adequate for dealing with a crisis of this magnitude. Initially, many doctors failed to recognize the symptoms of the illness, treated the sufferers as though they had contracted ordinary influenza and allowed infected persons to spread the virus to others. Beds and equipment were in short supply. A backbench M.P., Burdett-Coutts, visiting the area, saw enfolding before his eyes terrible scenes reminiscent of the dark days of the Crimean Campaign, and his startling exposures in *The Times* created a first-class political storm.[3]

The capture of Pretoria by the British and the formal annexation of the Transvaal in September, 1900, were widely taken to mark the end of the war. In the event, however, they ushered in a phase of guerrilla activity that was to last another eighteen months. Faced by unorthodox military resistance, the British Army could only 'pacify' disaffected areas by devastating large tracts of what had now become British territory and by adopting counter-measures that revolted humanitarian consciences without proving especially effective in forcing the 'hard liners' into surrender. The Peace of Vereeniging, when it was finally signed in May 1902, came as a relief to the British, for whom the war had long lost what glamour

---

[1] G. Arthur (ed.), *The Letters of Lord and Lady Wolseley*, 1870–1911 (1922), p. 380; Wolseley to Lady Wolseley, 26.1.00.

[2] D. James, op. cit., pp. 296–300

[3] E. Holt, op. cit., pp. 231–3. For Balfour's inept handling of the issue in the Commons, see *Annual Register* for 1900, pp. 148–151, 180.

or purpose it might once have possessed. The final balance sheet showed that the war had cost some £200 million. From start to finish, nearly half a million British and colonial soldiers had had to be employed against an enemy whose *total population*, women, children and old men included, amounted to scarcely one-fifth that number.

Even now the humiliations of the Boer War had not ended. Another scandal was soon to break over the disposal of the surplus stores that had been accumulating in massive quantities in South African depots. It was subsequently discovered that the authorities had been selling off goods to private contractors and then re-purchasing them at much higher prices; the contractors had thus been allowed to pocket extortionate profits, which bore no relation to whatever expenses they might have incurred through storage, wastage and deterioration. Certain high-ranking officers in the sales department of the Army Service Corps, responsible for these extraordinary business transactions, were almost certainly guilty of fraud;[1] not even the British Army was capable of inefficiency on this majestic scale.

From the start, it was agreed that the war had taught the nation valuable lessons that might otherwise have been ignored. Rudyard Kipling expressed the dominant emotion in verses printed in *The Times*:

Let us admit it fairly as a business people should,
We have had no end of a lesson: it will do us no end of good.
. . . It was our fault, and our very great fault—and now we must turn it to use;
We have forty million reasons for failure, but not a single excuse![2]

L. S. Amery wrote in a similar vein in his *The Times History of the War*:

[1] *Report of Committee on Sales and Refunds to Contractors in South Africa*, Cd. 2435, 1905.
[2] 'The Lesson, 1899–1902 (Boer War)', in *Rudyard Kipling's Verse* (1940), pp. 299–300.

. . . the war has not only shaken our military organisation. It has profoundly affected the whole nation in many ways. The Mournful Monday of Nicholson's Nek, the Black Week of Stormberg, Magorsfontein and Colenso, the alternate hope and disappointment of six weeks' fighting on the banks of the Tugela, the long anxiety for the fate of Ladysmith, Kimberley and Mafeking, have taught lessons that nothing else could have taught so well. . . The war has been the nation's Recessional after all the pomp and show of the year of Jubilee. It has transmuted the complacent arrogance and contempt of other nations begotten of long years of peace and prosperity to a truer consciousness both of our strength and of our defects, and has awakened an earnest desire to make those defects good.[1]

Perhaps it was here, in the very real blow dealt to feelings of national superiority, that the South African War made its principal impact upon British society. 'Whatever else the war may do or undo,' observed Bernard Shaw, 'it at least turns its fierce searchlights on official, administrative and military perfunctoriness.'[2] To ignore these things became impossible after 'Black Week', which had affected all classes of the community. Looking back on that period, Karl Pearson noted that 'the spirits of one and all, whatever their political party or their opinions might be, were depressed in a manner probably never before experienced by those of our countrymen now living'.[3] To Cecil Spring-Rice, on diplomatic duty in Persia, life in December 1899 had been 'a prolonged nightmare'. 'The daily telegrams are a horror,' he confided to a friend, 'and waking in the morning or late at night is a terrible thing; one lies alone with a living and growing fear staring one in the face.'[4]

The Government, through its very energy and determination in responding to the disasters of 'Black Week', helped contribute to popular alarms. For the decision to send out massive reinforcements to South Africa meant that the British Isles were denuded of regular troops at a time when the peoples and governments of most continental states were openly exulting over the British

[1] *Times History*, Vol. I (1900), p. 11.

[2] G. B. Shaw (ed.), *Fabianism and the Empire* (1900), p. 98.

[3] K. Pearson, *National Life From the Standpoint of Science* (1901), p. 9.

[4] S. Gwynn (ed.), *The Letters and Friendships of Sir Cecil Spring-Rice*, Vol. I (1929), pp. 303–4; Spring-Rice to Chirol, 20.12.99.

D

defeats. Although not taken seriously by the Admiralty or the Cabinet, an invasion scare was built up by a certain section of the Press during the spring and summer of 1900, and the imminent arrival of the French fleet off the South Coast was predicted.[1]

Hysterical though these fears were, they can readily be understood. The blunders committed by the British army in South Africa scarcely augured well for the likelihood of success in the event of Britain's involvement in hostilities with one of the European great states. The writing, it seemed, was on the wall: the Empire was passing through its Mexican expedition; would it soon be encountering its Sedan?[2] The vicious anglophobia which the Boer War had stirred up on the continent made many people brood in this kind of way. H. G. Wells later wrote that the war had confirmed his growing sense of unease at the gigantic dangers that were gathering against Britain across the narrow seas: 'it discovered Europe to me, as watching and critical.'[3] Many times the tranquillity of Edwardian England was to be shattered by fears of foreign invasion and by intimations that the 'day of national judgement—*dies irae, dies illa*' was at hand.[4]

However irrationally, these fears sharpened the alarm that was felt at Britain's loss of commercial supremacy. In November 1900 Lord Rosebery anticipated that the twentieth century would 'be a period of keen, intelligent, almost fierce, international competition, more probably in the arts of peace even than in the arts of war'.[5] Henceforward, Britain would have to *fight* to hold her own.

But were the British prepared for such a struggle? Some people doubted it, and solemn debates were held in the press about whether 'Britain would last the century'. Andrew Carnegie de-

[1] Arthur J. Marder, *The Anatomy of British Sea Power* (Hamden, Connecticut, 1940), pp. 375–9.

[2] e.g. Arnold White, *Efficiency and Empire* (1901), p. xiii. Such allusions to the collapse of the Third Empire in France during the Franco-Prussian War were not uncommon in this kind of literature.

[3] H. G. Wells, *The New Machiavelli* (1911, Penguin edition 1946), p. 100.

[4] *Fortnightly Review*, May 1902, Vol. LXXI, p. 780; W. S. Lilly, 'Collapse of England'.

[5] Lord Rosebery, *Miscellanies*, Vol. II (1921), p. 245; 'Questions of Empire', Rosebery's Glasgow University Rectorial Address, delivered 16.11.00.

tected in 1901 a wave of pessimism sweeping over the country.[1] But equally in evidence was a grim determination to 'learn the lessons of the war': a mood captured in the much quoted speech of the Prince of Wales on 5 December, 1901 which the newspapers summarized under the headline, 'Wake Up, England!'[2] Cecil Spring-Rice took comfort after 'Black Week' in the reflection that Britain might 'be the better' for the reverses: 'we were perhaps too fat and prosperous, and now the chastisement has come.'[3] The Bishop of London, Mandell Creighton, drew a similar moral:

The war news is terrible. Never have we been so low. No one can foresee the future. We have been for a long time much too arrogant and insolent, and we must repent and learn humility... We must think and pray and humble ourselves. Life is becoming a very serious matter to us all, and we must learn to face its seriousness.[4]

When the war was all but over, the *Daily Telegraph*, surveying the past two years, noted that the ordeal in South Africa had wrought a 'profound transformation' in the political temper of the nation. 'A change has come over the spirit of our dream,' it said, 'and all that is earnest, strenuous and determined in our national character is unmistakably working to the top . . .'[5] Fabian Ware, the editor of the *Morning Post*, thought that in the five years that followed the Boer War the British people had learned to recognize their defects and now desired to remedy them. 'I know many . . . who are forming themselves informally into a sort of *Jugendbund*,' he wrote, 'depriving themselves unostentatiously of all sorts of little luxuries, believing that the necessary sacrifice should begin in this way . . .'[6]

Although the Edwardian Court can scarcely be said to have set a good example in this respect,[7] patriotic earnestness was much in

[1] *Nineteenth Century*, June 1901, Vol. XLIX, pp. 901–12; Andrew Carnegie, 'British Pessimism'.

[2] H. Nicolson, *King George V* (1952), pp. 73–4.

[3] S. Gwynn, op. cit., Vol. I, p. 304.

[4] L. Creighton, *Life and Letters of Mandell Creighton*, Vol. II (1904), p. 405; Creighton to his niece, 16.12.99.

[5] *Daily Telegraph*, 6.1.02.

[6] C. Headlam, op. cit., Vol. II, p. 549; Ware to Milner, 28.6.05.

[7] See Curzon Papers, Vol. 181; Clinton Dawkins to Curzon, 24.5.01: f. 271.

vogue. 'We have to fight hard for our position among the nations,' wrote Milner to Haldane in 1901. 'A great effort is required all round, and great *seriousness*. We cannot afford, as we have been able to afford, when we had the field all to ourselves, to play with these big external problems.'[1] He feared that the British people, sheltered for so many years from keen competition in trade or war, had developed the bad habit of approaching their work as if it were a game, often sacrificing work altogether for the pleasures of sport. Were the battles of the next generation being lost on the playing fields of Eton? In January 1902 *The Times* printed 'The Islanders', Kipling's furious indictment of a nation which devoted so much time to sport, yet refused to master the arts of warfare.[2] At once leader writers and politicans, with Rosebery to the fore,[3] took these verses as their text, and for many months no after-dinner speech was complete without some reference to the dangers of substituting sport for more 'serious' pursuits.

It was easy enough to moralize about the war in this general fashion, but when it came to particularizing the 'lessons of the war', one entered on contentious ground. Naturally, the men who had been personally involved, in one capacity or another, put forward conflicting explanations for what had gone wrong. Arthur Balfour, the First Lord of the Treasury, greatly angered the Conservative Press in January 1900 by telling his constituents in Manchester that it would have been impossible to reinforce the South African garrisons well in advance of the Kruger Ultimatum, because public opinion would not have agreed to it; and he added, in an unfortunate phrase, that the Government had had no more idea than the 'man in the street' about the likelihood of war.[4] Privately, Balfour was expressing the opinion that Ministers had been grossly let down by their military 'experts', of whom he took an understandably poor view.[5] On the other hand, within the

[1] C. Headlam, op. cit., Vol II, p. 263; Milner to Haldane, 1.7.01.

[2] *Rudyard Kipling's Verse*, pp. 301–4.

[3] *The Times*, 19.12.02; Rosebery in speech to the Great Northern Railway Athletic Association.

[4] B. Dugdale, *Arthur James Balfour*, Vol. I (1936), p. 303.

[5] ibid., pp. 306–7.

War Office, the Commander-in-Chief, Lord Wolseley, interpreted the set-backs as a vindication of his ineffectual stand against the subordination of his office to civilian control; he even took a certain gloomy satisfaction in the guilt and remorse which he imagined that Lansdowne, the War Secretary, must be feeling. In fact Lansdowne had been cast in the role of scapegoat by an enraged public opinion. To such lengths were vituperative attacks on him carried, that Lord Roberts wrote to his friend, the famous war correspondent, Spenser Wilkinson, in an attempt to restrain him from attributing all the army's short-comings to errors committed by the civilian Minister. The drift of Roberts's letter was that the worst blunders had been made by Wolseley and the Generals whom Wolseley had selected for command at the start of the campaign.[1] Behind these strictures lay the bitter rivalry within the army between the 'Wolseley ring' and the 'Roberts ring', which was a continuing source of friction and factionalism.[2]

Lord Salisbury tried to raise the debate to a more philosophic plane by musing out loud about the unsuitability of the British Constitution as an 'instrument of war'. But when he went on to criticize Treasury parsimony, he became involved in a bizarre public altercation with the Chancellor of the Exchequer, Hicks-Beach, who much resented this slur on his Department.[3] The attacks on Treasury 'cheese-paring' were taken up by the Press, and for a while Hicks-Beach was almost as unpopular with indignant patriots as Lansdowne. Salisbury's remarks about the inadequacies of the British Constitution also encouraged certain journalists to launch an assault on the very conception of popular and representative government, which was not quite what Salisbury had intended.[4] Finally, there was a revival of the demand heard during the Crimean War for 'a government of business men'.[5]

To unravel the rights and wrongs of all these charges and

[1] H. Spenser Wilkinson, *Thirty Five Years, 1874–1909* (1933), p. 245; Roberts to Wilkinson, 23.1.00.

[2] J. Symons, op. cit., Part I.

[3] Hansard, 4th Series, Vol. 78, col. 30: 30.1.00., ibid., col. 32: 30.1.00., ibid., cols. 239–40; 1.2.00.

[4] See below, Ch. III, pp. 93–4.

[5] See below, Ch. III, pp. 87–9 and Ch. IV, p. 113.

counter-charges, the Government set up numerous official inquiries, which scrutinized nearly every aspect of the war. In 1900
a departmental committee looked into ways of improving the administrative procedures of the War Office.[1] In July of that year
Burdett-Coutts' agitation led to a Royal Commission of inquiry
into the medical arrangements.[2] The break-down of the remounts
department necessitated yet another investigatory committee.[3]
Chamberlain seems to have been the first Minister to urge that
when peace came, a Royal Commission should be set up to look
more generally into the preparations for the war and its conduct.[4]
His advice was acted upon in due course, and in August 1903 the
Elgin Commission submitted a massive report, the conclusions of
which have never been seriously contested.[5] The Butler Committee into the disposal of war stores did not finish its labours
until 1905.[6] Incidentally, the appearance, at periodic intervals, of
a succession of Parliamentary Papers, all, to a greater or lesser
extent, chronicling official ineptitude and administrative chaos,
helped to keep alive the emotions of 'Black Week' and to sustain
the demand for fundamental reforms in all branches of public
life, long after the military situation had been retrieved.

What, then, were the lessons to be derived from a perusal of all
these various inquiries? The conclusions drawn by contemporaries
alone concern us in this chapter. It may indeed be true that in the
spasm of despair and anger that swept the country after 'Black
Week', pessimistic evaluations were made of government and army
which failed to do justice to the difficulties involved in engaging an
elusive enemy over vast empty spaces in a distant theatre of war.
Besides which, much in the conduct of the war, as the official
inquiries show, reflected great credit on the British military
machine; the mobilization and marine transport arrangements
were particularly efficient. Yet people at the time naturally

[1] *Report of Committee on War Office Organisation*, Cd. 580; 1901.
[2] *Report of Royal Commission on the Care and Treatment of the Sick and Wounded
During the South African Campaign*, Cd. 453: 1901.
[3] This Committee produced a 'whitewashing' report in October 1902, to
the fury of most newspapers, e.g. *The Times*, 10.10.02.
[4] B. Dugdale, op. cit., Vol. I, p. 313; Chamberlain to Balfour, 21.10.00.
[5] *Report of Royal Commission of Inquiry into the South African War*, Cd. 1789; 1903.
[6] Cd. 2435.

brooded over the things that had gone wrong. They noted that a whole consignment of rifles had been wrongly sighted, and that many of the maps proved to be inaccurate and inadequate. And they marvelled at the uncanny skill shown by the British generals in so often manoeuvring their troops into untenable positions, where they lost the advantages which greatly superior numbers should have given them.

L. S. Amery, *The Times*'s war correspondent, put much of the blame upon the stultifying regime established by Wolseley's predecessor as Commander-in-Chief, the Duke of Cambridge. The influence of the Royal Duke was still being felt in the importance attached to ceremonial and parades and in a misplaced concern for the 'traditions of the service', which hampered most attempts to improve the army's fighting efficiency. Amery described some of the consequences of this. 'The preserving of mathematically straight lines and fixed intervals, the wheeling of a line of men through an angle with all the precision of a clock dial—this and much other eighteenth-century frippery ruled paramount at inspections and even at manoevres. Cavalry and artillery tactics were dominated by the same idea.'[1] In all, only two months of the soldier's life were devoted to military training as such: the rest was occupied in parades, military guards, in general domestic tasks and in looking after the uniform, which, at home, was the old elaborate red and blue uniform, retained, thought Amery, 'from some notion that in its absence the soldier would cease to have that attraction for servant maids which was believed to be the chief stimulus to recruiting'.[2] As for the officer class, the poor standard of education offered in the military academies, together with the low pay and absence of promotion by merit in the lower ranks, 'shut out not only the less wealthy but also the majority of those who were conscious of their ability and wished to give it scope. The Army did not get the best brains of the country. . .'[3]

The penchant for precision drill, close-rank formations and firing in volleys, which the Duke of Cambridge had encouraged, dominated British military operations in the opening months of the war with disastrous results. By contrast, the Boer irregulars realized the importance of cover, and fired as individuals with

[1] *Times History*, Vol. II (1902), p. 32.   [2] ibid., p. 34.   [3] ibid., p. 36.

deadly marksmanship. Moreover, the British generals tended, in their exaggerated respect for rank, tradition and protocol, to exhibit a lack of enterprise and imagination. It is interesting to note, however, the opinion of the Elgin Commission that 'junior officers very rapidly developed in the actual war their natural power of initiative, and that the deleterious effects of a system based upon a passed-away mode of warfare were more apparent among the senior officers'.[1]

When Milner looked back in 1907 on the events of the Boer War, he felt that its main lesson was that one could not' improvise soldiers, and that no amount of patriotism, willingness, or devotion (would) save a militarily untrained nation from disaster in any great struggle.'[2] The hastily devised arrangements for raising volunteer units were paralleled by the improvisation in staff arrangements and the absence of any carefully conceived plan of campaign. When Sir George White was sent out to command the British forces in Natal in September 1899, he received nothing but the vaguest instructions from the War Office about the part he was expected to perform. 'In no other line of life,' commented the Elgin Commission, 'would an agent be entrusted with a difficult and responsible task without some attempt at precise and careful definition of the object in view, and there seems to be no reason why military duty should be a solitary exception.'[3]

The rejection of the Hartington Commission's recommendation that a General Staff be created, on German lines, to act as the 'brain of the Army',[4] meant that there was no central directing intelligence within the War Office to guide the generals on the spot. Admittedly, an Intelligence Division existed, but it numbered a mere 18 officers, operated on a ludicrously small budget, and had no real *status*, since it was little more than an information bureau.[5] Within the limitations imposed upon it, the branch did good work, estimating with some accuracy the force that the Boers were likely to put into the field; but Wolseley, to whom the in-

[1] Cd. 1789, par. 99.
[2] Lord Milner, *The Nation and the Empire* (1913), p. 189; speech of 25.6.07.
[3] Cd. 1789, par 48.
[4] See above, Ch. I, pp. 23–4.
[5] *Times History*, Vol. II (1902), p. 40. See below, Ch. III, p. 73.

telligence officers were responsible, did not pass on these reports, and it was left to Chamberlain, at the Colonial Office, to draw Lansdowne's attention to their existence.[1] At the highest levels of policy-making, these shrewd assessments of the South African situation were never given proper consideration.

On the field of battle there was the same disregard for the *intellectual* side of warfare that prevailed in Whitehall. Few generals appreciated the importance of staff work or knew how to use the few good staff officers they possessed. Buller showed no particular dismay when General Hunter, who had been nominated as his Chief of Staff, became invested at Ladysmith.[2] Moreover, the staffs were suddenly thrown together on the eve of war without having gone through a prior period of training. As Amery noted, 'Englishmen, who would not dream of sending a crew to Henley Regatta whose members had never rowed together before, were quite content that a general's staff should be hastily improvised at the last moment from officers scraped together from every corner'.[3]

The absence of efficient staff work meant that once battle was joined, the commanding generals more often than not lost effective control over the course of the fighting, and, in certain instances, like Spion Kop, there was a catastrophic break-down in communications. This war was justly dubbed 'an absent-minded war',[4] since offensives were frequently mounted without adequate preparation; yet the notorious lack of maps should have focused attention on the paramount need for thorough reconnaissance. Typical was the attitude of General Methuen, who failed to carry out proper reconnaissance before the Battle of Modder River, because, as he later explained, he 'didn't know the enemy was there'.[5] All the more surprising, then, was the enthusiasm for ambitious night marches, which led Gatacre to disaster at Stormberg and Methuen to an even worse disaster at Magorsfontein.

Displays of high courage were not wanting during the Boer War. For their heroism in the Battle of Colenso five soldiers received the

---

[1] Cd. 1789, par. 45. [2] J. Symons, op. cit., p. 110.
[3] *Times History*, Vol. II (1902), p. 38.
[4] W. E. Cairns, *An Absent-Minded War* (1900).
[5] E. Holt, op. cit., p. 129.

V.C. and eighteen the D.C.M. But the battle was a major defeat for the British. Buller epitomized all that was wrong, as well as much that was admirable, in the army of his day. The courage which had won him a V.C. in the Zulu campaigns, was again in evidence at Colenso. Exposing himself to enemy fire with foolish bravura, as he munched his sandwich lunch, he saw his staff surgeon killed beside him and was himself bruised in the ribs by a fragment of shell. With stiff-upper lipped restraint, he refrained from mentioning his injury to anyone, but the fact that he was wounded, however slightly, may possibly have affected his judgement and caused him to send his panicky telegram to White. In any case, no amount of personal bravery could compensate for Buller's deficiencies in the elementary skills of his profession or his ignorance of the scientific aspects of modern warfare.

If the training and command of the Army showed alarming weaknesses, the poor quality of the equipment and the dangerously low state of the reserves gave equal ground for concern. Here the blame was reasonably enough placed on the over-centralized system of financial control enforced by the Treasury. In February 1899, the able Director General of Ordnance, General Brackenbury, had put in an order to increase the reserve stock of clothing; but his request did not reach the Finance Branch until May; it was then held back for consideration until the autumn; in consequence, when the war began, the reserves consisted largely of red and blue uniforms totally unsuitable for service in South Africa, or indeed anywhere else.[1]

Instances could be multiplied of this sort of obstructionism. The departmental heads at the War Office did not always press strenuously for equipment they knew to be essential to the army's fighting efficiency, aware as they were of the impossibility of obtaining Treasury sanction for increased estimates. And when the War Office itself *did* take up their demands, the Chancellor of the Exchequer and his senior officials could be relied upon to object, and as often as not nothing would be done. When the Under-Secretary at the War Office, George Wyndham, put in an order for reinforcements, Hicks-Beach inquired the reason. 'The

[1] Cd. 1789; par. 178.

defence of the country,' said Wyndham. 'Fiddlesticks,' snapped Beach.[1]

On this occasion, in October 1899, the War Office carried the day, but only because by then hostilities were in progress. In fact, the system of financial control proved so impossible to operate in war-time conditions that much of the purchasing had to be entrusted to officers in the field who had had little or no previous training. Almost overnight unreasonable economizing gave way to gross extravagance and uncontrolled expenditure, which sometimes reached scandalous proportions: for example, in the remounts department. As for the cumbrous administrative system which had been in force before 1899, Amery felt it to be a throw-back to 'the days when kings might use armies for the suppression of public liberties or misappropriate the funds for their mistresses'. Not only was it anachronistic, but in the long run it did not even save money, since the unpreparedness of the army cost the tax-payer more in one year than the most cheese-paring economy could save in a generation.[2]

The 'tyranny' of the Treasury,[3] in setting itself up as a final arbiter of military policy, illustrates the relative decline in the importance of the Cabinet, whose true functions it was partly usurping, and also the failure to co-ordinate general policy with the requirements of the military 'experts'. The struggle for supremacy within the War Office between Lansdowne and Wolseley was but one instance of a wider problem. In 1895 an attempt had been made to overcome the difficulty by setting up a Defence Committee of the Cabinet, which Service Chiefs could be invited to attend; but this body was held in justifiable contempt by the military and did little or nothing to prepare for or prosecute the South African War.[4] This left responsibility in the hands of a

[1] Mackail and Wyndham, op. cit., Vol. I, p. 368; G. Wyndham to brother, 27.10.99.

[2] *Times History*, Vol. II (1902), p. 41.

[3] One should in fairness add that, though the Committee on W.O. organization criticized the over-centralized system of financial control within the army and the referring of very small items of expenditure to the Treasury, they absolved the Treasury from the charge of interference in matters outside its competence (Cd. 580, pars. 41–3; 1901).

[4] See below, Ch. VII, pp. 218–19.

large Cabinet which lacked the means of informing itself adequately before reaching decisions. Therefore, the Boer War had
revealed organizational weaknesses, not only in the army, but in
the whole machinery of government.

In the series of army reforms that were carried through in the
following decade, the 'lessons of the Boer War' played their part in
the formulation of policy—not always with the happiest results.
Certain of the military experiences which might profitably have
been taken to heart were forgotten; for example, the demonstration at Magorsfontein that frontal assaults on barbed-wire protected trenches could only lead to slaughter. But so different was
the kind of fighting that took place against the Boers from what
the British army was to encounter during the First World War,
that military reformers who made a close study of the events of
1899–1902 often became convinced of the merits of measures that
later proved to be irrelevant, if not positively harmful. On the
South African veldt British soldiers had engaged in a mobile,
open war, in which small groups of men were obliged to assume a
large amount of responsibility for their own actions. As the Elgin
Commission saw it, 'the conditions of modern warfare with long-
range arms and smokeless powder involve an immense extension of
lines of battle, diminish the power of control by Commanding
Officers, and increase the degree of individual intelligence required in each individual private, both in attack and defence'.[1]
In short, South Africa did not provide the best possible preparation for the battle fields of northern France and Flanders.

But the 'lessons of the war' had an application to areas of life
other than the military. The type of explanation given above for
the blunders of the army also supplied a cogent critique of Britain's
entire political and administrative arrangements and the liberal
values underpinning them, and could therefore be appealed to by
reformers, of differing interests, who shared a feeling of dissatisfaction at the functioning of their 'model liberal state'. A good
example of the way in which men with an axe to grind could use

---

[1] Cd. 1789, par. 80. L. S. Amery made the same point about the need for
greater mental alertness in the private soldier, for 'the active, conscious discipline of the mind and of the will' in his *The Problem of the Army* (1903), pp.
181–2.

recent events in South Africa to emphasize the urgency of change is provided in this excerpt from a symposium on 'National Education', published in 1901. 'Whether we shout it in the newspapers or confess it in our secret communings,' wrote the editor of this book, 'we have had our "lesson" in this South African war. We have learned, in circumstances which came within measurable distance of being fatal, the folly of blind self-confidence and the paramount wisdom of self-searching and self-preparation.' 'Conquest is good,' he went on, 'but self-conquest is better; and whatever the benefit of our victory over the Boers, the best result of the empire's war in South Africa will be in the nation's resolve to expel from all its departments the habit of "muddling through". And witness after witness may be quoted to show that the Board of Education is the department of departments in this respect. The supreme lesson of our national experience during the past two years is the need of educational reform . . .'[1]

Other prophets preached a different sermon on this same text, so that the 'man in the street' (to use the abstraction so favoured by the Edwardians) must at times have felt bewildered at the quantity and variety of the good advice he was receiving. There was, moreover, a considerable resistance to the very spirit of all this moralizing about 'the lessons of the war'. The continued popularity of Buller, up to the time when the 'surrender telegram' was published and even *after* this disclosure, seemed to suggest the prevalence of an altogether false order of national priorities, which had, at all costs, to be destroyed; that, and not personal vindictiveness, was why Amery was so concerned to discredit Buller and to deprive him of the Aldershot Command, which he had assumed on his return from South Africa.[2] In the next chapter, we will examine the new code of values that was designed to keep the Buller type of person from ever reaching positions of authority in the future.

The need for a complete change in national purpose, upon which men like Amery insisted, seemed, somehow, to be reinforced by the advent of a new century. As one journalist put it: 'we stand upon

[1] L. Magnus (ed.), *National Education: A Symposium* (1901), pp. 21–2.
[2] See L. S. Amery, *My Political Life*, Vol. I (1953), pp. 153–7.

the threshold, not so much of a new century—for that merely signifies a mechanical calculation of time—as of a new era in political and social life. . .'[1] The death of Queen Victoria in January 1901 and the resignation the following year of Lord Salisbury could also be regarded as symbolic breaks with the immediate past.[2] The Queen and her Prime Minister had occupied the centre of national life for so long, that when they departed, there disappeared two of the few stable and reassuring landmarks in a rapidly changing scene. But deeply revered by all sections of the community though the Queen and, to a lesser extent, her Prime Minister had been, many people were not sorry to see them replaced. Sir Henry Birchenough, explaining to Milner the reactions at home to the Queen's death, admitted that 'the new generation which has not quite our feelings [was] longing for a new era'.[3] And the opinion in all parties was that Salisbury had outstayed his welcome by acting in the last years of his premiership as a drag on those younger members of the Cabinet who were more responsive to the challenges of the hour.[4] In private, Salisbury himself admitted that issues were arising which his past experience did not equip him to understand.[5]

This feeling that a new era had dawned was reflected in the popularity of utopias and other imaginative exercises in prophesying the future.[6] It found outlet, also, in a tendency to mock at the values and principles of 'the Victorian period': 'That age of nasty sentiment, sham delicacy and giggles', as Wells dubbed it in 1903.[7] Already the Queen's reign was receding into history and becoming enveloped in myth.

---

[1] *Nineteenth Century*, May 1901, Vol. XLIX, p. 843; Harold E. Gorst, 'The Blunder of Modern Education'.

[2] See Amy Strachey, *St Leo Strachey: His Life and His Paper* (1930), p. 118; Maisie Ward, *The Wilfrid Wards and the Transition*, Vol. I (1934), p. 390.

[3] Milner Papers, Vol. 39, Birchenough to Milner, 27.1.01: f. 7.

[4] See below, Ch. IV, pp. 107–8.

[5] Salisbury to Curzon, 9.8.02, quoted in J. A. S. Grenville, *Lord Salisbury and Foreign Policy* (1964), p. 439.

[6] e.g. H. G. Wells's *Anticipations* (1901) sold out in its first edition, before it could be reprinted (H. G. Wells, *Experiment in Autobiography*, Vol. II, pp, 645–6).
This craze for utopian speculation is amusingly satirized in the opening chapter of G. K. Chesterton's *Napoleon of Notting Hill* (1904).

[7] H. G. Wells, *Mankind in the Making* (1903), p. 68.

Combined with the impact of the Boer War, the arrival of a new century and of a new monarch stimulated the general impatience for change: for scrapping obsolete industrial machinery and methods and, still more, for re-testing antiquated political ideas, so that whatever was irrelevant to twentieth-century circumstances might be speedily discarded.

But only young men, it was claimed, could do this: hence, the agitation in the Press, or, to be precise, in certain Unionist journals, for an infusion of fresh blood into the Cabinet.[1] 'An assemblage of sexagenarians, most of whom have little knowledge or conception of the problems to be solved, who are bound by the shibboleths of a bygone era . . . who are blind to the salient tendencies of modern life . . . is not the kind of body to reorganize the nation.' So fulminated the *National Review* in November 1900.[2] A few years later Bernard Shaw was off on the same tack: 'old men are powerful in England, where reputations are made so slowly that it seems almost impossible for anyone to become a popular hero before the age of seventy, by which time the idol is succumbing to the facile enthusiasms of old age, and losing all touch with contemporary realities.'[3] Surveying the political scene from South Africa, the High Commissioner, Milner, agreed with such indictments. He pinned his hopes upon the younger Ministers and the Under-Secretaries, not on the more famous leaders: 'All these past-60 politicians, *bar Joe* . . . must go,' he wrote in a private letter. 'Go—with Hicks-Beach. He is one of the worst of the worn-out old gang.'[4] This outburst, like Kipling's sneers at the 'eavy-sterned amateur old men'[5] in the army who had bungled their jobs in South Africa, sprang from a desire to see all important departments of national life staffed by earnest young men, aware of the demands of 'National Efficiency'.

[1] e.g. *Daily Mail*, 8.1.00; editorial, 'The Oldest Government on Record'.
[2] *National Review*, Nov. 1900, Vol. XXXVI, p. 331; 'An Englishman': 'Reconstruction or Catastrophe'.
[3] Fabian Tract, no. 116, *Fabianism and the Fiscal Question; An Alternative Policy*, February 1904, p. 5.
[4] Milner Papers, Vol. 28, Milner to Clinton Dawkins, 5.4.02: f. 13.
[5] 'Stellenbosch' in *Rudyard Kipling's Verse*, p. 477.

CHAPTER III

THE IDEOLOGY OF
NATIONAL EFFICIENCY

'NATIONAL EFFICIENCY' was not a homogeneous political ideology. It served as a convenient label under which a complex of beliefs, assumptions and demands could be grouped. At its periphery, the agitation for Efficiency shaded off into programmes and ideologies, like Tariff Reform, Compulsory Military Service and Eugenics, which had the support of some members of the 'efficiency group' but were emphatically rejected by others. And naturally the ideas associated with Efficiency were expressed with varying degrees of sophistication. A fastidious and intelligent politician like Rosebery might wince at the journalistic excesses of an Arnold White; but, as Rosebery himself admitted, he was 'in substantial agreement' with White's opinions.[1]

The German and Japanese Models

If one were to sum up its meaning in a single sentence, one might describe the 'National Efficiency' ideology as an attempt to discredit the habits, beliefs and institutions that put the British at a handicap in their competition with foreigners and to commend instead a social organization that more closely followed the *German* model. It was contended by one journalist that the key to

[1] 'I have been reading . . . *Efficiency and Empire*', wrote Rosebery to White. 'With much of it I am in substantial agreement, and admire the pungency of the epigrams and the vigour of the style. If I might point out blemishes, I should say that the book lacks a sense of proportion, and carries some of its views to an extreme which will repel many who would agree, as I do, with the spirit of it.' (dated 24.10.10: Rosebery Papers, Box 88, Letter Book I, f. 284).

the internal policy of the German Empire was 'this central idea of national efficiency', just as the key to British national life was to be found in 'the idea of personal liberty'.[1]

If this were indeed the case, a dedication to national efficiency clearly brought impressive results, as a cursory glance at Germany's material achievements would have shown. After all, Britain, for all her 'personal liberty', boasted of nothing that could rival Germany's model army, the Bismarckian network of social insurance, or the highly organized educational system, with its organic links with the expanding science-based industries. Many intelligent Englishmen at the turn of the century were convinced that the competitive position of the British would suffer, unless they could emulate the Germans in these areas of life.

But this was not going to be easy. For, or so it seemed, the admirably systematic and orderly habits of conduct of the German people were the outcome of the widespread respect for Science and *Wissenschaft* to be found in that country. They also sprang out of the German belief in the state as a creative and moral agency. Unfortunately, as the 'efficiency group' admitted, in Britain the dominant national attitudes were quite different. Without an intellectual revolution, then, the British would have difficulty in matching the Germans in the practical affairs of life. Indeed, in Haldane's view, Germany's lesson to the modern world was that science and statesmanship were interdependent:

Since the days of ancient Greece there has been no such spectacle of the intimate blending of the life of the Statesman with that of the Thinker. The spirit of the Germany of today is highly concrete and practical. But it is based on foundations of abstract knowledge, and that is why it is well-ordered. For orderliness becomes easy when first principles have been clearly defined. The country that has produced a Kant and a Goethe can later on produce a Bismarck; *Aus dem Lernvolk soll ein Thatvolk werden!* . . .[2]

Haldane was to be cruelly punished during the First World War for the lectures which he had delivered to his fellow countrymen

---

[1] *Round Table*, Nov. 1910, Vol. I, p. 10.
[2] In the preface to J. H. Rose etc, *Germany in the Nineteenth Century*. (Manchester, 1912), pp. vii-viii.

E

over the last two decades, extolling German culture and science. Even during the Edwardian period, to be known as a Germano-phile had its dangers. For from the start of the twentieth century, if not earlier, Britain and Germany had been drifting into mutual estrangement and conflict. In fact, if the comments of the Press give any accurate indication of popular feeling, it would seem that German methods of diplomacy, the tactless behaviour of the Kaiser and the Anglo-German trade rivalry of the 1890s[1] had between them caused large sectors of British society to view German policy with deep distrust, even before the significance of Tirpitz's two naval laws had been properly appreciated. This distrust naturally intensified as the two countries embarked upon a naval arms race. 'Yes, we detest the Germans, we detest them cordially and they make themselves detested by all Europe,' said Harmsworth, the newspaper proprietor, in an interview with *Le Matin* in 1904. 'I will not permit the least thing that might injure France to appear in my paper, but I should not like . . . anything to appear in it that might be agreeable to Germany.'[2]

Yet there is a sense in which this extravagant Germanophobia can be seen as a grudging tribute to German military might and national organization. It is no coincidence that Chamberlain, with his vaguely racialist belief in the inherent superiority of the Anglo-Saxon and Teutonic peoples, should have swung round on the failure of his project for a German Alliance in 1901 to a strongly *anti*-German position. For if Germany was not to work out her destiny in co-operation with Britain, then her very efficiency, it seemed, would sooner or later bring her to challenge the British Empire for world supremacy.

Jumping ahead eight and a half years, we find Sir Edward Goschen, British Ambassador at Berlin, countering the Kaiser's complaints about the abusive anti-German speeches being made in England with the remark: 'he had not noticed abuse so much as endeavour to stimulate people to imitate German activity and go-aheadness, and to make people realize that England must

[1] On the Anglo-German trade rivalry, see R. J. S. Hoffman, *Great Britain and the German Trade Rivalry, 1875–1914* (Philadelphia, 1933).

[2] O. J. Hale, *Germany and the Diplomatic Revolution: A Study in Diplomacy and the Press, 1904–1906* (Philadelphia, 1931), p. 17.

bestir herself if she was not to be left behind. This could scarcely be regarded as abuse of Germany, rather the contrary. . .'[1]

This double response to the German challenge was well expressed by the ebullient editor of the *Observer*, J. L. Garvin, who simultaneously commended the example of his 'beloved Germans' and warned his readers of the inevitability of war against them.[2] Others, who refused to believe that an Anglo-German war was inevitable, nevertheless saw in progress a relentless trade competition between the two nations, of which the outcome might be equally fateful. Whichever of these two views was adopted, Germany assumed the dual role of model and enemy: a state whose threat to vital British interests could be fended off only through an adoption of her own methods and institutions. This was assuming that Britain still had time to catch up with a nation that had, as Wells put it, 'attended sedulously to her collective mind for sixty pregnant years'.[3]

Another paragon of National Efficiency was thought to be *Japan*. In 1902 the Japanese became allies of Britain, and as such they could be admired without the shudder of apprehension that a contemplation of German efficiency so often evoked. Yet the values which the Japanese state embodied seemed to resemble, in many respects, those of Germany. In consequence, Japan's victory over Tsarist Russia in 1904–5 was widely cited as a vindication of organization, dedicated patriotism and scientific method in the supreme test of war. The Webbs were not alone in interpreting the events of the Russo-Japanese War as a triumph for collective regulation and action over the old laisse-faire creed.[4]

For a short time, under the impact of events in the Far East, there was an extravagant cult of Japan in Britain, partly fostered by *The Times*'s military correspondent, Colonel Repington, who popularized 'bushido' (the code of honour of the Samurai) and 'did much to create the legend of a people inspired by a more than medieval sense of knightly chivalry and by a superhuman

---

[1] Sir Edward Goschen to Hardinge, 28.1.10: F.O. 371, Vol. 900.
[2] .eg. *The Observer*'s editorial of 19.12.09.
[3] H. G. Wells, *The New Machiavelli* (1911, Penguin, 1946), p. 257.
[4] Passfield Papers, II 4 c, B. Webb to M. Playne, 2.9.05: f. 111. See also, *National Review*, July 1904, Vol. XLIII, p. 709.

contempt for death'.[1] While *The Times* urged its readers to emulate the self-abnegation practised by their Asiatic allies,[2] comments
can be found in private correspondence reflecting a similar outlook. Thus, Philip Lyttelton Gell wrote to Milner in May 1904: 'I
shall turn Japanese, for they at least can think, and act and be
reticent! . . . I fail to see any Western people in a position to set
the Japs an example in their diplomacy . . . their organization,
their strategy, their virile qualities, their devotion and self-control.
Above all, their national capacity for self-reliant self-sacrifice and
their silence . . .'[3]

One might have expected Conservative imperialists, like Gell,
to approve of the Japanese soldier's fanatical suppression of his
individuality in the service of the state: but at first sight it seems
odd that some soi-disant Socialists and Liberals should have followed suit. Yet H. G. Wells chose to call his ruling elite in *A
Modern Utopia* the 'Samurai'. To Beatrice Webb he laughingly
remarked: 'the chapters on the Samurai will pander to all your
worst instincts.'[4] This suggests that Beatrice Webb had already
developed that infatuation with the social and political organization of Japan, which in later years was to excite the mild ridicule of
her friends.[5] Rosebery, too, joined in the chorus of admiration,
writing a preface to a book significantly entitled, *Great Japan: A
Study of National Efficiency*, in which he praised the Japanese highly
for their patriotism, their thoroughness and their rejection of the
party system.[6]

The 'efficiency group' especially admired the Japanese for
their ascetic way of life and their puritanical ethic. H. G. Wells
celebrated these values in his portrayal of the 'Samurai', a self-
recruiting caste, who voluntarily submitted to a harsh code of
discipline, abstaining, for example, from regular sexual intercourse.[7] Admittedly, Wells hardly conducted his own life by these

---

[1] L. S. Amery, *My Political Life*, Vol. I (1953), p. 218.
[2] *The Times*, 12.2.05.
[3] Milner Papers, Vol. 41, P. Lyttelton Gell to Milner, 6.5.04: f. 85.
[4] B. Webb, *Our Partnership* (1948), p. 305; 17.4.05.
[5] e.g. Hugh Dalton, *Call Back Yesterday* (1953), p. 131; 11.2.22.
[6] Alfred Stead, *Great Japan: A Study of National Efficiency* (1905), pp. vii–xiii.
[7] They had to sleep alone at least four nights out of five: H. G. Wells, *A
Modern Utopia* (1905, Thomas Nelson, n.d.), p. 286.

admirable principles. In a private letter to Graham Wallas he even ventured the opinion that 'a man or woman ought to have sexual intercourse. Few people are mentally, or morally or physically in health without it. For anyone there is a minimum and maximum between which lies complete efficiency. Find out your equation, say I, and then keep efficient . . .'[1] Beatrice Webb, who would have been shocked to the core by this letter, preferred to keep mentally, morally and physically efficient by undergoing a course of dieting so rigorous that at times it amounted to fasting. She even disapproved of Haldane, for indulging his taste for good food and wine, though Haldane drove himself to the limits of his endurance and got through a punishing amount of public work. For Haldane, in his own way, also attached great importance to earnestness and self-denial; and, again, the Japanese provided him with an example of his ideal. On one occasion, he urged an undergraduate audience to pay less attention to sport, but instead to take inspiration from the fierce disciplinarianism that had led the Japanese army to victory at the Battle of Mukden.[2]

Far from rejecting the values of an autocratic, military state, the Fabian leaders, Rosebery and Haldane were thus actually attracted by the streak of silent, calculating ruthlessness they detected in the Japanese national character. This cult of Japan shows, in fact, how far the 'efficiency group' was prepared to go in its contempt for the traditions of liberal humanitarianism. But here was merely one reflection of a powerful preoccupation, that finds many different expressions in their writings. Wells had predicted in *Anticipations*, in tones of something like complacency, that the ruling elite of the future would 'have little pity and less benevolence'.[3] The rather self-conscious brutality of such utterances must be seen as a reaction against the sentimental kind of liberal idealism which seemed to be preventing the British people from following the German and Japanese example and dedicating themselves to a purposeful pursuit of national objectives.

'It is indefiniteness of aim which is at the root of our troubles,'

---

[1] Wallas Papers, Box 2, Wells to Graham Wallas, 19.9.02.
[2] R. B. Haldane, *Universities and National Life* (1911, 2d. ed.), pp. 87–8; Edinburgh University Rectorial Address, 10.1.07.
[3] H. G. Wells, *Anticipations* (1901, Chapman & Hall ed., 1902), p. 299.

wrote Milner in 1913. 'At present it is really very difficult to say what we are driving at with all this immense expenditure of money and energy, or why, having gone so far as we do go, we suddenly stop. Up to a point everything is carefully regulated, then, at the most critical moment, all the rest is left to chance'.[1] The disasters into which the British army had drifted on the South African Veldt fourteen years earlier seemed in Milner's eyes only too likely to be repeated in the near future, unless every aspect of national life was reorganized according to some clearly formulated *plan*. Piecemeal reform, the gradual removal of particular injustices and governmental weaknesses, no longer sufficed.

The Improvement of the National Physique

It might be thought that this insistence on a Germanic policy of 'Thorough' would have offered little encouragement to humanitarians, anxious to improve the lot of their deprived fellow citizens. In fact, however, the concern with organization, with eliminating all elements of waste, brought a new urgency to the work of social reform. The Christian virtue of compassion was perhaps a little out of fashion, but there were other approaches that could be adopted to the problems of human distress. In the view of the 'efficiency group', men and women formed the basic raw material out of which national greatness was constructed: hence, they argued, the statesman had a duty to see that these priceless resources were not squandered through indifference and slackness.

That much needed to be done was dramatically highlighted by the physical unfitness of the slum denizens of the big cities who had come forward for recruitment during the Boer War; in Manchester, to give a frequently cited example, 8,000 out of 11,000 would-be volunteers had had to be turned away and of the remainder 2,000 were declared fit only for the militia.[2] No wonder fears were abroad about the possibility of the physical stock of the nation degenerating. It was in vain that the inter-departmental committee

[1] Lord Milner, *The Nation and the Empire* (1913), p. xliii.
[2] See *Nineteenth Century*, May 1903, Vol. LIII, p. 802; George F. Shee, 'The Deterioration in the National Physique'. For the uses made by the Webbs of this sort of evidence: Sidney and Beatrice Webb, *Industrial Democracy* (1919 ed.), p. liv (from the introduction to the 1902 edition).

set up to investigate such alarming allegations reported that the health and physique of army recruits gave no accurate reflection of the physical state of the population as a whole, where standards were probably being slowly but steadily raised.[1] Journalists and politicians continued to discuss the problem of 'physical deterioration' in language which often bordered on panic.

This concern for the physical efficiency of the British population became intermingled with the problem of the declining birth rate. The evidence showed that it was among the professional and upper middle classes that birth control was most practised and that the further down the social scale one went the fewer were the restraints on reproduction.[2] Thus, on the (fallacious) assumption that the working classes were made up of people of weak physique and low intelligence, it logically followed that Britain was breeding a race of degenerates. In this mood of hysteria, the Eugenic Movement made considerable headway and catch-phrases, like 'the sterilization of the unfit', found their way into general political controversy.

In 1905 Cecil Chesterton, then a Fabian Socialist with Tory leanings (after the manner of Bernard Shaw), was writing: 'in the last resort, all progress, all empire, all efficiency, depends upon the kind of race we breed. If we are breeding the people badly neither the most perfect constitution nor the most skilful diplomacy will save us from shipwreck.'[3] As it happened, most of the Fabian leaders were at one time attracted to eugenics.[4] But naturally they would have nothing to do with the class-biased view that poverty resulted from some inherited physical or moral failing, as

[1] *Report of the Inter-Departmental Committee on Physical Deterioration*, 1904; Cd. 2175; Amended Reference.

[2] Arthur Newsholme, *The Declining Birth-Rate: Its National and International Significance* (1911, 'New Tracts for the Times' Series).

[3] Cecil Chesterton, *Gladstonian Ghosts* (1905?), p. 195.

[4] After seeing *Man and Superman*, in which Shaw plays with the idea of eugenics, Beatrice Webb wrote, '*We* cannot touch the subject of human breeding—it is not ripe for the mere industry of induction, and yet I realise that it is the most important of all questions, this breeding of the right sort of man. . .' (B. Webb, *Our Partnership* (1948), p. 257; 16.1.03). Shaw and Wells took a keen and not unsympathetic interest in Francis Galton's original exposition of the principles of eugenics to the Sociological Society in 1904 (*Sociological Papers*, Vol. I (1904), pp. 58–60, 74–5).

many eugenists were prepared to assert.[1] That poverty sometimes *caused* degeneracy the Fabians did not deny; but the remedy for that lay in a policy of social reform, just as the solution to the problem of the differential birth-rate was 'to alter the balance of considerations in favour of the child-bearing family' by the 'endowment of motherhood'—in other words, by family allowances.[2] As H. G. Wells argued: 'people rear children for the State and the future; if they do that well they do the whole world a service, and deserve payment just as much as if they built a bridge or raised a crop of wheat.'[3] The country which wanted a larger number of babies born to healthy working-class families, wrote the Webbs, should be prepared to pay 'a small part of the cost of production'.[4]

From the tone of these remarks one can appreciate the difference between the standpoint of the advocate of efficiency and that of the humanitarian social reformer, moved by pity, or that of the 'labour representative' demanding justice for 'his class'. Proud of his detached, unemotional and 'scientific' approach to social problems, such a person tended to despise other radical and socialist agitators for being swayed by sectional and class resentments that made them incapable of seeing society as a totality. In the interests of efficiency he wanted remedial action that avoided setting class against class and that did not threaten the rights of property or carry with it the risk of social turmoil; he wanted a policy imperial in its scope which would strengthen the nation as a unit in its competition with rival states. Appealing to the self-interest of his audience, a predominantly Conservative one, Milner could claim:

[1] Not all eugenists by any means discounted the importance of environmental factors or were hostile to social reform. But their arguments were used to the full by those who wanted to find a stick with which to beat the Liberal Government in the years after 1905; see *Fortnightly Review*, August 1909. Vol. 86, pp. 207–22; E. B. Iwan-Muller, *The Cult of the Unfit*.

[2] Sidney Webb, *The Decline in the Birth-Rate* (1907), Fabian Tract, no. 131, pp. 17–19.

[3] *Independent Review*, Nov. 1906, Vol. XI, p. 172; H. G. Wells, *Modern Socialism and the Family*. But neither in this article nor elsewhere did Wells make it clear whether he proposed to endow *unmarried* mothers (see H. G. Wells, *Experiment in Autobiography* (1934), Vol. II, pp. 478–9). Thus, the question of family allowances and free infant welfare services became confused with the emotional issue of 'free love'.

[4] Sidney and Beatrice Webb, *The Prevention of Destitution* (1911), p. 318.

'the attempt to raise the well-being and efficiency of the more
backward of our people . . . is not philanthropy: it is business'.[1]

The Fabians had much more drastic ideas than Milner about
how far social reform should go, and they did not share the
tenderness of many of the 'efficiency group' towards property
rights. Yet throughout the Edwardian period and up to 1911 or so,
the Webbs and Shaw had to all intents and purposes dropped their
former commitment to socialism, striving instead for the much
more limited objectives contained in the National Efficiency ideology. It was not simply on tactical grounds that Shaw justified a
legal minimum wage by the argument that the country would as a
result 'reap a much handsomer (saving) in national soundness and
reduced disease bills, crime bills, and inefficiency bills (the heaviest
of the three) . . .';[2] this represented his considered opinion on
social policy. But, of course, the transfer of wealth, power and social
esteem from the owners of capital to the working classes has
almost been lost sight of in the pamphlet from which this quotation
has been taken.

So, too, with the article in which Sidney Webb called for 'the
formulation and rigid enforcement in all spheres of social activity,
of a National Minimum below which the individual, whether he
likes it or not, cannot, in the interests of the well-being of the
whole, ever be allowed to fall'. The sick, the underpaid and the
ill-educated had to be taken in hand by the community, not just
for their own good, but equally for the advantage of the efficient
members of society. Far from such state interference leading
inexorably to Socialism, Webb argued, it merely provided the
'necessary basis of society', the foundation of national survival and
prosperity.[3]

This philosophy, which was to inspire the Webb's Poor Law
Minority Report, was shared by Morant. In a speech at the
annual dinner of the Medical Officers of Health in 1909. Morant
explained how, in the same way that compulsory education
had now become accepted as a social necessity, so the state was

---

[1] Lord Milner; op. cit., p. 161; speech at Wolverhampton, 17.12.06.

[2] G. B. Shaw (ed.), *Fabianism and the Empire* (1900), p. 65.

[3] *Contemporary Review*, June 1908, Vol. XCIII, pp. 665–7; S. Webb, *The Necessary Basis of Society*.

beginning to recognize its obligation to prevent the outbreak of sickness, where practicable, by sweeping measures of public health. This duty could not be shirked, he said, since the country which 'neglected the health of the race' would 'lose in the racial competition of the world'.[1]

No doubt Morant's audience received these remarks favourably. Many M.O.H.s, we know, warmly embraced the Poor Law Minority Report, attracted, presumably, by its emphasis on the need to apply the techniques of preventive medicine to new areas of social experience.[2] Certainly, Arthur Newsholme, the Chief Medical Inspector at the Local Government Board, was only too eager to accept such additional responsibilities on behalf of his profession. 'With wider and more exact knowledge of hygiene,' he wrote, 'it is being increasingly realized that the whole range of the physical, mental, and to a large extent of the moral life of mankind may be brought within the range of preventive medicine; and that as medical knowledge grows the number of diseases that can be regarded as preventable will increase, and public administration will extend beyond its present limits.' 'Disease is always more expensive than measures for its prevention,' Newsholme explained; or, to put it another way, prevention would always be cheaper than a policy of unconditional doles which relieved the symptoms of illness and destitution without getting at their root cause.[3] How, then, could any government *afford* the luxury of laissez-faire principles that allowed disease to advance unchecked?

Although it would be misleading to place a Quaker philanthropist and humanitarian reformer, like Seebohm Rowntree, within the movement for greater National Efficiency, Rowntree did, in fact, base much of his analysis and argument on these 'practical' considerations, when he came to write his famous survey of York, *Poverty: A Study of Town Life*, first published in 1901. The novel aspect of this social survey was its attempt to relate social policy to the science of nutrition. Himself an employer

---

[1] *Public Health*, Nov. 1909, Vol. XXIII, p. 67.
[2] See below, Ch. VII, pp. 243–4.
[3] *Public Health*, Aug. 1909, Vol. XXII, pp. 403–14; Arthur Newsholme, 'Some Conditions of Social Efficiency in Relation to Local Public Administration'.

of labour, Rowntree wanted to find out 'the amount of calories, proteins and fat necessary to maintain persons in a state of physical efficiency'. Actually, the existence of vitamins was only discovered on the eve of the First World War, so Rowntree could not benefit as much as he had hoped from the assistance of the dietician. Nevertheless, he felt confident enough to inform his readers that 'the labouring class receive upon the average about 25 per cent less food than has been proved by scientific experts to be necessary for the maintenance of physical efficiency': a fact to ponder upon in view of 'the stress and keenness of international competition' and the widespread concern over 'the conditions of commercial success'.[1] This line of argument was pursued by W. T. Stead, who reviewed *Poverty* under the title, 'How The Other Half Lives: The Way We Undermine Our National Efficiency'.[2]

The scare of racial deterioration had, as we have seen, grown up largely as a result of the exposure of the poor physique of recruits during the Boer War, and great emphasis was always placed upon the dangers to the State of having to rely for its soldiers upon an anaemic slum population. It comes as no surprise, therefore, to find many people looking to a military solution of a problem, which had such grave military implications.

Those who called for universal military training or conscription almost invariably dwelt on the physical health argument: taking the poor working-class lads from the big cities and giving them regular good food, exercise and wholesome country air would quickly improve their health. It was easy to show statistically that army recruits developed in strength and girth after even a few weeks of service life. In addition to this, Germany and other continental countries were cited to show how beneficial military training was in inculcating habits of neatness, order and discipline and thereby increasing the efficiency of the national labour force.[3] A friend and political intimate of Milner's, Sir Henry Birchenough, put a familiar case tersely when he wrote: 'Discipline

[1] S. Rowntree, *Poverty: A Study of Town Life* (1901: 1910 ed.), pp. 303, 261. See also A. Briggs, *Social Thought and Social Action: A Study of the Work of Seebohm Rowntree, 1871–1954* (1961), pp. 32–3.

[2] *Review of Reviews*, Dec. 1901, Vol. XXIV, pp. 642–5.

[3] e.g. *Nineteenth Century*, Oct. 1904, Vol. LVI, p. 620; J. L. Bashford, 'The German Army System and How it Works'.

and physical fitness lie at the very root of national efficiency, and it is because we see in universal compulsory military training one of the main routes which lead to national efficiency that we should continue to advocate it, even if our military requirements were less pressing than they are.'[1]

With anything at all resembling conscription ruled out as politically unacceptable, many advocates of efficiency tried to devise ways of combining the advantages of a military training with a regard for Britain's traditions of liberalism. For example, the Physical Deterioration Committee made an ingenious, but vain, plea for compulsory drill and physical exercises in continuation classes, from which exemption would be given to members of clubs and cadet forces which submitted to inspection and conformed to certain specifications.[2] Rejecting compulsory military service, on political and technical grounds alike, Haldane, when he became War Secretary, could at least agree with the National Service League on the importance of providing the youth of the nation with physical training that would foster 'self-restraint and co-operation in a common endeavour which is the outcome of discipline.'[3] To accomplish this desirable end was Haldane's purpose when he organized the Officers Training Corps and also when he encouraged Baden-Powell to leave the army and launch the Boy Scouts Movement. 'I feel,' he told Baden-Powell, 'that this organization of yours has so important a bearing upon the future that probably the greatest service you can render to the country is to devote yourself to it.'[4] For in its way the Scout Movement was yet one more response to the cry that British youth needed 'organizing', and as such it met with the approval of Wells, who wrote in 1911: 'I liked the Boy Scout, and I find it difficult to express how much it mattered to me, with my growing bias in favour of deliberate national training, that Liberalism hadn't

[1] ibid., July 1904, Vol. LVI, p. 22; H. Birchenough, 'Compulsory Education and Compulsory Military Training'.

[2] Cd. 2175 (1904), par. 380.

[3] In the preface to Ian Hamilton, *Compulsory Service* (1910), p. 39.

[4] William Hillcourt and Lady Baden-Powell, *Baden-Powell* (1964), p. 302. Baden-Powell had commanded the Northumbrian Division of the Territorial Army between 1908 and 1910 and had seen much of Haldane in this connection.

been able to produce, and had indeed never attempted to produce, anything of this kind.'[1]

A disciplined population could overcome any kind of material handicap. As Shadwell wrote in his comparative study of the industrial efficiency of Germany, America and Britain: 'The habits of the people! There lies the real reason why the German working classes with lower wages, longer hours and higher costs of living yet maintain a superior standard of physique' to their British counterparts.[2] But if, as most observers agreed, the German streets were almost free of those undersized, ill-developed, sickly-looking people who thronged in every large British town,[3] credit for this had to be given, not only to the German system of military service, but also to the Social Insurance Scheme and ultimately to the administrative system which made its operation possible. A study of this impressive scheme convinced Sir John Gorst of 'how much more efficient the Governments of Germany, central and local, (were) in promoting the welfare of the people than our own'.[4] T. C. Horsfall reached the same conclusion in his comparison of housing and 'town planning' in the two countries.[5] 'The Germans are governed by skilled experts: we by ill-informed amateurs,' wrote Gorst.[6] This indictment takes us to the heart of the case for National Efficiency: the demand for improvements in Britain's whole machinery of government.

The Machinery of Government

In fact, the Edwardian decade was a period when Britain's administrative arrangements, at local, central and imperial level, were causing grave and widespread dissatisfaction. Of late, new responsibilities had been forced upon the public authorities, which their administrative structures seemed unable to accommodate. Local government, in particular, still presented a picture of con-

---

[1] H. G. Wells, *The New Machiavelli* (1911; Penguin ed. 1946), pp. 245–6.
[2] Arthur Shadwell, *Industrial Efficiency: A Comparative Study of Industrial Life in England, Germany and America* (1906), Vol. II, pp. 250–1.
[3] e.g. T. C. Horsfall, *The Example of Germany: The Improvement of the Dwellings and Surroundings of the People* (Manchester, 1904), pp. 161–2.
[4] W. T. Stead (ed.), *Coming Men on Coming Questions* (1905?), p. 314.
[5] T. C. Horsfall, op. cit., *passim*.   [6] W. T. Stead (ed.), op. cit., p. 314.

siderable confusion at the start of the century. Even though the
country had by this time been covered with a network of popularly
elected county, borough, urban and rural district councils, 643
Poor Law Boards and some 2,500 School Boards, each with its
own administrative boundaries and rating powers, were operating
independently of the 133 county and county borough councils
which covered the same area of England and Wales. Too small to
carry out their responsibilities efficiently, except in the big cities,
these *ad hoc* bodies stood in the way of administrative uniformity
and led to duplication of effort and wasteful rivalries. So it was
natural for the 'efficiency group' to wish to sweep away the *ad hoc*
authority as an anachronism and unite all public services under the
control of the county and county borough councils, in order that
they could be properly co-ordinated.

Educationalists might rejoice that at last there was 'a likelihood
that a theory of local government (would) be abandoned that ha(d)
long since become antiquated'. '*Ad hoc* election,' argued Laurie
Magnus, 'is an instance of what the Germans expressively call an
überwundener Standpunkt; it is a sign of an "historical accident", in
the phrase of the Fabian tract . . .'[1] Not all the Fabians agreed with
these sentiments. It was in vain that Shaw tried to detach Graham
Wallas from what he castigated as 'that foolish democratic mistake, the adhocious School Board'.[2] But most of the 'efficiency
group' were agreed that 'in the face of the imperative demand of
modern times for simplicity of organisation and economy of
effort', the future of local government lay with the county councils
and the municipalities.[3]

Yet even warm believers in 'municipalization', like the Webbs,
were soon wondering whether these units of local government did
not belong to a receding social and economic order. Such doubts
increased after Wells had read them his paper on 'Scientific
Administrative Areas'. The provision of gas, electricity, water and
public transport, Wells demonstrated, could only be efficiently
organized on a larger scale. Traditional local boundaries had

[1] L. Magnus (ed.), *National Education: A Symposium* (1901), p. 14. From the
editor's introductory chapter.
[2] Wallas Papers, Folder 9a; Shaw to Wallas, 24.8.99.
[3] Fabian Ware, *Educational Reform* (1900), pp. 118–19.

anyhow lost most of their meaning, he argued; faster methods of locomotion were 'delocalizing' the population, so that people often lived in one administrative area, worked in another, and had their children educated in yet a third. Wells suggested that a more functional arrangement of local government areas would be one based upon the available means of transport or perhaps one which followed the course of natural watersheds.[1]

An argument about the proper allocation of functions between different institutions was also in full spate at central level. The structure of government in the nineteenth century had been largely departmental, co-ordinated through the Cabinet and supervised by the Treasury. But the government had of late acquired responsibility for new areas of policy, which cut across existing divisions between Ministries: for example, Imperial Defence. And the Cabinet, operating as it did without a formal agenda or secretariat, could no longer co-ordinate departmental work at all adequately.

Fleet Street tended to lay the blame for such shortcomings on the excessive size of the contemporary Cabinet. (Salisbury's Cabinet at the end of 1900 contained twenty ministers, as compared with the fifteen of Palmerston's day). Professing great anger at this state of affairs, many people called instead for a small executive council, ignoring the Parliamentary and party pressures that made for large Cabinets, or dismissing this consideration as of no importance. There were those who thought it feasible or desirable for Britain to be governed by the centralized, authoritarian methods that had proved their worth in India and the dependencies. A more practical suggestion came from people who accepted the inevitability of large Cabinets, but wanted more duties to be delegated to Cabinet Committees, to which civil servants and other appropriate 'experts' could be co-opted. Haldane, for one, favoured such an arrangement, which also provided a remedy to another organizational weakness disclosed by the Boer War: the poor liaison between ministers and their permanent advisers.[2]

---

[1] Wells' paper is printed in his *Mankind in the Making* (1903; Chapman and Hall ed. 1904), pp. 399–417. This issue is discussed in A. M. McBriar, *Fabian Socialism and English Politics, 1884–1918* (Cambridge, 1962), pp. 232–3.

[2] See above, Ch. II, pp. 46–7.

A strong argument in favour of strengthening the Cabinet in any of these ways was that this would curb the power exercised by that bug-bear of the 'efficiency group', the Treasury. The disparaging tone adopted towards the Treasury was itself part of a more general reaction against 'Gladstonianism' in all its forms: a reaction so violent that it moved Lord Salisbury himself to complain in Parliament about the harm produced by 'the exaggerated control of the Treasury', which took away 'the freedom and (diminished) the initiative of the respective departments' and reduced them to 'immobility'.[1] Naturally, no-one denied the importance of economy, but as Lyttelton Gell argued: '*Nothing is so cheap as efficiency: nothing is so inefficient as cheapness.* Substitute for the Treasury control which seeks *cheapness* the Administrative control which seeks *efficiency*, and the nation will be the gainer, even pecuniarily.'[2]

Another step in the direction of efficiency would be a 'grading' of the issues which came before Parliament and the Cabinet, so that broad problems of imperial policy would not become intermixed with 'parish pump' disputes.[3] Essentially, this had been the justification advanced in favour of Federal Home Rule since the time of Isaac Butt; and it was also an idea with which the Imperial Federation League had once made great play. Anything which suggested a way of more closely integrating the component parts of the Empire had an additional appeal to the advocate of efficiency, preoccupied as he was with threats to British security. From Seeley he had learned that the technological developments which made possible larger political units would soon reduce to second-rate status those European nations which did not expand their scale.[4] In economic and military rivalry, as Chamberlain forcefully argued, victory would go to the big battalions;[5] and

[1] Hansard, 4th Series, Vol. 78, cols. 239–40; 1.2.00. This statement was made in the course of denying that an earlier speech of his (ibid., col. 32: 30.1.00) reflected personally on the Chancellor of the Exchequer and his officials.

[2] *Nineteenth Century*, July 1900, Vol. XLVIII, p. 50; P. Lyttelton Gell, 'Administrative Reform in the Public Service'.

[3] C. Headlam (ed.), *The Milner Papers: South Africa, 1899–1905* (1933), Vol. II, p. 448. Milner to Lady Edward Cecil, 16.5.03.

[4] J. R. Seeley, *The Expansion of England* (1883), pp. 86–9.

[5] See speech of Chamberlain at the Guildhall, 19.1.04: *The Times*, 20.1.04.

England could only avoid decline by mobilizing the vast material and manpower resources of the Empire. Yet the literature of national efficiency shows that large-scale political units also found favour for less tangible reasons, such as the belief that they lifted their subjects out of a narrow parochialism into a loftier conception of the duties of citizenship.[1] In self-defence traditional liberals fell back upon an even more exaggerated cult of 'littleness' in international affairs.[2]

Innumerable were the projects for creating a 'Greater Britain' that would bring together people of British stock scattered throughout the globe. But they all foundered ultimately upon the rock of Colonial Nationalism. Chamberlain's failure to convert the Colonial Premiers in 1902 to his Imperial Council Scheme should have shown the impracticability of even an *advisory* authority to coordinate the policies of states otherwise free and self-governing. And Imperial Federation itself stood no chance at all of being seriously entertained. Yet Milner and the 'Round Table' group, not content with the modest advances being made in the sphere of Imperial Defence, were as late as the 1910–14 period still hoping to weld the British Empire into a single unit of power. If, so ran their reasoning, Bismarck and Alexander Hamilton had overcome particularist interests and created new nations out of previously warring elements, was it too much to hope that a British 'statesman' of comparable ability might come forward to save the Empire from disintegration? Such analogies, of course, were misleading in the extreme, and the self-delusion practiced by the 'Round Table' group shows how the concern for efficiency sometimes led to an undue reliance upon machinery and organization, to the neglect of more important factors.

[1] e.g. 'Political corruption, place-hunting, and party intrigue have their natural home in small communities, where attention is concentrated upon local interests. Great public causes call into being the intellectual and moral potentialities of a people' (*The Round Table*, June 1913, Vol. 11, p. 497).

[2] Much of the sentimental support given to the Boer Republics during the South African War sprang from this sort of feeling. See also: George Moore, *Hail and Farewell: Salve* (1912), p. 58. G. K. Chesterton, *What's Wrong With The World* (1910), p. 34.

F

Education

Political organization, well contrived and adapted to its purpose, may do much to offset the failings of individual human beings. It was on that score that the 'efficiency group' favoured the attachment of a secretariat to the Committee of Imperial Defence, in order to safeguard the national interest against the possibility that a Prime Minister who was incompetent to deal with defence problems might come to power. But the subsequent history of this body shows only too clearly that political machinery can be stultified by the incapacity or lethargy of those who operate it.[1]   In the last resort, as Rosebery observed, national efficiency depended upon a supply of 'first-rate' men, equal to the task of governing the mightiest empire in the world.[2] In the opinion of Professor Armstrong, the one raw material which Britain had in abundance was 'brains', and 'the manufacture of brains into a highly finished and efficient product' ought to be a task engaging the full energies of the community.[3]

But this was just what the British seemed to be neglecting to do. It was widely conceded that brains and science had replaced swords and sinews in the fierce relentless struggle for national survival and supremacy, with the consequence that the country most imbued with the scientific spirit would triumph every time over rivals with inferior intellectual equipment, as the Japanese had triumphed over the Russians. But despite this warning of the imperative importance of specialized training in all departments of life, the British seemed content to rely upon 'rule of thumb' methods and 'muddling through'.

Forced back again and again on courageous improvisation through inadequate preparation and forethought, the British army had paid the appalling price of 'Black Week'. The moral, as one contemporary pamphleteer put it, was that courage, though still a necessary attribute in the soldier, led, unless scientifically directed, more certainly to loss of life than to success.[4] The Elgin Commission

[1] See below, Ch. VII, p. 231.

[2] Lord Rosebery, *Miscellanies* (1921), Vol. II, p. 245; Glasgow University Rectorial Address, 16.11.00.

[3] *Quarterly Review*, Oct. 1903, Vol. 198, p. 464; Henry E. Armstrong, 'The Reign of the Engineer'.

[4] W. E. Cairns, *An Absent-Minded War* (1900), p. 4.

into the South African War substantiated such complaints; in 1899, it reported, the full strength of the Army Intelligence Department had been 18 officers, a total which had risen to only 20 by October 1902.[1] Arnold-Forster noted that the two Intelligence Departments in Britain together employed a mere forty-one men, whereas the Intelligence Department of the German Army alone numbered 250.[2] Moreover, on the eve of the Boer War a paltry 0.22 per cent of the army estimates was being spent on military education proper;[3] and this education was found, on investigation, to be in a most unsatisfactory state.

On the other hand, the blunders of the British army in South Africa seemed to be the consequence, not merely of the defective system of *military* education, but to reflect deficiencies in the mental training of a people incapable of reasoning, arguing or applying the 'scientific method' to the practical problems of life. For the standards of military education could merely follow the standards that ran through the whole of public education; they could sink below the general level, but never rise above it.[4] Witness after witness told the Elgin Commission of the difficulty of training British private soldiers, whose mental qualifications were not up to the general run of soldiers coming from countries where a higher premium was put on education.[5]

If this by itself were not enough to jolt politicians into reforming Britain's ramshackle system of public education, there was the constant harping on the amateurishness that reigned in office and factory. From 1885 onwards the newspapers were full of gloomy

---

[1] *Elgin Commission Report*, (1903), Cd. 1789; par. 257.

[2] Cabinet Memorandum of 20.10.02: Cab. 37/63/145. In a chapter of his *The Problem of the Army*, L. S. Amery described, under the heading of 'Brain Starvation', the Intelligence Division: Section 1.2 (D), which included in its scope the whole of Asia, except Turkey and French Indo-China, plus Russia. Amery calculated that to do its work adequately, this division would have required 100 officers in London, whereas its actual strength was only 4 (L. S. Amery, *The Problem of the Army* (1903), pp. 146–9).

[3] *Military Education Committee Report* (1902); Cd. 982: par. 6.

[4] See *Nineteenth Century*, Dec. 1901, Vol. L, p. 900; Charles Copland Perry, 'Our Undisciplined Brains—The War-Test'. Also Professor Henry Armstrong's Address to the Educational Science Section of the British Association, 1902; printed in his *The Teaching of Scientific Method*. (1903, 2nd ed., 1925), p. 56.

[5] *Elgin Commission Report*, par. 77.

talk about Britain's stagnating exports, lost markets and technological obsolescence, contrasted with Germany's superiority in business methods, salesmanship and industrial research.[1] By the turn of the century, Britain probably compared not unfavourably with other countries in the lower and intermediate grades of technical instruction, but she had nothing equivalent to the German Technical High Schools, in which technology was pursued at a university level.[2]

This, thought the advocate of efficiency, was something which had to be remedied, if Britain were not to lose, first her industrial supremacy, then the bulk of her foreign trade, and finally sink exhausted to the rank of an impoverished third-rate power. 'The expenditure cannot but be great,' Haldane admitted, 'but it will be salvage expenditure and cannot be stinted, however desirable economy in other directions may be. For it goes to nothing short of the sources which our people have to look to for the future of that commerce which is their life-blood as a nation.'[3] The scientist, Sir Norman Lockyer, employing an analogy much used at the time, declared to the British Association in 1903 that 'our Universities must become as much the insurers of the future progress as battleships are the insurers of the present power of States.'[4]

This type of propaganda certainly made an impression. *The Times* could write in October 1902 that it had become 'a sort of mark of intelligence' to join in the 'fashionable cry' about the nations' backwardness in technical education.[5] Even members of the Royal Family began to make speeches on the subject:[6] infallible proof that this viewpoint had attained the status of a platitude. However, the enthusiasm for expanding teaching facili-

[1] See R. J. S. Hoffman, op. cit., especially Chapters III and VI.
[2] *Report of the Departmental Committee on the Royal College of Science* (1906), Cd. 2872, par. 27.
[3] R. B. Haldane, *Education and Empire* (1902), p. 38.
[4] Sir Norman Lockyer, *Education and National Progress* (1906), pp. 189–90. A slightly different version of the same idea appears in Michael Sadler's slogan, 'The very existence of the Empire depends on sea-power and school-power' (*Unrest in Secondary Education in Germany and Elsewhere: Special Reports on Educational Subjects*, Vol. 9, 1902, Cd. 836, p. 163).
[5] *The Times*, 16.10.02.
[6] e.g. the Prince of Wales' speech on opening the new National Physical Laboratory buildings (*The Times*, 20.3.02).

ties in technology, theoretical science and higher commercial studies coincided with a reaction inside the educational world against technical instruction of a narrowly utilitarian kind and against premature specialization in the sciences in the secondary and higher grade schools. Thus, while reformers worked to bring the universities into closer relation with industry and commerce, there was a counter-movement in the schools away from a technical and vocational education in favour of a more literary syllabus: a trend encouraged by Morant in his famous Secondary School Regulation of 1904.[1]

Amongst the 'efficiency group', there were those like Shaw who called for a school course which would be 'as obviously useful and helpful as good clothing and fresh air'.[2] And the classics-centred education of the public schools came in for heavy criticism, especially from scientists.[3] Yet it was widely felt that a general secondary education of the grammar-school type provided the best grounding for an advanced and specialized training in science and technology. Even the staff at the higher technical institutions sometimes complained that their students lacked the general educational attainments to take full advantage of their courses.[4]

On the other hand, a practical and utilitarian approach seemed to be appropriate at the level of *higher* education. In Rosebery's view, the newly founded universities and university colleges possessed definite advantages over Oxford and Cambridge; 'these practical universities,' he said, 'are the universities of the future, for the average man, who has to work for his livelihood, cannot superadd the learning of the dead to the educational requirements of his life and his profession'.[5] The assumption embedded in Rosebery's remarks was made explicit by Sidney Webb, when he drew a sharp line between Culture, which was 'the all-round cultivation of the individual mind, the continuous appreciation of the finest literature that has been written, the balanced judgement due to a scholarly criticism of the past achievements of

[1] Olive Banks, *Parity and Prestige in English Secondary Education* (1955), Ch. 3.
[2] G. B. Shaw (ed.), *Fabianism and the Empire* (1900), p. 90.
[3] *e.g.* Oliver Lodge, 'School Reform' in *Contemporary Review*, Feb. 1904, Vol. LXXXV, pp. 153–64. Also, the copious writings of Professor Henry Armstrong.
[4] See O. Banks, op. cit., p. 35.
[5] Lord Rosebery, *Miscellanies* (1921), Vol. II, p. 256.

mankind'; and Science, which Webb defined as 'the discovery of facts and laws hitherto unknown, new conquests of man over his environment'. Like Rosebery, Webb apparently regarded culture as something of a luxury, suited to Oxford and Cambridge, maybe, but superfluous in a 'modern' univeristy. Webb wanted London's university to be in close intellectual contact with, as well as in close physical proximity to, the bustling world of commerce, politics and practical activities.[1] New courses, like the one run by Professor Ashley in the Faculty of Commerce at Birmingham University, the first of its kind in the country, were meant to demonstrate that practical training and high academic standards were in no way incompatible.[2]

The proper *content* of education might give rise to certain differences of opinion; but the efficiency group as a whole could unite in deploring the *attitude* to intellectual effort of any kind among a ruling class that seemed to have acquired from its public school background a positive aversion to systematic thought. 'Some of our finest schools,' wrote Rosebery, 'are content to turn out lads of admirable character and temper, I admit, but equipped for the keen competition of our modern world with a thin varnish of dead languages. Even that disappears in a very short time, leaving little to show as the intellectual result of the educational springtime.'[3] The notion that 'character' was a substitute for knowledge or intelligence had to be demolished, along with the belief that an English 'gentleman' brought up on sport and a smattering of the classics was a match for the trained 'expert'. Lord Esher made the point well in explaining why he considered the old gentleman-sportsman type of soldier to be a national liability: 'the laws of historical and ethnographical evolution . . . require that we shall fight one of the most powerful military empires that has ever existed . . . I fear that proficiency in games, or in the hunting-field, will not help our poor lads much when they have to face the carefully

[1] *Nineteenth Century*, June 1902, Vol. LI, esp. pp. 918–19; S. Webb, 'London University: a Policy and a Forecast'. S. Webb, *London Education* (1904), Ch. II, esp. pp. 59–60.

[2] See article by Professor W. Ashley, 'The Enlargement of Economics' in *Economic Journal*, Vol. 18, June 1908, pp. 181–204.

[3] Rosebery Papers, Box 76; Rosebery to the Incorporated Assoc. of Headmasters, 31.1.00.

trained and highly educated German officers. *Our* difficulty is that our lawyers and physicians are professional men, but until quite lately our soldiers have been amateurs—and soldiering a pastime and not a "business".'[1] What Esher said about the need for greater 'professionalism' could also have been applied to politics, administration and all branches of the public service. At the moment, complained George Brodrick in the *Nineteenth Century* for October 1900, we were a 'nation of amateurs'.[2]

This charge was taken up by Sidney Low in his famous survey of the British Constitution in action, *The Governance of England*, first published in 1904. Whether the Unionists or the Liberals were in power, he noted, the political oligarchy, the Ministers with Cabinet rank, came overwhelmingly from the landed classes and the legal profession. Honest, public-spirited and conscientious these men undoubtedly were, but, he warned, 'a different kind of leadership may be required in the future, and it may or may not be forthcoming'. In Low's words: 'administrative and legislative functions cannot be discharged, in a complex society, without something more than good intentions and a respectable character'; and it was therefore disconcerting that while government had become more technical than ever before, the governors were, relatively speaking, less expert than at any previous period. 'Government in England,' Low asserted, 'is government by amateurs. The subordinates, in their several grades, are trained; the superiors, the persons in whom rest responsibility and power are untrained.' Nor could the House of Commons redress the weaknesses of the Cabinet, since it shared them in large measure: 'Its members, though generally upright, and sometimes able, are too apt to regard politics as a pastime, and the House itself as a club.'[3]

At first sight it would seem that the effect of this kind of criticism would be to undermine the prestige of the ruling social groups by exposing the limitations of men whose traditional functions had been eroded by scientific and technological progress. It was, in-

[1] M. V. Brett (ed.), *Journals and Letters of Reginald Viscount Esher*, Vol. II (1934), pp. 183–4; Esher to the Duchess of Sutherland, 7.9.06.

[2] *Nineteenth Century*, Oct. 1900, Vol. XLVIII, pp. 521–35; George C. Brodrick, 'A Nation of Amateurs'.

[3] Sidney Low, *The Governance of England* (1904), esp. Ch. XI and pp. 197, 304.

deed, generally conceded that, if Britain were to bring her finest intellects to bear on the work of government, many of the social and financial impediments that stood in the way of political advancement would have to go. The same consideration applied to other branches of the public service. This point was underscored in 1902, when a scandalized public learned that certain crack cavalry regiments were effectively barred to officers who did not possess a private income of £400 a year, and in some regiments £700 a year.[1] It was precisely because wealth and 'connections' played so large a part in army promotions, according to one government report, that junior officers in the military academies affected an indifference to military knowledge and 'keenness was out of fashion'.[2] In the interests of efficiency, aristocratic privilege of this kind had to yield to the principle of *la carrière ouverte aux talents*. Admiral Fisher, disgusted at the way in which 99 per cent of Britain's naval officers were drawn from the 'Upper ten', would have liked the state to have met the whole cost of a naval education.[3]

However, most advocates of efficiency regarded state provision of this order as a waste of limited resources. Although they wanted exceptional children of poor families to be given assistance, and deprecated narrow social prejudices that led to inefficiency, they felt that, in the short run at least, public money could more usefully be spent in improving the vocational training of those marked out by birth or wealth for a professional career.

That was why in both secondary and university education such people tended to think in terms of producing highly trained élites. Joseph Chamberlain went so far as to argue that primary education, important though it was, failed to meet the most urgent of Britain's needs; 'national progress of every kind depends upon certain individuals rather than upon the mass', he said; therefore, the role of universities was, if possible, to turn out 'geniuses', like Watt, Arkwright and Siemens, or at least their

[1] *Military Education Committee Report* (1902); Cd. 982, par. 153. See the angry comment in *The Times*, 12.6.02.

[2] ibid., pars. 131–2.

[3] A. J. Marder (ed.), *Fear God and Dread Nought: the Correspondence of Admiral Fisher*, Vol. II (1956), pp. 334–5; Fisher to Esher, 5.8.10 and to Spender, 8.8.10.

assistants and interpreters.[1] A contributor to the *Monthly Review* explained that technical education could only be for a few: 'to train our whole population in this manner would be about as wise as to give an army officer's training to every private who entered the ranks. In industries and manufactures, as in war, only a few can be leaders: the majority must simply obey.'[2]

A similarly hierarchical approach was adopted with regard to secondary education. The demand for 'secondary education for all' was beginning to be heard from organized labour and from the N.U.T. But the 'efficiency group' mostly felt that, since the available resources were limited, it was better to restrict education to fee-paying children from the middle classes, plus a handful of exceptionally able pupils caught by the offer of free places or by a 'scholarship ladder'.[3] Morant himself was anxious to integrate the different educational levels by bringing into the elementary schools, as inspectors and so on, men drawn from a 'higher' rung in the educational pyramid who presumably possessed greater knowledge and broader horizons. But at the same time Morant wished to draw a clearly defined boundary between the elementary and the secondary spheres, because he too believed that secondary education was only suitable for those who would enter the professions and the higher posts in industry and commerce. One can see why Morant was vilified by his many enemies as class conscious and 'undemocratic'; for his educational ideals gave only a low priority to considerations of social equality and tended, in their everyday consequences, to set stringent limits to 'upward mobility'.[4]

Although Sidney Webb had the reputation of being an 'advanced' thinker, he too wanted to separate the task 'of educating

---

[1] *The Times*, 18.1.01: at Annual Meeting of the Court of Governors of Birmingham University.

[2] *Monthly Review*, July 1901, Vol. IV, p. 39; John Kershaw, 'Some Fallacies and the Education Bill'.

[3] O. Banks, op. cit., pp. 51, 61. The Treasury was acting on the same principle when it made its grants-in-aid to University Colleges conditional upon their receiving a minimum of £1,500 from fees (Treasury Minute of 30.3.04: Cd. 2422).

[4] Asher Tropp, *The School Teachers* (1957), Ch. 11. On the other hand, Morant co-operated fully with the Liberal Government, when it brought in its Free Place Regulations in 1907 to enable more children from the elementary schools to receive a secondary education (See O. Banks, op. cit., pp. 68–9).

the *mass* of ordinary average children for the ordinary average life' from 'the other (educational) function, that of preparing the exceptionally clever boy or girl for exceptional work'.[1] Underlying this viewpoint was the same sort of assumption which led Webb's friend, Haldane, to emphasize the distinction between the upper division of the Civil Service and its clerical branches. To allow promotions from 'the ranks' into the upper division, said Haldane, 'would be detrimental to the highest interests of the State', because it would mean a lowering of standards. People who complained about the restricted class background from which senior civil servants were drawn were advised by Haldane to concentrate on democratizing the educational system and not seek to whittle away Whitehall's educational qualifications.[2] Haldane's viewpoint, of course, assumed that the highest administrative posts should still be reserved for an exclusive élite, although this élite was to be gradually enlarged and diversified.

The Cult of the Expert

All this shows that the campaign for national efficiency proved in practice to be suprisingly accommodating towards hereditary privilege. Arnold White, in his book, *Efficiency and Empire*, could actually argue that gentlefolk would always win in a crowd, whenever they took the trouble: 'for aristocracy is nothing more than the most efficient people in the nation, whose efficiency has been graded up by generations of training. . . Homage to efficiency is the secret of the respect paid by the Anglo-Saxons to aristocracy.'[3] The upper classes, in short, had got into slack ways and were being 'let down' by the 'smart set', but they remained fundamentally 'sound'.[4]

Much of this may read like special pleading. For, it must be remembered that the call for greater national efficiency came primarily from within the ranks of the privileged. Rosebery was a wealthy landed aristocrat, with a traditional Eton-Christchurch

---

[1] Wallas Papers, Box 2; S. Webb to Graham Wallas, 6.9.00.

[2] Haldane's evidence (19.4.12) to the Royal Commission on the Civil Service; Appendix to First Report (1912–13), Cd. 6210, pp. 79–92.

[3] Arnold White, *Efficiency and Empire* (1901), p. 23.

[4] ibid., p. 75.

background, a classical education and a passion for horse-racing: superficially, the very type of 'amateur gentleman' he spent so much time in denouncing. Haldane was a natural aristocrat, by social class and temperament, delighting in his contacts with the City and the Court and possessing little first-hand knowledge of the way of life of the urban working man. And so in a way the agitation for national efficiency was an exercise in self-criticism conducted from *within* the 'ruling classes'.

Moreover, even those advocates of efficiency who were social 'outsiders', like Wells, chose to collaborate with the traditional political 'leadership groups'. Perhaps because the demand for efficiency postulated the existence of an élite, they felt more attracted to *any* élite, whatever its faults, than to, for example, the Labour Party, with its egalitarian structure and programme. Besides, they had hopes of 'permeating' this restricted world of politicians and inducing its members to take a changed view of their responsibilities. Wells, for all his contempt for the trappings of hereditary privilege, believed that little could be achieved by 'transferring power from the muddle-headed few to the muddle-headed many';[1] and like the hero of his novel, *The New Machiavelli*, he was for a while inclined to look for effective political leadership to a reinvigorated aristocracy which had combined its old traditions of public service with an altogether new deference towards knowledge and trained intelligence. For the twentieth century was to be the era of the 'expert', in politics as in all departments of national life.[2]

---

[1] H. G. Wells, *The New Machiavelli* (1911, Penguin ed. 1946), p. 255.

[2] Wells, however, combined a respect for expertise with a contempt for most of the professional groups that then existed, scientists and engineers alone excepted. Later, during his period of alienation from the Webbs, he came to doubt many of the assumptions upon which the cult of the expert had been built and argued that specialization was being confused with division of labour and that, contrary to popular belief, technological advance was *destroying* expertise; 'The trained man, the specialized man, is the most unfortunate of men; the world leaves him behind, and he has lost his power of overtaking it. Versatility, alert adaptability, these are our urgent needs'. Progress was mainly due, not to experts, who were tradition-orientated, but to amateurs and to professional men who had carried over their skills and techniques into a field outside their original specialism. (*An Englishman Looks At The World* (1914), pp. 90, 241-4).

Nothing so irritated the orthodox party Liberals as this adulation of 'experts'. How, asked the radical intellectual, L. T. Hobhouse, scornfully, were these impressive people to be identified? Was the proposal simply that greater discretionary power should be conferred on the 'man on the spot'? Or was the 'expert' supposed to possess a special sort of knowledge that marked him off from ordinary mortals, like politicians? 'Sometimes,' wrote Hobhouse, 'it seems to be thought that the art of governing men is as mechanical a matter as that of laying drain-pipes, to be acquired through a similar routine of instruction and apprenticeship. Having mastered this routine the expert, it would almost seem, is qualified to direct society as its natural governor.' But, argued Hobhouse, it was as necessary in public as in private life to keep a watchful eye on the experts one employed; the expert might be qualified to perform certain specialized tasks, but he worked to the orders of others and was not concerned with the ends of his action. In short, Hobhouse believed that those who lavished uncritical praise upon the 'expert' were guilty of confusing the quite distinct activities of politics and administration.[1]

In penning this indictment, Hobhouse has unwittingly drawn attention to a deficiency in the old Liberal creed; for one characteristic of modern government is that politics and administration shade off into one another and interact in a complex way. In making a 'political' decision, a Minister may be very largely guided by the advice of those whose function it will be to implement it, and in consequence the permanent adviser often finds himself to all intents and purposes participating in the process of policy-making. The 'efficiency group', far from taking fright at this apparent departure from 'democratic government', recognized it as natural and unavoidable, and rather felt that the role of the 'adviser' had better be taken into account and institutionalized. In this way, the quality of the advice tendered to ministers would be improved and the whole standard of government raised to a new level of efficiency. A close association of 'experts' and politicians could come about through a number of reforms, of which the most obviously attractive was the co-option of the relevant 'experts'—engineers, M.O.H.s, statisticians, Service Chiefs and

---

[1] L. T. Hobhouse, *Democracy and Reaction* (1904), pp. 119–21.

so on—onto departmental committees and even onto committees of the Cabinet: a device which would have the advantage of leaving the ultimate responsibility for what had been done in the hands of ministers accountable to Parliament and the electorate.

At local government level the same principle could be applied. The Webbs and Hewins went further and argued that the actual initiative in devising measures should lie with salaried officials, though it would still fall to the elected representatives to accept or reject their proposals.[1] Others cast jealous eyes on the German municipalities, where the posts of mayor and committee chairmen were usually filled for six to nine years by paid officials possessing stipulated qualifications, such as diplomas in law or finance.[2] 'Paid expert leadership (not subordinate expert advice) is the key to the efficiency and economy of German municipal administration of the modern type,' explained Michael Sadler, 'and this is only one of the social forces which render the career of an expert more attractive in Germany than here.'[3] Compared with this set-up, English local government could be portrayed as the ultimate in amateurishness.

Government and Science

To effect a closer union between Government and Science seemed one obvious way to break free from the slip-shodness and imprecision that plagued British life. This was a popular slogan in the Edwardian period, and like most slogans it covered a multitude of aims and meanings. When scientists used it, they were usually giving expression to their concern that politicians did not possess a greater awareness of the broader social implications of scientific advance. This complaint did not originate in the Edwardian period, of course. We have already noted the efforts of Sir Norman Lockyer to bring politicians and scientists together in recognition of their common interests.[4] The more favourable climate of opinion

[1] Passfield Papers, II 4 c, Hewins to S. Webb, 18.4.05: ff. 79–83.
[2] e.g. T. C. Horsfall, op. cit., pp. 22–3.
[3] Michael Sadler, *Unrest in Secondary Education. . .*, 1902, Cd. 836, p. 50. Not that Sadler felt that this state of affairs was altogether desirable; it was certainly not applicable to British conditions, he felt.
[4] See above, Ch. I, p. 14.

generated by the demands for greater national efficiency did, however, encourage Lockyer and his associates to step up their propaganda in the early years of the twentieth century. While holding the office of President of the British Association in 1903, Lockyer tried to set up in connection with it an organization which could pressurize governments in the interests of science; and, on failing to do so, he created an entirely new body, the British Science Guild, whose aim was to attract more public money to universities and other institutions where the bounds of science were being extended.[1]

Interestingly enough, when the Guild held its inaugural meeting at the Mansion House in October 1905, several prominent advocates of national efficiency were on the platform, and the main address was delivered by Haldane, who had been chosen as its first president.[2] Haldane, together with his friend, Balfour, were among the few Edwardian politicians to grasp the importance of spending public money generously in subvention of scientific research and involving scientists in the process of government; and it is perhaps significant that both men came from a distinguished family of scientists and tried to keep abreast of contemporary scientific developments.[3] So perhaps *The Times* was right when it urged that the next generation of politicians should all have received some scientific training, however rudimentary.[4] In the meantime was it asking too much of the government to show a deference to scientific expertise and a new readiness to utilize technology in the service of the state?

However, the natural sciences had another significance to those who talked of national efficiency, in that they provided an exemplar. Thus, Wells wrote that Socialism, as he conceived it,

[1] T. Mary Lockyer and Winifred L. Lockyer, *Life and Work of Sir Norman Lockyer* (1928), pp. 444–5.

[2] *The Times*, 31.10.05; *Nature*, Vol. LXXIII, pp. 10–13: 2.11.05; Joseph Chamberlain was one of the Vice-Presidents of the Assoc.

[3] A number of scientists have commented upon Balfour's remarkable grasp of current scientific developments; See Lord Rayleigh, *Lord Balfour in his Relation to Science* (Cambridge, 1930), pp. 16–17; Oliver Lodge, *Past Years* (1931), pp. 222–4; Lady Oxford, *More Memories* (1933), p. 157; Sir Almeric Fitzroy, *Memoirs* (1925), Vol. II, p. 491: 27.7.12; Sir Henry Tizard, *A Scientist In and Out of the Civil Service* (1955), p. 10.   [4] *The Times*, 24.1.00.

rested on the same fundamental idea as that by which all scientific
work was carried out, namely, 'the denial that chance impulse and
individual will and happening constitute the only possible methods
by which things may be done in the world.[1] He accordingly looked
forward to an orderly, planned society, based on forethought and
science. Sadler characterized the organization of German society
as one 'dominated by scientific conceptions, not, that is, by any
exclusive regard for physical science in its narrower sense, but by
those ideas of exact and co-operative inquiry and endeavour
which have been so brilliantly illustrated, and therefore so powerfully enforced, by the advance of modern science'.[2]

In this way the claim that governments needed to improve their
scientific intelligence service became confused with the belief that
politics and public administration could themselves be made an
exact science, in which key decisions would lie with 'experts'.
'The art of government cannot continue to be the one department
of activity for which no training is supposed to be necessary,'
wrote the eminent physicist, Oliver Lodge. 'We train doctors, we
train engineers, we are beginning to train teachers; some day
politicians must be trained too.'[3] When the Webbs founded the
London School of Economics, they had in mind the improvement
of the standard of government and administration by providing
a future generation of politicians and salaried officials with a
grounding in the 'science' of economics and politics. And the
Webbs saw their own research work as the start of a vast information service, which would in time remove the unsystematic and
random elements from political life. At the moment, complained
the Webbs, 'Our governing class . . . do not seem yet to have
realized that social reconstructions require as much specialized
training and sustained study as the building of bridges and rail-
ways, the interpretation of the law, or technical improvements in
machinery and mechanical processes'.[4] When this deficiency had
been put right, Britain would enjoy the benefits of an efficient

---

[1] H. G. Wells, *New Worlds for Old* (1908), p. 22.
[2] M. Sadler, op. cit., Cd. 836, p. 34.
[3] *Contemporary Review*, July 1905, Vol. LXXXVIII, p. 2; O. Lodge, 'Some
Social Reforms'.
[4] S. and B. Webb, *The Prevention of Destitution* (1911), p. 331.

bureaucracy, directed from above by an 'intelligence department' of 'experts'—social investigators, economists, scientists and statisticians.

The Business Man in Politics

A variant on the cult of the 'scientific expert' was the cult of the 'business man'. The distinction between commercial and political activity was blurred in much of this propaganda, and vague calls for more 'business men' in government often leave one uncertain whether the writer actually wanted to introduce industrialists into the public service, or merely to ensure that capable, efficient, *business-like* politicians, rather than rhetoricians, controlled the destinies of the nation.[1] In either case, the ethics and methods of business life were being put forward as an ideal by which the conduct of public policy should be guided.

Such vague talk reflected the widespread feeling that commercial affairs, serious, tough and demanding, developed qualities of hard work and orderliness, which were regrettably absent in the leisurely, sophisticated atmosphere of Westminster and Whitehall. Thus, Arnold White could attribute the nation's recent set-backs to the fact that the Cabinet contained only two business men out of twenty;[2] one of the Ministers to whom White was alluding was, of course, Joseph Chamberlain, and Chamberlain, having entered politics after a successful business career, was often credited in consequence with a quite exceptional practical shrewdness and organizing skill. Even the Fabians contributed to the perpetuation of this legend: 'The Colonial Secretary, because he had graduated in municipal business, and understands from commercial experience how to get things done and to deal with practical men, easily over-rides his colleagues.'[3] And Rosebery praised Chamberlain as 'a man of business with a keen eye for the real and the

---

[1] e.g. 'Great Britain is a business community, consequently it must be represented by a business House of Commons and a business Government . . .' (*Contemporary Review*, Aug. 1901, Vol. LXXX, p. 272). Also, Anon. (probably O. Eltzbacher), *Drifting* (1901), p. 68.

[2] A. White, op. cit., p. 129.

[3] G. B. Shaw (ed.), *Fabianism and the Empire* (1900), p. 94.

practical in matters of this life'.[1] Implied in all these remarks is the lack of 'business capacity' in the social classes from which most politicians were drawn. Here possibly was the explanation of notorious episodes of the Boer War, like the scandal over the supply of remounts to the army, which indicated an administrative ineptitude which would surely have led to the speedy dismissal of those responsible, had it occurred in any private business concern.[2]

Rosebery, in particular, made great play with this line of argument. 'After all,' he said in 1900, 'a State is in essence a great joint stock company with unlimited liability on the part of its shareholders. . . And a business depends on incessant vigilance, on method, on keeping abreast of the times. . . As in a business, too, a periodical stock-taking is necessary in a State.' Hence the urgency of putting the British Empire at once on a 'business footing'.[3] Once, at a dinner of the Edinburgh Merchant Company, Rosebery let himself be so carried away by this train of reasoning that he spoke aloud about a dream of his of forming a Cabinet entirely of business men. He would like to invite such tycoons as Sir Thomas Lipton and Andrew Carnegie, he said, to take over the administrative machinery of the state and see whether it met the standards of efficiency which they would exact in their own firms. These business men could examine the country's enormous expenditure and decide on whether the nation was getting 'twenty shillings for every pound of the 200 millions' being spent each year. Unfortunately for Rosebery, his audience chose to interpret these remarks, which had probably been seriously intended, as a passing jest, and, obviously annoyed, he had to explain away what he had said as a 'parable'.[4]

This facile equation of commercial success with the qualities necessary for administrative efficiency was not in any way new, since, as we have already seen, the Administrative Reform Association of 1855 had given such ideas wide currency during the

[1] at Edinburgh, 1.11.02: Liberal League pamphlet no. 33, *Administrative Efficiency*.

[2] e.g. H. O. Arnold-Forster, *The War Office, the Army and the Empire* (1900), pp. 73–4.

[3] Lord Rosebery, *Miscellanies* (1921), Vol. II, pp. 240–1; 16.11.00.

[4] *The Times*, 15.11.01.

G

Crimean War.[1] It is therefore interesting that in July 1900, when the blunders of the Crimean campaigns seemed to be repeating themselves, James Knowles, the editor of the *Nineteenth Century*, should have tried to organize a similar agitation. In his periodical he proclaimed the 'need for conducting the business of the country, as administered by all the various Departments of State, upon ordinary business principles and methods'.[2] These principles, it later transpired, could be defined as: the public accountability of all officials, payment by results and promotion by merit and efficiency.[3] To give effect to this programme, a vigilance committee was set up. The name it adopted was, inevitably, the Administrative Reform Association.

Equally inevitably, it failed. The sort of fierce anti-aristocratic resentment which had fuelled the campaign for administrative reform during the Boer War, was altogether lacking in 1900. Indeed, it is an interesting commentary upon the fusion between the business and landed classes that had taken place during the last half of the nineteenth century that the national figure who came forward to preside over Knowles's organization was none other than Lord Rosebery, a Whig aristocrat par excellence. It was simply a certain kind of administrative system, not an entire social class, that stood arraigned in 1900. This in turn altered the whole ethos of the agitation. In 1855 the outcry against aristocratic inefficiency and selfishness had given the movement for a 'business government' a progressive and radical tinge. The superficially similar movement of opinion during the Boer War seemed rather to be part of a 'reactionary' onslaught upon Parliamentary politics and the operation of the party system.

To people who had watched the rise and decline of the Administrative Reform Association in the 1850s, the activities of the new A.R.A. naturally did not inspire much enthusiasm. 'I am afraid Rosebery has got the "business man" fad on his brain,' wrote Lord Northbrook in 1901. 'I don't believe business-men, who know nothing of politics, and have no experience of administration, would do a bit better than our Selbornes and Brodricks, helped (or

---

[1] See above, Ch. I, pp. 17–19.
[2] *Nineteenth Century*, July 1900, Vol. LXVIII, p. 1.
[3] ibid., Aug., 1900, p. 184.

rather guided) by soldiers and sailors. I am old enough to remember the same cry—with much more reason for it—in the Crimean War, and nothing could be made of it. . .'[1]

All the same, before Knowles' vigilance committee had fizzled out, a fairly representative cross-section of the 'establishment' of the day had been eager to testify their approval of its objectives.[2] Moreover, several of the problems raised by the association were to recur frequently over the next fourteen years. For example, were the upper ranks of the Civil Service drawing upon people with a sufficiently wide range of social experience? Did a 'mandarin' class of senior officials, recruited by open examination from young men, most of whom had had their minds and characters formed by a study of the classics in the aristocratic environment of one of the older universities, possess the equipment to regulate the affairs of a 'business community'? Was it not in fact the case that government departments lagged behind the large joint stock companies in the techniques of personnel management, financial control and internal organization?[3]

In 1901 a committee investigating the functioning of the War Office, chaired by Clinton Dawkins, himself a retired imperial official currently employed by the American financial house of Pierpont Morgan, produced a report, in which it was asserted that 'a general, if not a precise analogy, can be established between the conduct of large business undertakings and that of the War Office.

---

[1] Curzon Papers, Vol. 181; Northbrook to Curzon, 12.12. 01: f. 42. Lord Selborne was the First Lord of the Admiralty, St. John Brodrick the War Secretary.

[2] *Nineteenth Century*, Aug. 1900, Vol. LXVIII, pp. 173–83. ibid., Nov. 1900, Vol. LXVIII, pp. 859–80. Heading the list of signatories was Rosebery himself. Other names included Mandell Creighton, the Bishop of London, Cardinal Vaughan, the Headmaster of Eton, Edward Grey, Arnold-Forster, and friends of Milner, like Henry Birchenough, Lyttelton Gell and Clinton Dawkins.

[3] One writer suggested the creation of 'Parliamentary Committees of business men, whose experience, if properly invited and utilised, might be of the greatest assistance to the spending departments'. This proposal, he said, had recently been voiced by the President of the Board of Agriculture, Hanbury, at a public speech at Colchester in Oct. 1901 (A. D. Provand in L. Magnus (ed.): op. cit., p. 166, footnote). Compare this with the account of Hanbury's speech which appeared in *The Times*, 25.10.01, which conveys the impression that the Minister had simply mouthed platitudes about the necessity for more business-like administration.

There are certain well-defined principles of management in all well-conducted business corporations, and the more closely the War Office can be brought into conformity with such principles, the more successful will be its administration.'[1] The committee's recommendations were a detailed working-out of this central idea.

Such a mode of reasoning was so prevalent that when the Royal Commission into the Civil Service went to work in 1912–13, it felt obliged to look closely into the charge that the affairs of the departments were 'not always conducted in a "business-like" manner, and that the application of "business methods" to the conduct of public administration (was) both practicable and necessary'. The commissioners eventually dismissed this complaint by showing the impossibility of comparing the operations of commercial companies, which were conducted for a profit, with government departments, which on the whole served a different purpose.[2] But to this, one of the commissioners replied, in a minority note, that though there was undeniably a difference in the *ends* pursued by private firms and public departments, the report ignored the essential similiarity in *means*: 'the teleological peculiarity cannot affect the methodological standard—the conception of efficiency.'[3]

This was certainly the assumption underlying the London School of Economics, with its courses designed for business men, as well as for prospective civil servants. The important thing, in the opinion of the people who ran such courses of study, was to make public officials more familiar with the techniques and complexities of commercial enterprise and the business community more knowledgeable about the political and institutional framework which circumscribed their activities. In fact, the expansion of government regulation into new areas of social life in the decade prior to the First World War inevitably did a great deal to break down the 'closed world' of Whitehall, increase contacts between officialdom and the commercial community and encourage the recruitment into the public service of men with a particularly useful or relevant kind of business experience.[4] The drawback to these

---

[1] *Report of Committee on War Office Organisation* (1901): Cd. 580, par. 11.
[2] *Fourth Report of Royal Commission on Civil Service* (1914); Cd. 7338, pp. 82–3.
[3] ibid., p. 116.
[4] e.g. the appointment of the new Labour Exchange Managers in 1910.

developments was that they re-awakened old fears of jobbery and corruption, especially when they involved the by-passing of the standard open competitive examination.

These problems were to be thrashed out thoroughly during the Edwardian decade. But at the height of the uproar over the Boer War scandals, it was hardly to be expected that the people who rushed to join the Administrative Reform Association should have taken all these circumstances into account. The professional politicians and the career civil servants seemed to have failed the nation: hence, this rather unthinking attempt to seek political salvation from the business magnates. When these people looked at the career of Cecil Rhodes and the activities of the Chartered Companies,[1] they could perhaps be forgiven for identifying the two distinct spheres of commercial enterprise and public administration and imagining that a successful practitioner in one sphere could be equally successful in the other.

Another powerful consideration was operating. Many people hoped that the huge aggregations of wealth that had been amassed in the 1890s in South Africa and elsewhere might be tapped for the endowment of higher education and scientific research.[2] Radicals might sneer at this 'touting among the millionaires',[3] but they

---

[1] The resort to rule by Chartered Company (the British North Borneo Company, the Royal Niger Company, the British South Africa Company and the British East Africa Company were all chartered in the 1880s) provided W. S. Gilbert with his main theme for his operetta, 'Utopia Limited' (1893). The King of a mythical South Sea Island, anxious to 'anglicize' his realm, is impressed by the part played by company promotion in England's commercial prosperity.

'And do I understand you that Great Britain
Upon this Joint Stock principle is governed?'
he asks one of his English advisers. He receives the reply:
'We haven't come to that, exactly—but
We're tending rapidly in that direction.
The date's not distant'.

Whereupon the King, determined to be in the vanguard of Progress, registers his Crown and Country under the Joint Stock Company Act of 1862, under the title of 'Utopia Limited'. (W. S. Gilbert, *The Savoy Operas*, 1926 ed., p. 602). What Gilbert conceived in jest was being solemnly discussed by a leading statesman only a few years later.

[2] Elizabeth Haldane, *From One Century to Another* (1937), p. 201.

[3] J. A. Hobson, *Imperialism: A Study* (1902), p. 233.

could scarcely deny its short-term effectiveness. The niggardliness of the state in recognizing its obligations in these fields forced many reformers in a hurry to pin their hopes on the enlightened self-interest of wealthy business men. Carefully handled, these people could perhaps be associated more generally with the work of 'national reconstruction'. Even the Fabians believed that this expedient was worth pursuing. 'What we have to do,' wrote Beatrice Webb in her Journal, 'is to detach the *great employer*, whose profits are too large to feel the immediate pressure of regulation and who stands to gain by the increased efficiency of the factors of production, from the ruck of small employers or stupid ones. What seems clear is that we shall get no further instalments of reform unless we gain the consent of an influential minority of the threatened interest.'[1]

Yet the attitude taken up towards the business community was more than a little ambivalent. The loss of markets to the more systematic Germans and Americans suggested that before British business men could come to the rescue of the state, they first needed to put their *own* house in order. In fact, those very people who were most vociferous in demanding the introduction of 'business principles' into the public service tended to be those who were also urging the Government to go to the aid of the business community by improving the educational system and transforming the consular service into a genuine 'intelligence department' for merchants and industrialists.

Party Politics

This emphasis on business-like management went with a disparaging attitude towards the Party System. For, if the principal function of government was indeed 'management', then what role were the parties supposed to perform? The divisions and ideals which had once sustained the party struggle seemed to have disappeared, depriving it of any *raison d'être*. The apparent redundancy of political principle meant that now the real choice before the electors no longer lay between Liberalism and Unionism, but

[1] B. Webb, *Our Partnership* (1948), p. 205; 2.1.01.

between competence and folly.[1] The one relevant principle, the one constructive ideal left in politics was that of national efficiency; but since this was subscribed to by both Unionists and Liberals, the party system seemed to be merely an artificial and damaging barrier to co-operation between men who were agreed on all the fundamental issues.

Again, so long as Britain was at war, many people naturally wished to suspend a party struggle which dissipated national energies and weakened the negotiating position of the Government. If not suspended, it could at least be limited, for example, through removing foreign policy and national defence from the party arena. A more generalized irritation with all aspects of party politics marked the utterances of Rosebery. 'The fact is,' he wrote, 'that party is an evil. . . Its operation blights efficiency. It keeps out of employment a great mass of precious ability. It puts into place not the fittest but the most eligible, from the party point of view—that is, very often, the worst'.[2] In violent language H. G. Wells dismissed the old party fabrics as 'dead rotting things, upon which a great tangle of personal jealousies, old grudges, thorny nicknames, prickly memories, family curses, Judas betrayals and sacred pledges, a horrible rubbish thicket (maintained) a saprophytic vitality.'[3]

Connected with this attack upon the party system was the demand for the introduction of 'outsiders' into the Cabinet: generals, admirals, administrators, Imperial proconsuls, men who had proved their title to be considered real rulers and governors of men.[4] The fact that such men had usually kept aloof from the party fight at Westminster was actually counted in their favour. The outside world of affairs, it seemed, provided a better apprenticeship for high ministerial office than a mere debating assembly.

[1] *Fortnightly Review*, June 1900, Vol. LXVII, p. 1082; 'Lord Rosebery and a National Cabinet'. The author was almost definitely J. L. Garvin. The *Daily Mail* said that it would support Parliamentary candidates on the basis of its judgement as to which 'from a practical point of view best fulfills the demands of the great principle—Efficiency'. (23.3.03).

[2] Foreword to A. Stead, op. cit., pp. ix–x.

[3] H. G. Wells, *Mankind in the Making* (1903; Chapman & Hall ed., 1904), p. 29.

[4] E.g. *National Review*, Jan. 1900, Vol. XXXIV, pp. 668–9; 'Carltonensis', 'Ought We To Have a Coalition?'.

Arnold White, as always intemperate in the expression of his views, alleged that Britain chose the majority of her rulers, not because they were organizers, administrators or men of affairs, but either because they could talk or because they were related to propertied politicians who formerly talked copiously.[1] It is easy to see how this line of argument shaded off in many cases into scarcely veiled pleas for an authoritarian government. Journalists who complained about the futility of endless Parliamentary debate which led to no action, invariably concluded with an appeal for a 'Statesman', for a 'Man' to come forward and save the Empire from disintegration and defeat.[2]

This mood of disillusionment with the functioning of the British liberal state was perhaps intensified by the more realistic description which political analysts were providing of the electoral process and of administrative procedures. Books like Ostrogorski's *Democracy and the Organization of Political Parties*, first published in 1902, made people increasingly aware of the role of party committees and caucuses, behind the façade of democracy, and threw doubt on the practicability of 'popular control', in the sense in which older radicals had used this expression. For if the initiating power rested with political leaders, administrators and 'experts', the electorate was relegated to the status of a 'foolo-meter', incapable of doing more than exercising a restricted, long-range control of government.

Elections did at least lead to smoother government by associating the population with national policy and securing popular consent. H. G. Wells for a time was hoping great things from an extended jury system,[3] but, as Beatrice Webb argued, juries, useful though they were for certain functions, did not secure *consent*. 'Moreover,' she added, 'it is only consent that is needed, not understanding or

[1] A. White, op. cit., p. 15.

[2] e.g. 'What the Empire needs now, and even after this war is over to give us a reformed and efficient army, is not a politician and a talker, not a middle-aged gentleman without the zeal and courage of a reformer, but a man, if possible, who has thought, who has seen and who knows—a man with an iron will' (*National Review*, Feb. 1900, Vol. XXXIV, p. 839; 'An Englishman'; 'The Causes of Reverse'). Cecil Chesterton pinned his hopes on a 'constructive', patriotic labour leader establishing a 'popular Caesarism' (C. Chesterton: op. cit., p. 230).

[3] H. G. Wells, *Mankind in the Making* (1903), Ch. VII.

intellectual appreciation, i.e., feeling not thought. All the defects of elections and the stupidities of voters—though they may detract from the intellectual value of the decision—do not detract from the feeling of consent.'[1]

All this, however, assumed that real responsibility was confined to a political-administrative élite. The Webbs, who thought that they belonged to the fringes of this élite, were able to view the existing state of affairs with a certain cynical complacency. But the proposition that 'Parliamentary democracy' was harmless because it simply did not operate in the way that its authors had intended, did little to allay antagonism to a system that was thought by many people to subordinate 'expertise' to the prejudices of an ignorant populace. One advocate of national efficiency, Bernard Shaw, contended that universal suffrage had put power into the hands of the 'riff-raff', with consequences that threatened 'national suicide'.[2] No real progress was likely, in Shaw's opinion, until a selectively bred race of Supermen had been reared; social improvement would have to wait upon the necessarily lengthy process of *racial* improvement.[3]

National Darwinism

This concern with race was no mere personal fad of Shaw's. During this period of imperial expansion much discussion centred round the question of what characterized a progressive and ascendant racial group. In November 1899 Chamberlain spoke at Leicester of the possibility of a triple alliance between 'the Teutonic race and the two branches of the Anglo-Saxon race'. 'The character, the main character of the Teutonic race,' he explained, 'differs very slightly indeed from the character of the Anglo-Saxon'; therefore, an alliance between Britain, the United States and Germany would be a 'natural alliance'.[4] Here was an important member of the Government seriously proposing that Britain should choose her allies on the basis of alleged racial affinities, rather than

---

[1] Wallas Papers, Box 1; B. Webb to Graham Wallas, 23.7.08.
[2] G. B. Shaw, *Man and Superman* (1903, Penguin ed. 1946), p. 268.
[3] ibid., p. 264.
[4] See J. A. S. Grenville, *Lord Salisbury and Foreign Policy* (1964), p. 281.

reach agreements with states which had similar material interests.

What were those qualities which people like Chamberlain believed to distinguish a 'progressive' racial group? One gets the impression that they included scientific knowledge and methods,
technological sophistication and an efficient military machine:
those very qualities, in fact, which contributed to national
efficiency. Not surprisingly, therefore, people who swelled the cry
for efficiency tended to be imperialists, and vice-versa. For it
seemed axiomatic that an advanced, 'efficient' nation or race was
entitled to control, or even if need be to crush, an inferior race
which blocked its interests, which were ultimately those of civilization itself. Indeed, in Arnold White's view, true religion enjoined
'self-surrender to the law of efficiency' which ran through the
universe; inefficient nations had sinned against the Divine Will
and would be justly punished.[1] These somewhat nebulous ideals
Karl Pearson elaborated into a so-called 'scientific theory' of
racial strife, according to which races tuned up to a high pitch of
external efficiency 'naturally' destroyed those which had fallen
below the necessary level of physical and mental fitness.[2]

Although this cold-blooded kind of racialism never met with
more than a very limited acceptance in Britain, many of its
assumptions did enter into the political vocabulary of imperialism
and the cult of efficiency. Tariff Reformers and Liberal Imperialists
alike dwelt on the terrible fate reserved for nations that were weak
and ill-organized, and Chamberlain's speeches, in particular, were
full of references to the 'struggle for existence'. The tendency was
to see all human activity in terms of warfare, and warfare was presented, not only as an unavoidable feature of international life,
but also as something inherently desirable, since it helped to
develop a courageous and resourceful community.

Tariff Reform later attracted many people's support precisely
because Chamberlain's policy would have given the state the
means to direct and control the channels of trade and manufacture
and in that way to mould the lives of its citizens. This was deemed
desirable by all the 'efficiency group', whether or not they hap-

[1] Arnold White, *The Views of Vanoc* (1910), p. 166.
[2] For the writings of this school, see Bernard Semmel, *Imperialism and Social
Reform* (1960), Ch. II.

pened to agree with the Tariff Reform programme. Garvin pointed to an antithesis 'between the passive and the active conceptions of the State, between the static and the dynamic ideas of public policy, between a theory of structure and a theory of energy; or, in one word, between "laisser faire" and "savoir faire" '. The 'active' conception of the state, which Garvin held, postulated that 'the economic progress, no less than the political preservation of a State, must largely depend upon the conscious purpose and efficient action of the State itself. Government, in a word, should be the brain of the State, even in the sphere of commerce'.[1]

The popularity of Hegelianism added credibility to this political philosophy; the writings of the German 'national economists'[2] were a more immediate source of inspiration. But theories about the nature of the State counted for little beside what many Edwardians thought to be a matter of simple observation: that Gladstonian Liberalism had failed when faced by German Realpolitik. It was Bismarck who had shown how power could best be organized and concentrated upon the advancement of the nation state, and it behoved British statesmen to emulate his methods and objectives.

The Role of the Churches

The sort of 'national government' which the advocates of efficiency were anxious for Britain to have would be one that, by ignoring all factional and sectional agitation, could take a 'strong line' in its dealings with foreign powers. Discontented 'have-not' groups, like Labour, the Irish Nationalists and the Nonconformists, all suffered from the prevalence of this consensus approach to politics. The label, 'anti-national', could so easily be tagged on to these divisive elements within the community. Particularly favoured as a whipping-boy by those who extolled efficiency was the provincial chapel-going radical, engaged in his implacable vendetta against the Established Church, the brewers and the landed interest; with

[1] J. L. Garvin in 'Compatriots' Club Lectures, 1st Series (1905), pp. 9, 2–3.
[2] The academics and economic historians who supported Tariff Reform were particularly indebted to the German 'National economists': see B. Semmel, op. cit., Ch. XI, for the views of Sir William Ashley.

his atomic conception of society, this sort of Dissenter seemed to express all that was most negative and factional in the national life. No wonder that after being pilloried in this unjust way, few Nonconformists were prominently identified with the national efficiency movement and that many staunchly opposed it.

By contrast, the Church of England found it much easier to come to terms with the cult of efficiency, perhaps because of its traditional concern with the problem of 'authority' and 'discipline'. Another reason for this, however, may be the continuance within Anglicanism of that 'Broad Church' tradition of thought which we have already encountered.[1] The most eminent Broad Church-man at the turn of the century was perhaps Mandell Creighton, the Bishop of London; and many of the ideas associated with the ideology of national efficiency, dressed up in suitably theological language, of course, can be found in Creighton's sermons and letters.[2] It was natural, then, that the Webbs, having secured the co-operation of Creighton in their educational ventures and realizing that here was a man whose cast of mind closely resembled their own, should have begun to view the Church of England as organizationally equipped to serve a modern function as 'the home of national communal aspirations' and its spiritual leaders as possible agents of 'national reconstruction'.[3]

Beatrice Webb was also attracted by the ceremony and ritual of the Church; she thought they contributed to 'mental hygiene'. Thus, although rejecting the actual dogmas of Christianity, at least at a literal level, she and Sidney found themselves being drawn into social contact with the High Church Bishops as well as with the Creightons. In the first few years of the twentieth century Talbot and Cosmo Lang were both frequent visitors to 41 Grosvenor Road.

Some of the 'efficiency group' were orthodox Christians; Hewins, for example, was a devout Roman Catholic. But many more were like Haldane and the Webbs, 'religious-minded agnos-

---

[1] See above, Ch. I, pp. 31–2.
[2] Louise Creighton, *Life and Letters of Mandell Creighton* (1904), 2 Vols, passim.
[3] B. Webb, *Our Partnership* (1948), pp. 205–10; 15.1.01. Passfield Papers, Vol. 25; B. Webb's Journals, 20.2.05; ff. 11–12. But Beatrice Webb also admired Roman Catholicism; see A. Fitzroy, op. cit., Vol. I, p. 289; 4.4.06.

tics', people unable to accept orthodox dogma but appreciating the social importance and the psychological value of the Christian faith. H. G. Wells stood very much apart from those who shared his other social and political opinions, with his self-assured eighteenth-century brand of secularism and anti-clericalism. His seemed a futile stance to adopt, in the absence of an alternative social code or philosophy suitable for the broad mass of people.

This suggests a further reflection. The 'efficiency group' may have been appealing for greater intelligence in the conduct of public affairs, with the argument that 'character' alone was no longer adequate. Yet their awareness of the complexity and technicality of the statesman's task, and their often perceptive and subtle political analysis, contrast strangely with the somewhat simple-minded moralizing, which was another strand in their propaganda. Clearly, many of these people were bewildered and upset by the 'moral pluralism' of life in the large conurbations and feared that modern civilization was weakening the moral fibre of the population and producing an effeteness and slackness of character that portended national ruin. In their dislike for the distractions and complexities which they saw besetting the ordinary citizen, one can detect a certain nostalgia for an earlier and simpler age, when Englishmen knew what their duties were and performed them in a manly way. Surely, therefore, one reason why the 'efficiency group' viewed organized Christianity with such sympathy was that the Churches were the traditional custodians of a homely moral code. Moreover, the social and moral values which the Churches emphasized were precisely those which, allied to scientific method, could be counted upon to propel a nation to greatness and prosperity.

All these considerations predisposed the 'efficiency group' to treat the Churches indulgently. There might even be occasions, they argued, when the State could advantageously step forward to subsidize particular religous organizations which provided the community with certain beneficial services—always on the condition that the churches, for their part, submitted to a minimum of public control. This principle could be extended to enable the state to distribute grants-in-aid among a whole range of semi-private associations and corporations. True, this would mean that the taxpayer might have to contribute money to the furtherance of causes in which he had no personal stake—even to causes which he might deeply dislike. Yet, as Sidney Webb argued, corporate action of any sort would become impossible, unless people were occasionally prepared to 'subsidize error' in this way.[1]

Radicals might object to this departure from the principle of 'public accountability'. Yet in answer to their complaints, one could contend that it was both unrealistic and retrogressive to cling to abstractions, like 'the people' and 'the will of the majority', when in fact society consisted of a multitude of minorities, each with its own beliefs and its own needs. Traditionally, governments may have provided services 'in the gross'; but in future there would have to be a classification of the population according to need and status, so that quite small minorities could be accorded specialized, scientific treatment. As Sidney Webb provocatively put it: ' "Class legislation" . . . is not only not bad, or wicked, or undemocratic, but actually the only good, the only useful and the only really effective legislation.'[2]

Thus, the kind of collectivist state, for which Haldane and the Webbs were striving, would clearly have been pluralistic in structure, containing within itself numerous subordinate organizations, associations and social and economic groups. Nineteenth century radicalism, they believed, had erred in working to destroy these intermediate groups in the name of 'freedom', and in attacking the last vestiges of the aristocratic order, without any serious thought about what was to take its place. To this 'destructive' view of politics, Beatrice Webb opposed her own 'constructive' philosophy:

We want to stamp out the notion that the world can be bettered by the abolition of some of the existing institutions; we want, on the contrary, to set people to work to build up new tissue which may in time take the place of the old. . . We do not want to unfetter the individual from the

---

[1] *Nineteenth Century*, Sep. 1901, Vol. L, pp. 369–70; S. Webb, 'Lord Rosebery's Escape From Houndsditch'. For Beatrice Webb's views, see Bertrand Russell, *The Autobiography of Bertrand Russell, 1872–1914* (1967), p. 194; B. Webb to Russell, 16.10.04.

[2] *Contemporary Review*, June 1908, Vol. XCIII, pp. 658–64; S. Webb, 'The Necessary Basis of Society'.

obligation of citizenship, we want on the contrary to stimulate and constrain him, by the unfelt pressure of a better social environment, to become a healthier, nobler and more efficient being.[1]

Rather than beginning with an attack on all given institutions, it seemed better to 'permeate' these institutions whenever possible with people under whose guidance they might in time be brought to play a useful, positive role in that scientifically ordered society towards which the world was moving.

The Opponents of Efficiency

But the quiet insidious infiltration of positions of power and influence recommended by the advocates of national efficiency was unlikely to take place without opposition. Inertia and the deadweight of tradition apart, the quest for efficiency quickly ran into open political resistance; since the aim was to undermine the liberal values and practices upon which British government rested, this could hardly have been avoided.

The opposition to efficiency no more came from a single political party, than did its support; for although the radical wing of liberalism led the way, many of the older Conservative politicians, like Salisbury and Hicks-Beach, had an equal distrust of this new ideology. Where the radicals had the advantage, however, was that, whether they were 'Gladstonians', like Morley, or belonged to the social reform group which was associated with the *Daily News* and *The Speaker*, they possessed a consistent political philosophy, in which they had utter faith. To them representative government, popular control, individual rights, the will of the people, and so on were not discredited or outdated catchcries, but constituted a body of political truths whose validity transcended time and circumstance.

G. K. Chesterton, a liberal, though an eccentric one, hazarded the opinion that only people who had become weak and ineffective talked incessantly about efficiency:

So it is that when a man's body is a wreck he begins, for the first time, to talk about health. Vigorous organisms talk not about their processes,

[1] B. Webb, *Our Partnership* (1948), pp. 228–9; 28.2.02.

but about their aims. . . There can be no stronger sign of a coarse material health than the tendency to run after high and wild ideals. . . None of the strong men in the strong ages would have understood what you meant by working for efficiency. . . Even if the ideal of such men were simply the ideal of kicking a man downstairs, they thought of the end like men, not of the process like paralytics. They did not say, 'Efficiently elevating my right leg, using, you will notice, the muscles of the thigh and calf, which are in excellent order, I— . . .[1]

But most radicals were too shocked by the ideology of national efficiency to see the humorous side of it. A virtual denial of mankind's common humanity, they felt, was involved in the cult of expertise. Already they had before them one concrete example of what happened when 'efficiency' became the dominating preoccupation. As early as the 1890s certain British workshops had been employing 'efficiency engineers' and operating time and motion studies, 'speeding up', incentive payments, and so on. But it took the publication in 1911 of the famous treatise, *Scientific Management*, by the American F. W. Taylor, to dramatize for a wider audience the big *moral* problems which these new industrial techniques brought in their wake. The fears of most radicals were expressed by J. A. Hobson, when he anticipated that these methods, by destroying the 'creative' element in work, might in time produce a situation where there would be, on the one hand, 'small bodies of efficient taskmasters carefully administering the orders of expert managers', and, on the other, 'large masses of physically efficient but mentally inert executive machines'.[2] But, mused some radicals, would not the whole community be divided on similar lines, if the cult of expertise made further political headway? What future, in that case, would there be for 'political democracy' and all the hopes that it had inspired?

In their dislike for the 'efficiency group', radicals were tempted to seize upon their opponents' arguments and stand them on their head. There was an especially interesting inversion of the position

[1] G. K. Chesterton, *Heretics* (1905), pp. 17–18.

[2] See *Sociological Review*, July 1913, Vol. 1, pp. 197–212; J. A. Hobson, 'Scientific Management'. ibid., vol. 7, April 1914, pp. 99–125; 'Some Principles of Industrial Organisation: The Case For and Against Scientific Management'. E. H. Phelps Brown, *The Growth of British Industrial Relations* (1959), pp. 92–8. Asa Briggs, op. cit., pp. 118–19.

taken up by the 'efficiency group' towards Germany. The radicals, of course, preached friendship and co-operation with the German people, dismissing the 'German threat' as a hysterical scare. Yet at the same time they were concerned to belittle the achievements of the German state by a careful selection and presentation of evidence which the advocate of efficiency usually preferred to ignore. Could the country with the largest Social Democratic Party in the world, asked the radical, really be such a haven of social harmony and national unity?

An implacable hatred of compulsory military service and protection was enough by itself to turn the radical against the organization of the German *state*; but even German *culture* was not immune from attack. Thus, L. T. Hobhouse denounced Hegelianism as 'one expression of the general reaction against the plain, human, rationalistic way of looking at life and its problems'. It had confused people, he claimed, by making all truths relative and so providing a spurious cloak for injustice, as well as encouraging a mood of fatalism in which individuals were absolved from rational and moral behaviour. And so 'Hegelianism had its political sponsor in Bismarck', the statesman who 'first showed the modern world what could be done in the political sphere by the thoroughgoing use of force and fraud'.[1]

Assuming for once the role of self-righteous patriot, Hobhouse rebuked those fellow-countrymen of his who looked to Germany for their ideas and inspiration. 'Perhaps even, recovering from our present artificially induced and radically insincere mood of national self-abasement,' he wrote, 'we shall learn to take some pride in our own characteristic contributions as a nation to the arts of government, to the thought, the literature, the art, the mechanical inventions which have made and are re-making modern civilisation'.[2] The radical cosmopolitan, Norman Angell, in *The Great Illusion*, also poured scorn on 'the German superstition': 'With the curious perversity that marks "patriotic" judgements, the whole tendency at present is to make comparisons with Germany to the disadvantage of ourselves and of other European countries.' 'Do we not run some danger,' he asked, 'that *

[1] L. T. Hobhouse, *Democracy and Reaction* (1904), pp. 77–83.

[2] L. T. Hobhouse, *Liberalism* (1911, Galaxy ed., New York, 1964), pp. 121–2.

H

with this mania for the imitation of German method we may Germanize England, though never a German soldier land on our soil?'[1] Other high-minded liberals were not above attempting to discredit Milner in 1906, by pointing to his German origins and mental dispositions, presumably in the hope of mobilizing xenophobic prejudice against a politician for whom they had an understandable aversion.[2]

But basically both socialists (the Fabian leadership expected) and radical liberals refused to go along with the cult of efficiency because they wanted to alter the *quality* of social life, not simply to increase its efficiency and competitiveness within the existing institutional framework. An intellectual liberal monthly, the *Independent Review*, reacted to the demand for improved technological instruction with the argument that what Englishmen first needed was 'training in the real values of life', which could best be acquired by a study of Greek literature.[3]

Moreover, radical aims could obviously not be realized without a frontal assault on 'privilege' in its many manifestations. So, the claim that it was possible to carry out important reforms by manipulating the big business community, the Anglican Bishops and so on struck them as a highly dangerous delusion. Indeed, from the radical vantage point, this defence of 'privilege' was of a piece with the glorification of the 'expert', the disparaging of popular rights, the insistence on national solidarity and the obsession with the imminence of a major war. Together these things had brought down on Britain a period of 'black reaction'.

This sense of self-righteous outrage is frequently encountered in the utterances of radicals at the turn of the century. When the fortunes of war went against the British forces in South Africa, the famous Baptist minister, Dr. John Clifford, could interpret this as divine retribution on a people which had undergone 'a deterioration of moral fibre, a depraving of the conscience, a blinding of the judgement'.[4] No doubt it was understandable that 'Pro-Boers',

---

[1] Norman Angell, *The Great Illusion* (1909, Heinemann ed., 1912), pp. 209, 213.

[2] e.g. *Speaker*, 22.12.06. See A. M. Gollin, *Proconsul in Politics* (1964), pp. 80–1.

[3] *Independent Review*, March 1905, Vol. V, p. 138.

[4] Sir James Marchant, *Life of Dr John Clifford* (1921), p. 147.

like Clifford, subjected to the unscrupulous electioneering tactics of Chamberlain, should have taken solace in the reflection that they at least were the only sane and sober men in a nation that had temporarily taken leave of its senses. In general, radicals and socialists saw themselves at this time as the sole guardians of the sacred ark of liberal principle and thus morally superior to those who followed the dictates of efficiency: a mere euphemism for expediency, they sneered.[1] They found difficulty, all the same, in keeping up their spirits, as they saw their political universe crumbling all round them. England was sinking even more rapidly than America, wrote James Bryce sadly to his friend, Goldwin Smith.[2]

This air of gloomy self-righteousness was bound to irritate the 'efficiency group' and provoke a counter-stream of abuse. 'Sentimentalists', 'old women', 'pedants' and (a particularly favoured expression) 'mandarins': these were some of the epithets hurled at the heads of liberal purists who refused to adapt their political principles to changing circumstances. Radicals of the old school, like Francis Channing, who could write in 1904: 'The Liberalism of the Reform Bill, of the Corn Laws, of the Gladstone age, contained all that was necessary to salvation',[3] laid themselves wide open to such taunts.

But Campbell-Bannerman, too, by his somewhat inflexible adherence while Leader of the Opposition to Gladstonian principle earned himself the reputation among his enemies, both Liberal and Unionist, of being the greatest conservative in the House.[4] The *Daily Telegraph* wrote of his 'curious morbid Toryism',[5] and the *National Review* dubbed him a 'Chinese Conservative.[6] But this may be taken as a kind of backhanded compliment to a politician who, whatever his other deficiences, was very quick to spot the intrusion of measures reflecting the philosophy of national

---

[1] e.g. L. T. Hobhouse, *Democracy and Reaction* (1904), p. 119.

[2] Bryce Papers, Vol. 17; Bryce to Goldwin Smith, 27.12.00: f. 186.

[3] F. A. Channing, *Memories of Midland Politics, 1885–1910* (1918), p. 292.

[4] Arnold-Forster agreed with Rosebery, who told him that he considered Campbell-Bannerman to be ' "the greatest Conservative" in the House' (Arnold-Forster Papers, Add. Mss. 50, 341; Journals, 16.11.04: f. 88).

[5] *Daily Telegraph*, 18.5.03.

[6] *National Review*, April 1904, Vol. XLIII, p. 192.

efficiency and who seldom shrank from opposing them, regardless of the unpopularity he might incurr. Campbell-Bannerman's attitude was one reason among many why the quest for national efficiency in the Edwardian period became a political issue of the first magnitude; that the two major parties were not neatly arrayed against one another greatly added to its complexity.

CHAPTER IV

LORD ROSEBERY AND THE QUEST FOR EFFICIENCY 1900–1902

THE MILITARY REVERSES of 'Black Week' dealt the Unionist administration a blow from which it never fully recovered. Initially, there was the sort of patriotic rallying round behind the government of the day which usually occurs at a moment of national crisis. But with the successive disclosures of administrative ineptitude and political indecision, grave doubts were soon being expressed as to the competence of the Salisbury Cabinet to manage the affairs of the Empire. By one of those oddities of political life, Joseph Chamberlain, the Colonial Secretary, the Minister largely responsible for landing the country in this emergency, succeeded in giving the impression that he stood apart from his other colleagues and would have put a stop to the mismanagement, had he been given a free hand; and so he was exonerated from the most of the blame incurred by the rest of the Cabinet.

No minister's reputation suffered more catastrophically from the turn events had taken than Lord Salisbury's. Even from usually sympathetic quarters one finds baffled and exasperated comments about the Prime Minister's tactlessness and lofty unconcern for public opinion. Edward Hamilton thought Salisbury's defence of Government policy in the Lords debate of January 1900 'particularly feeble. . . There was a sort of helplessness about it which angered people very much'.[1] The fact was that the Prime Minister had had his doubts about the wisdom of the policy which had culminated in the Boer War,[2] and his determination to see the thing

[1] Hamilton Papers, Add. Mss. 48,676; Journals, 31.1.00: f. 10.
[2] See his famous letter to Lansdowne of 30.8.99, printed in Lord Newton, *Lord Lansdowne* (1929), pp. 156–8.

through to a victorious conclusion went with a pessimistic assessment of its likely long-term consequences. A negative and defeatist tone crept into many of his public speeches, which people at the time naturally resented. So long as the war was in progress, a show of vigour and pugnacity was expected of the Prime Minister, and the rapidly ageing statesman was totally incapable of projecting this sort of public image of himself.

Unfortunately for the Unionist government, Arthur Balfour, the Leader of the Commons, was running into heavy criticism at just this very time, because of the philosophic nonchalance which he chose to affect when addressing his constituents in Manchester.[1] For a while Balfour even lost his usual control over the Commons; and to the dismay and astonishment of his well-wishers, he began to treat any opposition or criticism in a querulous and peevish spirit.[2]

What saved the Government was the sad state of disarray into which the Liberals had fallen. Divided over the merits of the war, in low morale and weakly captained by Campbell-Bannerman, who was still widely regarded as a mere stop-gap leader, the Liberals were scarcely credible contenders for office. Consequently, when in the late summer of 1900 the Government, flushed with optimism at Lord Roberts' entry into Pretoria and doubtless confident that the end of the war was in sight, dissolved Parliament and went before the country, beating the imperial drum, they won a comfortable enough electoral victory, being returned with a majority of 134 over their opponents. Long before the polling booths opened, the Liberals had tacitly admitted defeat.[3]

Yet the Unionist Party's electoral triumph of October 1900 was not widely interpreted as an expression of strong confidence in the Government, certainly not as a popular endorsement of the Government in its existing form. And so in response to the clamour of the Unionist Press, Salisbury soon afterwards reshuffled his Cabinet. But the outcome was not the smaller and younger Cabinet that

[1] See above, Ch. II, p. 42.

[2] e.g. in his reluctance to set up a Commission of Enquiry into the military hospitals in South Africa. Even Salisbury was surprised by Balfour's stand on this issue; see Viscountess Milner, *My Picture Gallery, 1886–1901* (1951), p. 224.

[3] A notable feature of this election was the unusually large number of constituencies which the Liberal Party failed to contest, over 150 in England and Scotland.

was being demanded, but one very similar in composition and outlook to its predecessor—in fact, the Cabinet was slightly larger than the one which had first been formed in 1895 and the average age of ministers fractionally higher. Moreover, the reshuffle brought office to a disproportionate number of Cecils, as the newspapers did not fail to observe. And, after Salisbury had been induced to give up the Foreign Office, there was understandable indignation when this post went to Lord Lansdowne, the ill-fated War Secretary. No-one could have predicted at the time what a successful Foreign Secretary Lansdowne was eventually to make; to many contemporaries it simply seemed as though, to quote the *National Review*, Salisbury had 'perpetrate(d) a first-rate joke' on the nation.[1] All in all, as the Duke of Devonshire privately admitted, the Cabinet reconstruction had been badly handled and the Government did not seem to have been appreciably strengthened by it.[2]

But the unpopularity of the Government and the demoralized state of many Unionist backbenchers did nothing to revive the spirits of the Opposition. On the contrary, as the war dragged on into this guerrilla phase and the army was obliged to adopt measures that pressed heavily upon enemy civilians, the ideological fissure within the Liberal Party widened still further. The nadir of Liberal fortunes was reached in the middle of 1901. On 4 June Campbell-Bannerman felt impelled to speak out publicly against the Government's policy of farm-burning in South Africa; in doing so, he uttered the fateful words, 'methods of barbarism', and came near to destroying his party. A week later Asquith publicly dissociated himself from his leader's observations, to the joy of his imperialist followers, who marked the occasion by staging a dinner for Asquith at the Liverpool Street Hotel on July 19th. So developed what has gone down to posterity as 'the war to the knife and fork': an unhappy episode in Liberal history which convinced many contemporaries that the party had come to the end of the road and faced complete disintegration.

The situation, then, was a puzzling one. The Government did not even command much confidence amongst its own supporters

---

[1] *National Review*, Dec. 1900, Vol. XXXVI, pp. 462–3.
[2] Hamilton Papers, Add. Mss. 48,677; Journals, 24.12.00: f. 75.

and members. Yet this same government, showing many signs of
fatigue and disarray, had been given an extension of power at the
election of October 1900, and there was the strong possibility that,
with no effective opposition to challenge it, it might survive until
as late as 1906 or 1907, unloved and unwanted.

Only this abnormal situation can explain why it was that between 1900 and 1902 so many hopes should have been pinned on
Lord Rosebery. True, the aura of theatricality which always
surrounded Rosebery's activities, ensured that his views would be
well publicized. A hostile radical journalist, Massingham, complained that the Press reported and commented upon Rosebery's
every utterance, 'as though he were a new soap or a member of the
Royal Family'.[1] But the basic reason for his political prominence
was that, standing aloofly above party, he escaped the unpopularity which enveloped both Government and Opposition. He would
anyhow have enjoyed great prestige as an ex-Prime Minister and
imperialist of many years' standing, but this prestige was considerably enhanced by the position he assumed during these years as
the acknowledged high priest of the cult of 'efficiency' and 'business
principles'. At the same time that he was diagnosing the nation's
ills, Rosebery was offering an alternative political leadership to that
of the two Front Benches. It was common to regard him as the
Chatham of his age,[2] the one man who could rally the Empire in
its hour of crisis and provide strong war-time leadership.

The war correspondent and political commentator, Spenser
Wilkinson, was a Unionist and wrote mainly for Conservative
journals, but Salisbury's 'confession of impotence' in the Lords in
January 1900 made him so angry that he began to look for a possible replacement. At once his thoughts turned to Rosebery.

'Lord Rosebery at least sees the situation and understands the
position' he told his readers.

There is no other public man who commands such general confidence,
and it is practically certain that if the Cabinet were compelled to resign
by an adverse vote of the House of Commons Lord Rosebery would be
the first statesman to be consulted by the Queen. Lord Rosebery could

---

[1] *Speaker*, 24.1.03, p. 415.

[2] Rosebery's book on Chatham was not published until 1910, but it was
common knowledge that he was working on a study of the great war leader.

make a Government tomorrow if he would ignore parties and pick out the competent men wherever they are to be found. . .[1]

This was one of the sources of Lord Rosebery's strength. The other was his role as spokesman for the ideas of national efficiency. Speeches, like the eloquent Rectorial Address which he delivered at Glasgow University on 16 November 1900,[2] won him the confidence of many Conservative organs of opinion, not least of them *The Times*, whose manager, Moberly Bell, was a confessed admirer.[3] Among many sectors of the community, Unionist as well as Liberal, Rosebery had established himself as 'the advocate of the Nation'.

Yet Rosebery could not have thrown off his Liberal Party past, even had he so desired; and in fact he continued to exercise great influence over a sizeable faction within that party. In particular, the Liberal Imperialist leaders in the Commons, Asquith, Grey, Fowler and Haldane, looked to Rosebery for guidance, inspiration and moral support, and repeatedly urged him to lead them into battle against the 'Little Englander' radicals and Campbell-Bannerman.

It was clear to all that the Liberal Party was split over the war. But Liberals were also at odds over the question of how far their domestic policy needed to be adapted to the circumstances of a rapidly changing world. Rosebery and his admirers in the Liberal Party wished to throw over the Newcastle Progamme, partly because they considered it to be an electoral liability, partly because they thought a radical programme of that kind an anachronism in the twentieth century. Rosebery's advocacy of efficiency seemed to indicate the lines along which the badly battered Liberal Party might be reformed and 'modernized'.

From the start, therefore, Rosebery's position was ambiguous. Willingly or otherwise, he was drawn into the internal disputes of the Liberal Party, while at the same time appealing to a much broader sector of the public as a statesman who stood outside and

[1] Spenser Wilkinson, *Lessons of the War* (1900), pp. 152, 158–9 .These observations were made in a commentary, dated 1.2.00.

[2] Printed in Lord Rosebery, *Miscellanies* (1921), Vol. II, pp. 229–63.

[3] See the numerous letters from Moberly Bell to Rosebery in the Rosebery Papers, Box 76.

above the party struggle. On occasion Rosebery and his closest
followers expressed their hope of influencing and ultimately controlling the historic Liberal Party; yet they also realized that the
ideology of national efficiency provided the possible foundation for
a new political grouping which would cut completely across the
existing party divisions. It was perhaps because Rosebery could
never clearly decide in his own mind between these two alternatives that his behaviour in the Boer War period so often appeared
wayward and perverse.

Most historians have put forward a very different interpretation.
In their accounts Rosebery is shown as attempting in a half-
hearted and ineffectual way to oust Campbell-Bannerman from
the Liberal leadership and to resume his former position with the
aid of the Liberal Imperialist faction. But if that had indeed been
his chief purpose in 1900 and 1901, then his political strategy was
inept to the last degree. In fact, Rosebery in his speeches laid
great stress on the obsolescence and harmfulness of the British
party system—hardly the line to be expected from an aspiring
party leader.[1] One might be cynical about Rosebery's frequent
protestations that he had no wish to re-enter the inner councils of
the Liberal Party, but for the fact that on several occasions when
events were playing into his hands, he acted, as we shall see, in
such a way as to make his resumption of the Liberal leadership
impossible. Rosebery's character doubtless contained a certain
streak of self-destructiveness, but to account for his failure to re-
unite the Liberals under his leadership by reference to the peculiar-
ities of his temperament is to miss the significance of this phase of
his career.

Although the disasters of 'Black Week' induced Rosebery to return
to the political stage from his semi-retirement, the Cassandra-like
orations which he delivered in 1900 and early 1901 were not likely
to revive Liberal Party fortunes. Nor were they even intended to do
so. For Rosebery during this period was mainly anxious to flaunt
his freedom from *all* party ties. Thus, in the spring of 1900 he
suddenly resigned the presidency of two Liberal organizations, the

[1] See above, Ch. III, p. 93.

Scottish Liberal Association and the Midlothian Association, explaining that retention of these honorary posts was at variance with the decision he had made in 1896 to abstain from party politics. In his letter to the Scottish Liberal Association, he spoke of resuming 'his absolute independence unfettered even by the slight bonds of nominal office'.[1]

Although Rosebery did intervene in the Khaki Election in the autumn of that year, there was a certain ambiguity in his utterances. Captain Lambton, a minor war hero who was standing as a Liberal candidate of the imperialist persuasion, was sent a public letter of support, in which Rosebery took the Unionist government to task for its general inefficiency and its inadequate preparations for the South African crisis. Yet, as in all his pronouncements of this time, he spoke as though from a great height, above the noise of party strife, impartially dispensing praise and blame to all whom it might concern.

Rosebery's status as a 'national' statesman was emphasized in the summer and autumn of 1900 by his connection with the 'Administrative Reform Association', to which reference has already been made.[2] This organization had no importance in itself and soon petered out, partly, it seems, because, just as its draft constitution was ready for discussion, the general election was held and all other political activities receded into the background.[3] But the aim of the proposed association, to draw attention to the lessons of the Boer War and to advertise the need for conducting the business of the country upon ordinary business principles and methods, met with an enthusiastic response from notable public figures belonging to both parties and to none. Heading the list of people who declared their support for it was Lord Rosebery.[4] The organizers of this venture were undoubtedly concerned to 'puff' Rosebery and to strengthen his bi-partisan appeal.

Rosebery himself wanted to safeguard his 'independent' position, because, like many contemporaries, he anticipated a break-

---

[1] *Liberal Magazine*, Vol. 8, p. 126.

[2] See above, Ch. III, pp. 87–9.

[3] Rosebery gave this explanation in a speech to the Wolverhampton Chamber of Commerce (*Times*, 17.1.01).

[4] *Nineteenth Century*, July 1900, Vol. XLVIII, p. 1. ibid., Aug. and Nov. 1900, Vol. XLVIII, pp. 173–83, 859–80.

up of the Unionist government when Salisbury retired, as he was shortly bound to do. Given this situation, Campbell-Bannerman would have had difficulty in forming an alternative administration, and this in turn might have obliged the Monarch to call in an elder statesman to head an emergency coalition for the duration of the war. The likelihood of Rosebery being summoned in this capacity would obviously be increased by his keeping free from all party entanglements.

In March 1901 Rosebery's friend, Edward Hamilton, a senior Treasury official, asked Edward VII's Private Secretary, Lord Knollys, to put these considerations before the King. Soon afterwards the King, again on Hamilton's prompting, did actually approach Rosebery in person; he appealed to his patriotism and public spirit and asked him to hold himself in readiness for a possible return to office.[1] This appeal certainly seems to have made an impression, since a few weeks later we find Rosebery discussing with his friends the very contingency which the King had mentioned. When Salisbury retired, he mused, the only alternative to a Conservative administration would be 'a sort of Coalition Government, formed of the best men of both Parties'. 'If I am right in my calculations,' he added, 'I shall be able to be turned to more useful account by maintaining my political independence.'[2]

Here, perhaps, is the explanation for Rosebery's failure to join the Imperial Liberal Council, a Liberal Party ginger group which he was known to view with benevolent interest.[3] Rosebery's speculations about the possibilities of a coalition may also lie behind his seemingly odd behaviour in June and July 1901, when the quarrel inside the Liberal Party over events in South Africa came to its climax. For throughout the period of the 'war to the knife

[1] Hamilton Papers, Add. Mss. 48,677; Journals, 24.2.01, 3.3.01, 8.3.01; ff. 128, 133, 138. But according to the King's account to Salisbury, he merely asked Rosebery to resume the leadership of the Opposition; see P. Magnus, *King Edward the Seventh* (1964), p. 293.

[2] Hamilton Papers, Add. Mss. 48,678; Journals, 17.3.01: ff. 9–10.

[3] Rosebery wrote to the Vice-President of the Council, Robert Perks, on June 29th; 'The less your new party is tainted with Roseberyism the better. My conviction is that I had better remain as I am and take no part. Later on as an independent coadjutor I may or may not be of use.' (Marquess of Crewe, *Lord Rosebery* (1931), Vol. II, p. 568).

and fork', Rosebery affected a studied detachment. He refused to attend the Asquith dinner, and, what is more, two days before this demonstration occurred, he released to the press an open letter, in which he argued that the divergent views to be found within the Liberal Party were irreconcilable; a few hours before Asquith made his big speech, Rosebery descended on the City Liberal Club and expanded on this theme, adding, in a phrase which soon became famous, that for his own part he intended to 'plough his lonely furrow'.[1]

Naturally Asquith was cross at this intervention,[2] which distracted attention from his own pronouncement and nearly upset his carefully prepared publicity arrangements. Even Haldane was estranged, and later bitterly reproached Rosebery for deserting Asquith and the other Liberal Imperialists when they were fighting for their political lives.[3] The outcome of Rosebery's actions in July 1901 was to drive Asquith, Grey and Haldane back on to their own resources, in the belief that Rosebery had finally retired from active politics. Consequently, when Rosebery again 'emerged' in December to deliver his well-advertised address at Chesterfield, the Liberal Imperialists who loyally joined him on the platform did so in complete ignorance of what he was about to say.

Possibly Rosebery's reasoning was that, since he could anyway count upon the ultimate support of the Asquith-Grey-Haldane set, he might as well concentrate his efforts on winning over sympathizers who stood outside the ranks of the Liberal Party: a course of action with which Haldane, though not Asquith, undoubtedly had a certain sympathy. At this point we must therefore examine Rosebery's relationship during 1901 with those non-Liberals who shared his general political outlook.

*

[1] R. R. James, *Rosebery* (1963), pp. 424–7. Roy Jenkins, *Asquith* (1964), pp. 123–8.

[2] Rosebery Papers, Box 24: Haldane to Rosebery, 22.7.01. The annoyance of the Liberal Imperialist group as a whole soon found public outlet in Grey's speech at Peterborough, in which Rosebery was taken to task for his refusal to participate in the political rough and tumble; *Liberal Magazine*, Vol. 9, pp. 386–7.

[3] Rosebery Papers, Box 24; Haldane to Rosebery, 11.11.01.

Of these, the most prominent was Sir Alfred Milner, the British High Commissioner in South Africa. Milner's political views had not yet fully crystallized, but even at this stage of his career he had begun to expound to a small band of devoted disciples his damaging criticisms of the British liberal state. Opponents like John Morley saw him as an 'imitation Bismarck'. There was certainly a doctrinaire and violent tone to Milner's opinions; not being a Parliamentarian or career politician, Milner had no incentive to compromise with 'the system'. But what he was saying about the importance of expertise in public life, the need to organize the resources of the Empire, the disastrous influence of party politics on national interests and so on, differed little in essence from Rosebery's version of national efficiency.

In view of this, it is interesting to find that while Milner was away in South Africa, a number of his close friends living in England, among them Sir Henry Birchenough and Philip Lyttelton Gell, were doing what they could with their pens to promote Rosebery's political prospects. Gell used the background negotiations over the founding of the Administrative Reform Association to play the role of intermediary between Rosebery and Milner,[1] passing on to Rosebery extracts from a letter which he had recently received from the High Commissioner. Rosebery, he discovered, was 'extremely interested and impressed by them and said they were exactly his own views—that he would almost have guessed (had the dates not been what they were) that Milner must have read speeches of his on the same subject before uttering what he did. . .'[2]

But this undoubted ideological affinity was not accompanied by any great personal warmth. In fact, Rosebery had his private doubts about the wisdom of Milner's diplomacy, as Campbell-Bannerman, for one, realized.[3] This was where the other Liberal Imperialist leaders—Asquith, Grey and Haldane—took leave of Rosebery. These men were all old friends of Milner's; they shared his ideas and came from a similar background; and so they were

[1] Lyttelton Gell Papers: Knowles to Gell, 11.6.00.

[2] ibid., Knowles to Gell, 28.7.00.

[3] Spender Papers, Add. Mss. 46,388; Campbell-Bannerman to J. Smith, 27.11.99: f. 33.

prepared to rely on his judgement and support his policies through thick and thin, even when he had apparently blundered.[1]

But this 'religio Milneriana', as Campbell-Bannerman caustically called it, was not a simple matter of hero-worship. As a price for supporting Milner's actions whenever they came under attack in the Commons, the Liberal Imperialists tried to exact concessions and impose conditions. Haldane, his most uncritical supporter among the group, wanted the High Commissioner to be 'gentle in the little things that do not matter', so that a truly 'national' approach to South Africa might emerge.[2] Haldane apparently entertained the idea that Milner might be got to exert a restraining influence over Chamberlain, whose truculent speeches tended to alienate Liberal M.P.s of *all* views.[3] Now, on this issue Milner cannot have been anxious to meet his Liberal Imperialist friends; for although he, too, disliked the 'electioneering streak' in the Colonial Secretary's political make-up, he could not afford to offend the minister who was the main prop of his South African policy. And grateful though he was to Asquith, Grey and Haldane, he well knew that their motives in supporting him were not entirely disinterested. Apart from wishing to prise Milner away from Chamberlain, Haldane, for one, had vague hopes of getting him to align himself, in some way or another, with Rosebery and the other Liberal Imperialist leaders. By risking everything in his friend's defence, he wished to put Milner under an overwhelming obligation, which would influence him, when the time came to leave South Africa and enter the domestic political fray.

When in May 1901 Milner returned to England on leave, Haldane made a determined effort to involve him in Liberal Party disputes, on the imperialist side. In mid-June he arranged for

[1] Notably in late 1901 at the time of the Concentration Camps fiasco. Milner admitted to Haldane that the herding of women and children wholesale in camps had been a 'military mistake', but he assured him that the civilian administration in South Africa was acting vigorously to remedy the blunder; C. Headlam (ed.), *The Milner Papers: South Africa, 1899–1905* (1933), Vol. II, pp. 230–1; Milner to Haldane, 8.12.01. For the Liberal Imperialists such a personal assurance was sufficient, and so they refrained from launching embarrassing attacks on the South African authorities.

[2] Haldane Papers, Vol. 5905; Haldane to Milner, 6.7.01: f. 82 (copy).

[3] ibid. See also Grey's complaint to Milner about Chamberlain's methods of party warfare; Milner Papers, Vol. 39; Grey to Milner, 24.5.01: f. 149.

Milner to have a quiet, confidential discussion with Asquith, Grey and himself at his London flat.[1] A week later he was introducing sixteen of the Liberal Imperialist M.P.s to the High Commissioner at another similar social gathering.[2] Renewal of personal contact convinced Haldane more strongly than ever before of Milner's benevolence, capacity and administrative genius.[3] With the concurrence of Grey and Asquith, he sent off an uncharacteristically emotional letter, assuring Milner that there was no danger of the Liberal Imperialists deserting him in the future.[4] He even tried to get the High Commissioner to attend the Asquith dinner. Courteously but firmly, Milner refused: 'of course,' he explained, 'you will understand that I would have asked to come to A(squith)'s dinner and have come hopping, had I not learned that what would have been merely an act of friendly admiration would be treated as an intrusion into the domain of party politics and would therefore hamper rather than help.'[5]

Rebuffed in this direction, Haldane adopted a more circuitous approach, seeking to ingratiate himself with Milner's political friends in England. One such person, whom Haldane singled out for attention, was Sir Clinton Dawkins. A brief summary of Dawkins' career will illustrate the kind of man who tended to be attracted to the national efficiency movement. In 1900 Dawkins had retired from the post of financial member of the Council of the Governor General in India to become the principal London partner in the American financial house of Pierpont Morgan. His ultimate ambition was to enter the House of Commons, but the Khaki Election had come too early for him to look for a seat; besides which, he first wanted to acquire experience of the City and to visit America.[6] Yet despite being outside Parliament, Dawkins soon had ample occasion to see British politics and public administration from close quarters.

In 1900 the Government made Dawkins chairman of a committee of business men which was set up to investigate the functioning

[1] Haldane Papers, Vol. 5965; Haldane to Mother, 13.6.01: ff. 213–14.
[2] ibid., Haldane to Mother, 20.6.01: f. 226.
[3] ibid., Haldane to Mother, 14.6.01: ff. 215–16.
[4] C. Headlam, op. cit., Vol. II, pp. 264–5; Haldane to Milner, 6.7.01.
[5] Haldane Papers, Vol. 5905; Milner to Haldane, 15.7.01: f. 86.
[6] Curzon Papers, Vol. 181; Dawkins to Curzon, 5.10.00: f. 174.

of the War Office, and which later submitted a report sharply critical of the existing administrative system. Dawkins was deeply shocked by the chaos he had uncovered and by the quarrelsomeness and ineptitude of the War Office generals.[1] Meanwhile Dawkins' position with Morgan was bringing him into contact with the Government for discussions on the floating of war loans in the City. These contacts left on him a strong sense of the mediocrity of nearly all Cabinet Ministers, compared with the great Imperial Proconsuls, Cromer, Curzon and Milner, under whom he had worked and with whom he remained friendly. Dawkins felt that there must be something fundamentally 'rotten' about all aspects of British public life, which only a political revolution could eradicate.[2]

In November 1901 Haldane concluded that Dawkins was ripe for conversion. Dawkins reported to Milner:

I had an interesting political evening last week (in a private room of the Cafe Royal) with Haldane, with whose views I sympathise, and for whose abilities and courage I have great respect. Haldane's object—but he threw his fly delicately—was to get me to join him and his group. I could not, of course, do so as an active politician or member of the House while with Morgan . . . but perhaps I could be useful in some ways—and there are subscriptions.[3]

Nevertheless, the evening's conversation did not lead to Dawkins making a definite political commitment.

The reluctance of men like Dawkins to join forces with the Liberal Imperialists would have quickly disappeared, if only they could have been reassured that there was no risk of their being involved in hostilities with their great political hero, Chamberlain. Now, in a community where the lines of political cleavage were determined by fundamental convictions and beliefs, this dilemma would clearly never have arisen. For so close were the points of view which

[1] Milner Papers, Vol. 39; Dawkins to Milner, 25.1.01, 22.3.01: ff. 37, 39.
[2] An interesting collection of letters from Dawkins to Milner can be found in the Milner Papers, Vol. 39–41.
[3] Milner Papers, Vol. 39; Dawkins to Milner, 17.11.01: f. 50.

Chamberlain and Rosebery held, that an alliance between them would have been logical.

Nowhere was this resemblance more striking than in the approach each man adopted towards higher education. Before proceeding further, we should briefly examine the problems thrown up in this field, if only to define the ideals with which Rosebery and Chamberlain were alike associated in the public mind. Common to both men, and to the national efficiency movement as a whole, was an urgent desire to create new technological universities for the training of 'captains of industry'. Germany and the United States of America were in this respect the models usually singled out by British reformers for emulation. But in fact these two nations had built up their impressive systems of higher education by very different methods. The German universities were largely state-financed and state-controlled, whereas American ones, although receiving state grants that were lavish by British standards, owed their prosperity principally to the endowments of the benevolent rich.[1]

Even Germanophiles, like Haldane, conceded that the degree of bureaucratic interference in German universities would be rightly condemned in Britain as an intolerable encroachment on academic freedom. Moreover, there was still a current notion, articulated by Hicks-Beach, the Chancellor of the Exchequer, as late as 1901, that grants-in-aid to universities and university colleges had the effect of demoralizing their recipients, as Poor Law relief was thought to do to the improvident pauper. This being the situation, it seemed that Britain had more to learn, at least in the short run, from the American experience. Once business men had been brought to understand the returns which would follow a generous endowment of new technological and commercial colleges—a point which their American counterparts had already grasped—then the state of British higher education would rapidly improve. That, roughly, was the conviction of men like Chamberlain and Rosebery: and on this conviction they were prepared to act.

As Chancellor of the newly chartered Birmingham University,

---

[1] 'The amount raised during 1871–1901 by private munificence for higher education was, in the United States, more than eight times that similarly provided in the United Kingdom.' (*Nature*, Vol. LXVIII, p. 28; 14.5.03).

Chamberlain proved very skilful at charming money out of the pockets of rich business men in the locality.[1] However, as he explained to Haldane, he could not, while Colonial Secretary, approach the South African millionaires: 'I should certainly be told by Mr. Lloyd George or some other gentleman of equally delicate morality that I had sold myself to them.'[2] Rosebery and Haldane, on the other hand, worked under no such limitation. Through his marriage to Hannah Rothschild, Rosebery had established himself on friendly terms with certain City bankers and Jewish financiers. This enabled him to promote new educational ventures, not only by publicizing them, but also by persuading his rich City friends to come forward with generous subscriptions. Pushed forward by Haldane, Rosebery associated his name, in one capacity or another, with nearly all the extensions of higher education facilities that were made in the first few years of this century. For example, he served as a trustee of the Rhodes Scholarship Scheme[3] and also helped administer the Carnegie endowment to the Scottish universities. He also participated in the building up of the London School of Economics and in the founding of a 'London Charlottenburg', as we shall see below (pp. 124–5). Closely parallel to these ventures was Chamberlain's work in establishing a large-scale civic university, on the American model, at Birmingham: a university which Chamberlain intended to energize the commercial and industrial life of the entire West Midlands region.[4]

Yet although they were advancing towards the same goal,

---

[1] Oliver Lodge, *Past Years* (1931), p. 319.

[2] F. Maurice, *Haldane, 1856–1915* (1937), p. 116; Chamberlain to Haldane, n.d.

[3] Rhodes had long admired Rosebery, and had taken him into his confidence when drawing up the preliminary drafts of the Will; W. T. Stead (ed.), *The Last Will and Testament of Cecil J. Rhodes* (1902), p. 39. *The Times* (7.4.02) thought that since Rosebery was the politician most in sympathy with the ideals of Rhodes, he should have been made President of the Trust.

[4] In a speech to the Court of Governors in 1905, Chamberlain denied that Birmingham had any desire to rival Oxford and Cambridge on the arts side; Birmingham's 'special *raison d'être*,' he said, was to 'teach, as it had never been taught before, science, and also to proceed in the work of scientific research' (*Times*, 15.5.05). More specifically, he wanted the University to systematize and develop the special training required by men of business, and to do for those engaged in commerce and manufacture what was already being done for the professions of law and medicine.

Rosebery and Chamberlain could not avoid bickering, even over university reform. Chamberlain, jealous of the fame of his Birmingham University, somewhat resented Rosebery's activities in London, fearing that they detracted from his own creation.[1] This pettiness sprang out of the more general personal dislike which Rosebery and Chamberlain had for one another.[2] Like his Liberal Imperialist friends, Rosebery could never forgive nor forget the Colonial Secretary's unscrupulous language and behaviour during the Khaki Election. After the election was over, he had retaliated against Chamberlain by joining in the outcry over the latter's connections with certain War Office contractors.[3] Always a 'bonny hater', Chamberlain was not the man to pass lightly over this incident. Neither then nor later did he have any faith in Rosebery's judgement or courage.[4] And Rosebery, for his part, sharply disapproved of Chamberlain's periodic incursions into diplomacy, thinking them to be, not only tasteless in the extreme, but reckless and foolhardy as well.[5] All these considerations help explain why a Rosebery-Chamberlain combination, the possibility of which was on many people's lips,[6] never actually materialized.

A common interest in university reform did, however, form a bridge between Rosebery and the Fabians, with Haldane, an old family friend of the Webbs, playing the part of bridge-builder. All

[1] See A. P. Thomson, 'The Chamberlain Memorial Tower . . .' (*University of Birmingham Historical Journal*, Vol. 3, 1951–2, p. 172).

[2] Esher noted how the two men 'bickered' on the Queen Victoria Memorial Committee in February, 1901; M. V. Brett (ed.), *Journals and Letters of Reginald Viscount Esher* (1934), Vol. I, pp. 286–7.

[3] Hansard, 4th Series, Vol. 88, col. 47; 6.12.00.

[4] See Julian Amery, *Joseph Chamberlain* (1951), Vol. IV, p. 19.

[5] At Chesterfield Rosebery called Chamberlain's amateur diplomacy 'a national inconvenience, if not a national danger' (Lord Rosebery: *National Policy*, p. 5; Liberal League Pamphlet, no. 1).

[6] e.g. *Fortnightly Review*, June 1900, Vol. LXVII, pp. 1069–1082, 'Lord Rosebery and a National Cabinet'. Edward Hamilton's response to this article was: 'The combination may be beautiful in theory; but, rash though it is to prophesy about the future of anything in politics, I would lay long odds at their ever coming together. Each distrusts the other, and neither is likely to give way to the other.' (Edward Hamilton Papers, Add. Mss. 48,676; Journals, 8.6.00: f. 93).

Haldane's bland diplomacy was needed to secure this collaboration. Indeed, when in March 1900 he first brought the Webbs and Rosebery together at a select dinner party at his London flat, the guests took an instinctive dislike to one another, and Rosebery could only be induced to sit next to Beatrice by Haldane insisting on changing places; even then Rosebery for some time pointedly avoided speaking to his neighbour.[1] Afterwards, Haldane tried to smooth things over by writing a note to Beatrice Webb, telling her of the conquest she had made of Rosebery; 'he spoke to me in a way that was alarming,' added Haldane coyly; 'You ought not to insist on spelling "Woman" with a capital. It is not safe!'[2] But Beatrice Webb was not that gullible, and she watched with cynical amusement her scheming friend's attempt to spread 'a Rosebery-Webb myth.'[3]

Despite their first unfavourable impressions, the Webbs continued to urge on Rosebery, through the good offices of Haldane, the idea of a 'national minimum of health, education and efficiency'.[4] It is an indication of how detached they had become from the fortunes of the British Socialist parties that they should have felt Rosebery to be a man worthy of cultivation. Nevertheless, the Webbs were convinced that, however vague Rosebery's references to social problems might be, they were entirely consistent with the philosophy of the 'national minimum'; and, encouraged by Haldane, they flattered themselves into believing that they might foist a 'constructive' social policy on to the wealthy Whig aristocrat. Besides this, the Webbs had the usual contempt of the national efficiency group for Campbell-Bannerman, and thought the school of liberalism associated with the pro-Boer radicals 'extremely distasteful in every respect'.[5] So, Rosebery, for all his limitations, struck the Fabian Society leaders as the likeliest person among the recognized national statesmen of his day to implement the sort of social programme in which they believed.

[1] Beatrice Webb, *Our Partnership* (1948), p. 198; 16.3.00.
[2] Passfield Papers, II 4 b; Haldane to B. Webb, 18.3.00: f. 17.
[3] B. Webb, op. cit., p. 198; 16.3.00.
[4] ibid., p. 203; 9.12.00.
[5] ibid., p. 228; 28.2.02. On another occasion she wrote of the usefulness of Rosebery as a force that would 'destroy Gladstonianism' (ibid., p. 220: 28.7.01.)

But in addition to these considerations there was a very genuine community of interest between Rosebery and the Webbs on the education question. When they again met, in February 1901, this common enthusiasm led to Rosebery's acceptance of the presidency of the London School of Economics.[1] This institution had been founded by the Webbs in 1895 to serve as a great training centre in the social sciences for 'captains of industry', politicians and administrators.[2] But shortage of funds had prevented the school from developing as fast as had been hoped, and for a time the Webbs were obliged to put £1,000 of their own money into it, a sacrifice they could ill afford to make.[3] This was where the enlistment of Rosebery proved to be so useful. He persuaded his cousin by marriage, Lord Rothschild, into becoming treasurer of the school, and the scene was thus set for Haldane to organize a big fund-raising appeal in the City.[4] When the meeting at the Mansion House was duly held on 21 March 1901, Rosebery was the principal speaker,[5] and though his speech for once was a disappointment and the meeting did not bring in as much money as the director, Hewins, had expected,[6] the first step had been taken to publicize the school's existence and present it as the sort of institution that was attracting, and deserved to attract, the support of 'practical' men. When Rosebery managed in the following year to get the manager of the Northeastern Railway Company, of which he was a director, to send employees to the school for instruction in business management in a newly founded railway

[1] Haldane was characteristically complacent about the success of the evening: 'We had good talk, and the minds of those present were, I think, brought on to converging lines in matters political'; Haldane Papers, Vol. 5965: Haldane to Mother, 9.2.01: f. 53. Beatrice Webb, on the other hand, thought that there had been so much frivolous gossip and chaff that no time had been left for serious political discussion; Passfield Papers, II 4 b: B. Webb to Mary Playne, 10.2.01: f. 41.

[2] For the history of the early years of the London School of Economics, see Janet Beveridge, *An Epic of Clare Market* (1960.)

[3] Passfield Papers, II 4 b; B. Webb to Mary Playne, mid-Feb., 1901: f. 43.

[4] Haldane Papers, Vol. 5965; Haldane to Mother, 4.3.01: ff. 91–2.

[5] The appearance of Rosebery before a very distinguished audience, which included the Lord Mayor and the American Ambassador, was, as Beatrice Webb noted, 'an audacious advertisement and appeal' (B. Webb, op. cit., p. 213, 22.3.01).

[6] B. Webb, op. cit., p. 214: 2.4.01.

department, the Webbs must have felt that their association with the Liberal Imperialist group was beginning to pay real dividends.[1]

This co-operation in educational matters continued long after the Webbs had finally despaired of Rosebery as a 'national leader', and one of its fruits was the public launching in June 1903 of a scheme for a 'London Charlottenburg', out of which grew the Imperial College of Science and Technology at South Kensington. Haldane's role was to encourage the financial house of Wernher & Beit to make the initial endowment. Webb worked as chairman of the Technical Education Board of the L.C.C. to ensure that the new technological university received an annual grant from the rates of £20,000. Rosebery was useful as a 'name': it was he who announced the scheme in the form of an open letter to Lord Monkswell, the chairman of the L.C.C., and who later became the president of the trust set up to administer the Wernher-Beit endowment. Webb and Haldane had, of course, quietly done the bulk of the preparatory work behind the scenes.[2]

As early as the summer of 1901 this co-operation in the field of higher education had put the Webbs under a debt of gratitude to Rosebery, and still more to Haldane. When Sidney Webb finally agreed to attend the Asquith dinner in July, he did so, not because he felt strongly about the conduct of the South African War, but principally to please Haldane and to re-pay him for his help in educational matters. Beatrice admits in her Journal that they had been 'to some extent manipulated' into becoming followers of Rosebery.[3] The fact was that the Webbs needed Haldane very much more than he needed them; nearly every single important contact which they made in the opening years of the century was obtained through an introduction from Haldane, and this indebtedness tended to affect their political outlook.

Moreover, from the start, Bernard Shaw succeeded in getting

---

[1] *The Times* was very favourably impressed by the support that the school was getting from 'practical' people (22.3.01, 30.5.02).

[2] I have described these background negotiations at some length in my doctoral dissertation, 'The Development of the Concept of "National Efficiency" and its Relation to Politics and Government, 1900–1910'(Cambridge University, 1965), pp. 89–97.

[3] B. Webb, op. cit., p. 218: 9.7.01. ibid., p. 228: 28.2.02.

on to good terms with Rosebery. The Fabian tract, *Fabianism and the Empire*, which Shaw had largely drafted, had proved to the liking of Rosebery, who sent its author 'various gracious messages'.[1] Shaw consequently saw an opportunity for the Webbs to exercise their skill as 'tool wielders', with Rosebery as the 'political tool . . . screaming for somebody to come and handle him'.[2] Later, after Sidney had committed himself by attending the Asquith dinner, Shaw wrote urging them both 'to plunge in with Rosebery as the best chance of moulding home policy'.[3]

This was the origin of the famous article in the *Nineteenth Century* of September 1901, 'Lord Rosebery's Escape From Houndsditch', in which the Liberal Imperialists were invited to discard the last vestiges of Gladstonianism and to create a live opposition party on the basis of Fabian collectivism.[4] The whole tone of the article was in harmony with the general propaganda about national efficiency, and reminiscent in parts of Rosebery's own speeches. Campbell-Bannerman wrote sardonically of 'admirable sentiments which I have heard enunciated by other and greater men: which may be master and which scholar I do not know', adding 'I fear I am too old to join that Academy'.[5]

But Rosebery was delighted and flattered. 'I hope you will keep Webb out of London, or have him protected by the police,' he wrote to Beatrice, 'for his life can hardly be safe since the publication of his article in the *Nineteenth Century*—the most brilliant article that I have read for many a day'.[6] And Haldane also sent a note, expressing the appreciation of Asquith and himself.[7]

---

[1] ibid., p. 203: 9.12.00.

[2] Shaw to Sidney Webb, probably in the autumn of 1900. Quoted in Janet Dunbar, *Mrs G. B. S.: A Biographical Portrait of Charlotte Shaw* (1963), pp. 191–2.

[3] B. Webb, op. cit., p. 220: 28,7.01.

[4] *Nineteenth Century*, Sep. 1901, Vol. L, pp. 366–86.

[5] Campbell-Bannerman to H. Gladstone, 12.9.01, cited in J. A. Spender, *Sir Henry Campbell-Bannerman* (1923), Vol. II, p. 4.

[6] Passfield Papers; II 4 b; Rosebery to B. Webb, 3.9.01: f. 72a.

[7] ibid., Haldane to B. Webb, 5.9.01: f. 76. The Fabian Society soon afterwards had this article re-published as one of their Tracts (no. 108). It was sent to members of the Society in December. 'A special effort should be made to secure for it at once a wide circulation,' explained the editor of *Fabian News*, 'because the present is a moment when political opinion is in a state of flux, and people are likely to be unusually ready to entertain the ideas which the Tract embodies' (*Fabian News*, Dec. 1901, Vol. XI, no. 10).

On 15 September Haldane felt the moment opportune for drawing the Webbs more deeply into the support of his 'group'. 'I think the success of the article . . . shews that the time is at hand when he (Sidney) ought to come into Parliament,' he wrote to Beatrice. 'This is also the strong opinion of E. Grey, who was speaking of it the other day when I saw him and I know it is that of Asquith also. What a lot of work he could do at the L(ocal) G(overnment) Board and in the Education Office!' The Liberal Imperialist movement, Haldane explained, had an expert in foreign affairs, Grey, an expert in constitutional law, himself, and an excellent all-rounder in Asquith. 'But you would bring in an expert element which only you can supply and which would give life to the whole business.'[1]

Beatrice Webb must have replied in a sceptical vein, for when Haldane next wrote to her, on 23 September, he admitted that for the present Sidney could do more valuable work *outside* Parliament. He claimed, however, that it was by no means an impossibility that the Liberal Imperialists would soon find themselves in power. In that contingency 'S.W. should at once come into the House and take a leading part in deciding his own part of the programme of Efficiency.' 'It is your word,' added Haldane, 'a large part of the items are yours. You have worked it out.'[2]

The Webbs could not help being influenced by such appeals. In early December 1901 Beatrice Webb wrote in her Journal that Sidney must complete his definitive study of local government as soon as possible, so that if circumstances should lead him into national politics, he could enjoy the reputation of being 'the "great authority on local government" as well as "the great authority on labour questions".' A later passage makes it clear that she was contemplating the prospect of her husband being 'the colleague' of the Liberal Imperialists.[3]

But how in the immediate future were the Liberal Imperialists to gain high office? It is difficult to determine what exactly was

---

[1] Passfield Papers, II 4 b; Haldane to B. Webb, 15.9.01: ff. 82–3.
[2] ibid; Haldane to B. Webb, 23.9.01: f. 85.
[3] ibid; Vol. 21, B. Webb's Journal, 9.12.01: ff. 58–9.

passing through the heads of Haldane and Beatrice Webb in late 1901. But during this period, as we have seen, Rosebery was at pains to detach himself from his Liberal Imperialist friends. All this while, moreover, he was busy establishing contacts with 'disaffected' backbench Unionist M.P.s, like Winston Churchill— to the jealous resentment of Haldane.[1] At this time Churchill was writing his father's biography, and Rosebery who was helping him in this task, was generous in his hospitality to the up-and-coming Conservative M.P. 'Politics provided additional links and ties,' Churchill later recalled. Rosebery 'was out of sympathy with the Liberals: I was soon quarrelling with the Tories. We could both toy with the dream of some new system and grouping of men and ideas. . . We had certainly that solid basis of agreement and harmony of outlook upon middle courses, which is shared by many sensible people and was in those days abhorrent to party machines.'[2]

Churchill was not the only young Conservative to be excited by the imminence of the Chesterfield speech. Others, flattered by Rosebery's attentions, actually attended the Chesterfield meeting, if Clinton Dawkins is to be believed. 'Their open talk,' Dawkins informed Milner, 'is of rallying round Rosebery, when the present Government falls to pieces. He is the hope of the young men who see no prospects before them under the existing family regime, as they call it, and also long for more vigour.'[3] Churchill himself was so carried away with enthusiasm for Rosebery's performance at Chesterfield that a fortnight after its delivery his friend, Lord Hugh Cecil, had to write him a cautionary letter. 'Joining a Middle Party' under Rosebery's leadership, was all very well, Cecil observed, and 'that may be a very proper course when there is a Middle Party to join'. Meanwhile, it was 'wise to play a waiting game and not to respond to the imperialist's invitations until he has built himself a house to entertain you in. . .'[4]

---

[1] Rosebery Papers, Box 24, Haldane to Rosebery, 11.11.01.

[2] W. Churchill, *Great Contemporaries* (1937, Fontana edition, 1962, p. 13).

[3] Milner Papers, Vol. 39; Dawkins to Milner, 20.12.01: f. 53.

[4] R. Churchill, *Winston Churchill: Young Statesman, 1901–1914* (1967), pp. 35–6. Probably Churchill was more attracted by the idea of a new combination of 'all we wretched unorganised middle thinkers' grouped under the command of an elder statesman he admired, than appreciative of the actual contents of the gospel of efficiency that Rosebery was preaching. Over the next few years he several

Cecil's words of caution were well justified. The prime difficulty that faced Rosebery, so far as putting himself at the head of some national combination was concerned, arose from the bad relationship between himself and Chamberlain. By the summer of 1901 Chamberlain had anyhow become reconciled to the fact that he would not have the Premiership on Salisbury's retirement and he had resolved to serve in a Balfour Cabinet. He as good as announced this to the public when he appeared with Balfour at a Unionist rally at Blenheim Park in August—using the occasion, moreover, to single out Rosebery for one of his wounding sneers.[1] At about this time, too, Chamberlain was wrecking Rosebery's delicate efforts to arrange peace negotiations between British and Boer emissaries: an action that initially provoked Rosebery into making his big speech at Chesterfield on 15 December.[2] 'Are you excited to know what Rosebery will say?', wrote Chamberlain to Morley in November. '*I am not*—and I think I know beforehand the ballad which the lonely one is likely to sing.' The Liberal Imperialists, he felt, were at heart only interested in giving 'Master Joe another fall.'[3]

Although Chamberlain's antagonism doomed any hope of a Rosebery-led coalition government, that does not mean that Rosebery was not thinking, however tentatively, of engineering some new political grouping which could give expression to the demand for national efficiency. The alternative, the replacement of Campbell-Bannerman as leader of the Liberal Party by Rosebery or some other Liberal Imperialist, was even less likely of fulfilment. Campbell-Bannerman, despite receiving a generally hostile press, enjoyed a much stronger position than surface appearances

---

times tried to create some such grouping: for example, in late 1903 and early 1904, when Balfour's Cabinet seemed on the verge of disintegration over the Tariff Reform issue, he was busily advocating a Free Trade Ministry which would include both Rosebery and the Duke of Devonshire (see Churchill's letters for this period in the Devonshire Papers). Filial piety may also have played a part; in 1887 Lord Randolph Churchill had dreamt of a 'central party', and Winston Churchill might well have been brooding over this idea, as he prepared his father's biography.

[1] *Liberal Magazine*, Vol. 9, p. 450.
[2] R. R. James, *Rosebery* (1963), pp. 427–9.
[3] Chamberlain Papers, Chamberlain to Morley, 10.11.01.

suggested. Thus, in June 1901, on the eve of the Asquith dinner, he had called the rebellious Liberal Imperialists M.P.s to heel, and there was nothing to prevent him doing the same thing again. Only a few days before Chesterfield the National Liberal Federation meeting at Derby had shown that the party machine was still stongly behind its leader. And within the Parliamentary Party the imperialist faction, however distinguished its personnel, was in a permanent minority.[1] Even after the Chesterfield speech, when for a moment Lloyd George and other 'Little Englander' radicals were loud in Rosebery's praise, the *Manchester Guardian*'s lobby correspondent calculated that if the Liberal M.P.s were given a chance to choose between Campbell-Bannerman and Rosebery, the former would win by a comfortable majority.[2] Doubtless, had Campbell-Bannerman 'stepped down' as leader and recommended Rosebery as his successor, this situation would have been accepted with a good grace by most Liberals. But for all his modesty, Campbell-Bannerman had a strong sense of obligation to his party and the traditions it embodied, and he knew that Rosebery's advocacy of efficiency involved the abandonment of many of the political principles he held dear. His determination to prevent Rosebery from re-entering the inner circles of the party can only have been strengthened by the sentiments that Rosebery expressed at Chesterfields on 16 December 1901.[3]

Lloyd George and other radicals welcomed the Chesterfield speech because in it Rosebery called for informal peace talks—something to which no other Liberal Imperialist had yet publicly committed himself. While dissociating himself from those Liberals who wanted Milner recalled from South Africa, Rosebery had actually poked a little fun at Milner's expense, over some remarks that the High Commissioner had made to the effect that 'the War might have no formal end'. In this way the possibility of Rosebery and Milner ever forming any kind of political alliance was effectively destroyed. In a high state of alarm, Haldane dashed off

[1] In October 1900 *The Times* thought that there were 81 Liberal M.P.s who 'supported the War'; see Heber Hart, *Reminiscences and Reflections* (1939), p. 208.

[2] *Manchester Guardian*, 23.12.01.

[3] Lord Rosebery, *National Policy*; Liberal League pamphlet no. 1.

explanatory letters to Milner and to Milner's friend, Clinton Dawkins;[1] but the damage had already been done.[2]

But if Rosebery's observations about the South African war brought him closer than before to the radical wing of the Liberal Party, his reflections on domestic affairs pointed in a different direction, and these were to have the more important long-term consequences. For at Chesterfield Rosebery spelt out what he had said on previous occasions: if the Liberal Party were to return to power, it must first clean its slate and abandon old programmes and watchwords for a bold policy of educational, administrative and social efficiency.

There was much here that recalled Sidney Webb's 'Houndsditch' article, as Haldane naturally pointed out to Beatrice.[3] The Chesterfield speech certainly delighted Beatrice Webb who sent Haldane a note of congratulation, which he passed on to Rosebery, as she must have hoped he would.[4] Neither Haldane nor the Webbs were to know that Rosebery reacted touchily when Campbell-Bannerman tackled him a few days later on his connections with the Webbs, saying, according to Campbell-Bannerman, that he 'thought the Houndsditch article very clever, but had no distinct recollection of it'.[5] The fleeting alliance between Rosebery's followers and the Webbs was undoubtedly a potential embarrassment

[1] Returning to London from Chesterfield, Haldane scribbled off a note to Dawkins at three in the morning, explaining that Rosebery had spoken much more to Milner's advantage than disadvantage. Dawkins, angry and contemptuous, left this note unanswered: Milner Papers, Vol. 39; Dawkins to Milner, 20.12.01: f. 55. He also sent two soothing letters to Milner; Haldane Papers, Vol. 5905, 22.12.01: f. 150 (copy); and Milner Papers, Vol. 40; Haldane to Milner, 26.1.02: f. 122.

[2] Milner protested that he bore Rosebery no grudge (C. Headlam, op. cit., Vol. II, pp. 289–90; Milner to Dawkins, 16.1.02). But his disclaimers do not ring true. Milner had in fact received an unpleasant shock from the Chesterfield speech; because of the confused telegraphic reports from England, wild rumours had been circulating for several days and no-one could make out precisely what Rosebery *had* said (Milner Papers, Vol. 28; Milner to Mrs Montefiore, 21.12.01: ff. 50–1). Milner's subsequent observations exude distrust of Rosebery: e.g. C. Headlam, op. cit., Vol. II, pp. 364–5; Milner to a Friend, 30.5.02.

[3] Passfield Papers, II 4 b; Haldane to B. Webb, 17.12.01: ff. 317a–317b.

[4] Rosebery Papers, Box 24; B. Webb to Haldane, 17.12.01, enclosed in letter from Haldane to Rosebery, 21.12.01.

[5] Campbell-Bannerman Papers, Add. Mss. 41, 211; Campbell-Bannerman to Bryce, 25.12.01: f. 182 (copy).

to both sides. The *Speaker*, a radical weekly, was not slow to point out the incongruities: 'Mr Webb had provided Lord Rosebery with "administrative efficiency" as a substitute for the programme and principles of Gladstone and Cobden. Sir Henry Fowler has enthusiastically adopted the Webb-Rosebery programme, but forgets that one of its chief points is that "there must be no more Fowlers or Chaplins or Longs".'[1]

Campbell-Bannerman, for once, was very blunt and forthright in his response: 'All that (Rosebery) said (at Chesterfield) about the clean slate and efficiency was an affront to Liberalism and was pure claptrap,' he complained to Herbert Gladstone. 'Efficiency as a watchword! Who is against it? This is all a mere rechauffé of Mr. Sidney Webb, who is evidently the chief instructor of the whole faction.'[2] Another old-school Liberal, Harcourt, found the Chesterfield speech 'insulting to the whole past of the Liberal Party and a betrayal of its growth in the future.'[3] This was fair comment. Clearly, efficiency of the kind Rosebery was advocating had nothing specifically Liberal about it, and actually conflicted head-on at many points with the Liberal creed of such men as Campbell-Bannerman and Harcourt. That is one more reason why Rosebery had no prospect whatever of re-uniting the Liberal Party under his leadership on the basis of the Chesterfield speech.

Rosebery is so enigmatic a figure that one can only speculate about what his motives might have been in December 1901. However, the Rosebery Papers contain an interesting letter written by Spender, the editor of the *Westminster Gazette*, dated 8 October 1901. It is a reply to a communication from Rosebery which unfortunately seems to have gone astray. In this missing letter Rosebery had apparently suggested writing to the press, giving his views on the political situation: views which Spender summarizes as follows:

1. Lord R. despairs of the Liberal Party, so far in entire consistency with his letter to the City Liberal Club.

---

[1] *Speaker*, 21.12.01: p. 323.
[2] J. A. Spender, op. cit., Vol. II, p. 14; Campbell-Bannerman to Herbert Gladstone, 18.12.01.
[3] A. G. Gardiner, *Sir William Harcourt* (1923), Vol. II, pp. 536–7.

2. Lord R. is prepared either to form or to take part in—both assumptions, I think, are necessary—a Govt. of affairs formed from both parties, in other words, a coalition government.
3. For this purpose he is willing to make the concessions which are necessary to reassure Unionists on the Irish question . . .

Perhaps surprisingly, Spender, who had previously objected to all talk of a Rosebery-led Coalition, now expressed his approval of this as an objective. He thought, however, that it would be a tactical mistake to publish such a manifesto while Parliament was in recess. He advised Rosebery to hold back until a more favourable moment had come. 'Speeches, however, are quite different things,' he observed.[1]

Is it reasonable to regard the Chesterfield speech as an elaboration of the thoughts that Rosebery had conveyed to Spender two months earlier? Admittedly, the speech was delivered from a Liberal Party platform; and, as the *Liberal Magazine* pointed out, this was actually the first time Rosebery had availed himself of such a means of expression since his resignation in 1896, 'a statement which is no less true because of his successive speeches at the City Liberal Club'.[2] (Rosebery more often addressed his words to business men at Chamber of Commerce banquets). Yet the Chesterfield speech was not directed at an exclusively Liberal audience, and it ended with an appeal from the strife of parties to the 'Nation', which, if words had meaning, seemed to suggest that Rosebery was thinking in terms of the creation of a new political movement or the formation of a non-party government. That, moreover, was the impression received by journalists of papers so varied in hue as the *Speaker*, the *Spectator* and the *Daily Mail*.[3]

The *Daily Mail* had no doubt as to the significance of the Chesterfield Speech:

Briefly, we may say that Lord Rosebery threw over both the Liberal and the Tory Parties and offered himself to a new party whose watchword will be Efficiency. . .[4]

---

[1] Rosebery Papers, Box 76; Spender to Rosebery, 8.10.01.
[2] *Liberal Magazine*, Vol. 9, Jan. 1902, p. 648.
[3] *Speaker*, 21.12.01: p. 324. *Spectator*, 4.1.02.
[4] *Daily Mail*, 17.12.01.

Next day it wrote:

Lord Rosebery has come forward with a policy which ought to unite
in his favour every man in the reputable section of the Opposition, and
which is bound to attach the most progressive elements among those of
the Government's adherents who are dissatisfied with the flabbiness of
the existing Ministry.[1]

Even more excited in tone was an article in the *Fortnightly
Review* written by 'Calchas', *alias* J. L. Garvin, who was trying his
hand for the first time at master-minding a coalition from his
Fleet Street office. It seemed to Garvin that the golden moment
had arrived for forming a Rosebery-Chamberlain Government:

The Imperial and social gospels of Chesterfield and Birmingham are
mere variants of one another. . . If Lord Rosebery is in favour of a
business cabinet, is not Mr. Chamberlain himself the most complete
example of the business man in politics that has yet been seen in the
public life of this or perhaps of any other country? . . . If Lord Rosebery
is in favour of efficiency, so is Mr. Chamberlain, and with an equal
opportunity would assuredly go much the straighter way to work to get it.

There was only one escape route from the impasse, concluded
Garvin dramatically: on Salisbury's retirement the King must
personally intervene to secure a reconstruction of the Government,
in which Rosebery would be Foreign Secretary and Chamberlain
Leader of the House under the Premiership of Devonshire.[2]

Of course, not everyone interpreted the Chesterfield speech as
a call for coalition. Many of Rosebery's admirers among the
Unionists wanted him to concentrate on building up a 'patriotic'
opposition.[3] And most Liberals naturally deplored any suggestion
that Rosebery was flirting with their political opponents. Some of

[1] ibid., 18.12.01. The proprietor of the *Daily Mail*, Alfred Harmsworth,
although a Conservative, greatly admired Rosebery at this time. He may
possibly have been influenced by his three Liberal Imperialist brothers, Cecil,
Leicester and Hildebrand, who were all strongly pro-Rosebery. Leicester was a
Liberal M.P. In Feb. 1901 Cecil and Hildebrand founded a new monthly, *The
New Liberal Review* to push Rosebery's claims; its opening number carried a
prefatory inscription from the Glasgow University Rectorial Address.

[2] *Fortnightly Review*, Jan. 1902, Vol. LXXI, pp. 1–12; 'Calchas'; 'Lord
Rosebery and Political Reconstruction.'

[3] Such was the view expressed, for example, in the *National Review* (Jan. 1902,
Vol. XXXVIII, p. 676).

the most doctrinaire Liberal Imperialists recoiled in horror from the very idea that they might break with the historic Liberal Party.[1] Haldane, it is true, was saying privately shortly before Chesterfield, 'that the only possible or indeed probably upshot of the present political impasse, so far as the opposition were concerned, was some sort of coalition of the best and youngest men of both sides.'[2] One suspects that Haldane, on whom party loyalties always sat lightly, would have welcomed such a dénouement, and the same might be said of Edward Grey, a very popular figure in Unionist circles.[3]

But Asquith's position and outlook were rather different.[4] Being more of an orthodox party man, he continued to consult and co-operate with Campbell-Bannerman and the Chief Whip, Herbert Gladstone, even when Liberal quarrels were raging most fiercely. Admittedly, there had been the Asquith dinner in July 1901; but Asquith himself had destroyed much of the point of this demonstration by apologizing to Herbert Gladstone for damaging party unity.[5] There may well be something to be said for Campbell-Bannerman's opinion that Asquith was fundamentally loyal, but had become so 'thirled' to Grey and Haldane that he had allowed himself to be dragged into factious intrigue.[6]

After Chesterfield Asquith was perturbed at the possibility of Rosebery capturing support from outside the ranks of the Liberal Party.[7] It is significant that three days after the great pronounce-

---

[1] The *Daily Chronicle*, at this time an outspoken Liberal imperialist newspaper, took this line.

[2] Hamilton Papers, Add. Mss. 48,678: Journals, 1.11.01: f. 122.

[3] Lady Frances Balfour noted in July 1900 that Grey's 'manner and method appeal so entirely to the Conservative party, he would be the man after their own heart, if only he would come over'; Lady Frances Balfour, *Ne Obliviscaris* (1930), Vol. II, p. 334.

[4] Heber Hart goes so far as to doubt whether Asquith was ever a real Liberal imperialist: Heber Hart, op. cit., p. 245.

[5] Herbert Gladstone Papers, Add. Mss. 45,989: Asquith to H. Gladstone, 27.6.01: ff. 49–50. Campbell-Bannerman commented: 'Poor Asquith has tried to put off the dinner, quite agreeing with me about it; but Grey and Haldane hold him to his bond!'; Spender Papers, Add. Mss. 46,388: Campbell-Bannerman to J. Smith, 13.7.01: ff.42–3.

[6] R. R. James, op. cit., p. 424.

[7] e.g. Herbert Gladstone Papers, Add. Mss. 45,989: Asquith to H. Gladstone, 5.1.02: f. 60.

K

ment he should have qualified his approval of Rosebery's views by telling his audience: 'I confess to you I am a party man. I was brought up in the Liberal Party, and in the Liberal Party I intend to remain. . .'[1] To Rosebery himself Asquith wrote on 31 December: 'The newspapers are full of every kind of folly and rubbish, to which I pay no attention.'[2] Was this not possibly a veiled warning from Asquith that his personal loyalty to the ex-Prime Minister came second to his loyalty to the Liberal Party?

For a month after Chesterfield the political situation remained obscure. The most diverse interpretations were placed upon the speech, according to the personal inclinations of the interpreter. Hoping to clarify this situation, Campbell-Bannerman interviewed Rosebery at Berkeley Square on 23 December. One must remember that at this stage many radicals were disposed to look with a more friendly eye on Rosebery after what he had said about South Africa. Yet at this very moment Rosebery, in his meeting with Campbell-Bannerman, chose to emphasize his disapproval of Home Rule for Ireland.[3] At Liverpool a few weeks later he publicly called for the abandonment of Gladstone's Irish policy.[4]

The outcry which greeted this Liverpool speech was a little irrational, since most of Rosebery's points had already been made by the other Liberal Imperialist leaders during the autumn of 1901.[5] But it was the categorical manner in which Rosebery expressed himself that made the difference. Rosebery must have been aware that in thus repudiating Home Rule he was destroying his chances of ever being accepted back as leader of the

[1] *Liberal Magazine*, Vol. 9, p. 642. Speech at Bilston, 19.12.01.

[2] Rosebery Papers, Box 1: Asquith to Rosebery, 31.12.01. Oddly enough, however, Campbell-Bannerman, who was in general well disposed towards Asquith, was so angry at Asquith's public support of the Chesterfield speech, that he declared that he could no longer consult with him. Herbert Gladstone was horrified at his attitude, and must quickly have persuaded him to take a more temperate view of Asquith's behaviour. See Bryce Papers, E. 17: H. Gladstone to Bryce, 22.12.01.

[3] R. R. James, op. cit., pp. 434–5.

[4] Marquess of Crewe, op. cit., Vol. II, p. 574.

[5] e.g. Asquith at Ladybank, 28.9.01 and at Edinburgh, 13.11.01; Haldane at Tranent, 3.10.01: Grey at Newcastle, 11.10.01.

Liberal Party. On the other hand, his declaration had removed a very serious barrier to co-operation between himself and the Unionists: a consideration that we know, from Spender's letter of October, to have been at the front of his mind.

The Liverpool speech hastened the final breach between Rosebery and Campbell-Bannerman. Challenged by the Liberal Leader at Leicester to say whether or not he stood 'inside the tabernacle', Rosebery proclaimed his 'definite separation'.[1] But did this mean 'definite separation' from the Liberal Party, or only from Campbell-Bannerman and his Irish policy? The *Manchester Guardian*, which took the former view, wrote Rosebery a sad valedictory address.[2] Great was that newspaper's astonishment, therefore, when shortly afterwards a new organization, the Liberal League, was founded, with Rosebery as its president, and Asquith, Grey and Fowler as vice-presidents: its only comment was that the new body was 'to have a Unionist leader and a Liberal name'.[3]

From the start, all the members of the Liberal League, Rosebery included, insisted that they had no intention of causing a schism within the Liberal Party and that their organization was only a 'defensive' one, to prevent Liberals of imperialist convictions from being drummed out of the party.[4] With characteristic perversity, Rosebery, who had for so many months insisted on his complete independence from all party connections, now chose to view Campbell-Bannerman's Leicester speech as a move to expel him from the Liberal Party: a move which, through the machinery of the League, he had resolved to thwart. All the same, the league occupied an ambiguous position, since its membership was 'in communion' with the official Liberal Party, except for the president, who had announced that he stood 'outside the tabernacle'— whatever that meant. No wonder that Asquith's adherence to the Liberal League was always so half-hearted.[5]

Other Liberal Imperialists were convinced that sinister developments were afoot. Heber Hart, the chairman of the old Imperial Liberal Council, which the Liberal League had displaced, felt

[1] R. R. James, op. cit., pp. 437–8.   [2] *Manchester Guardian*, 22.2.02.
[3] ibid., 27.2.02.   [4] J. A. Spender, op. cit., Vol. II, p. 35.
[5] J. A. Spender and C. Asquith, *Lord Oxford and Asquith* (1932), Vol. I, p. 143.

certain that the Chesterfield and 'definite separation' speeches indicated Rosebery's desire to encourage a secession from the Liberal Party. Hart had never wished to go beyond stimulating imperialist sentiment *within* the Party, and so he refused to join the League and communicated his suspicions of its purpose to the press.[1] The future Liberal Attorney-General, Robson, took a similar stand: Rosebery, he wrote, 'seems to think that by raising a banner with his name on it he can call into being a new national party which is to be neither Liberal nor Tory. It is a dream. . .'[2]

These fears soon proved unfounded. Even had Rosebery still been hoping to join up with a section of the Unionist Party, his plans would soon have been overtaken by events. For in the course of 1902 party politics began to revive in intensity. In April the introduction of the Corn Tax and the Education Bill drove the Opposition together in a mood of righteous indignation. The conclusion of the Boer War two months later removed the main cause of disunity within the Liberal Party. Henceforward, the public lost interest in an 'advocate of the nation,' standing aloofly above party, nor was there any obvious place in politics for a 'third force', which the Liberal League had for a time seemed to foreshadow.

Rosebery will make a few subsequent appearances in this narrative, but from the time that the Education Bill controversy began in earnest, his importance declined. No longer certain of what issues he should emphasize, Rosebery showed increasing signs of vacillation and opportunism, which alienated many of his former supporters. For example, although in the early months of 1902 the Webbs were participating in the Liberal League, with Sidney sometimes helping out on the committee which selected and distributed pamphlet literature, they soon became disillusioned with Rosebery and the whole Liberal Imperialist group.

As his bi-partisan position was eroded, so Rosebery seems to have given up interest in his slogan of efficiency, although perhaps

[1] Heber Hart, op. cit., pp. 225–42.
[2] ibid., pp. 229–31. Also, G. W. Keeton, *A Liberal Attorney-General* (1949), p. 105.

out of habit, he still contrived to bring it into many of his speeches. There was now some justification for the sneer of his enemies:

> Lord Rosebery was a most wonderful man,
> He had every species of scheme on his shelf.
> But 'efficiency' still formed the gist of his plan,
> And 'efficiency' meant nothing else than himself.[1]

In retrospect it may be a little difficult to understand how Rosebery could ever have thought it likely that he should return to office as leader of a non-party government, or form a new 'national' political group which would draw upon the talents of both major parties. With his pessimistic cast of mind, Rosebery was all along aware of the well-nigh insuperable difficulties; yet, having once taken his stand on the issue of efficiency, he had left himself with very few options. He must simply have been gambling on the off-chance of some unforeseeable but favourable development occurring, which he could then exploit to his advantage.

And so, following the example of his hero, Chatham, Rosebery waited to be called back to power as the saviour of his nation. But the call never came. In the end it was this passivity which proved his undoing. Heber Hart rightly says that the latter half of 1901 was the period when Rosebery's position was at its strongest;[2] but he let this period fritter away. By the time he took the initiative with his address at Chesterfield, it was, as we can now see, too late. Chamberlain had already come to terms with Balfour, the Boer War was nearly over, the traditional party struggle was about to resume in all its vigour.

Rosebery was anyhow handicapped by the diversity of views and interests to be found amongst his followers. Many, but not all of them, responded to his propaganda about efficiency. But others, while agreeing with his sentiments about the war and admiring his 'imperialism', ignored, or even disliked, the domestic side of his programme.[3] There were those who were simply attracted by a

---

[1] Campbell-Bannerman Papers, Add. Mss. 41,237: f. 57. The lines are by Wilfrid Lawson, the 'rhyming' Liberal M.P.

[2] Heber Hart, op. cit., p. 218.

[3] e.g. The Webbs' bugbear, 'Imperial Perks', the Wesleyan Liberal M.P., who later became the treasurer and chief wire-puller of the Liberal League,

famous name and an intriguing personality; others still more simply despaired of Campbell-Bannerman. It would have required a stronger will-power than Rosebery possessed to have carried this motley crowd with him in a constructive political crusade.

Moreover, Rosebery's own commitment to efficiency, and all that this entailed, was qualified. There is some truth in Beatrice Webb's view of him as a man who lacked strong convictions and cared mainly for appearances and for striking the popular pose.[1] In the years at the end of the Boer War there were strident demands for greater efficiency in all branches of national life; encouraged and advised by Haldane, Rosebery put himself at the head of this agitation, without having either the determination or the 'vision' to carry through his ideas to any practical conclusion.

Finally, Rosebery found it difficult to get on with other people, particularly with those who held strong views and possessed dominating personalities—and not all Haldane's smooth diplomacy could alter the fact. No-one who contemplates the sad history of Rosebery's Administration of 1894–5 can feel confident that he 'had it in him' to work harmoniously with men of the calibre of Chamberlain or Milner; yet this would perhaps have been necessary, if his ideal of a 'National Government' had been realized. In the end we are again brought back to the question of Rosebery's odd and 'impossible' temperament.

But Rosebery's personal failure did not involve the disappearance of the ideology of efficiency. Nor was the search for a 'National Government' altogether abandoned. In 1910, when the threat to the British Empire was immeasurably more acute than it had been during the Boer War, Lloyd George opened his abortive coalition talks with the Conservative Leaders, circulating among them a memorandum, certain parts of which read like a paraphrase of Rosebery's earlier speeches. On becoming Prime Minister in

---

wrote to Rosebery after the appearance of the 'Houndsditch' article: 'I have always felt that one of the reasons why Toryism has got hold of the middle classes and the artisans is that as these classes have prospered or acquired their houses they have inclined to the Conservative Party because they dread the doctrines which Sidney Webb thinks would be so popular. Personally I am no believer in municipal trading, or the municipal ownership of means of locomotion.' (Rosebery Papers, Box 39: Perks to Rosebery, 8.9.01).

[1] B. Webb, op. cit., p. 228: 28.2.02.

1916, Lloyd George did put some of these ideas of efficiency into practice. Writing in 1923, E. T. Raymond, one of Rosebery's first biographers, was struck by the similarity between the attitudes of Rosebery and Lloyd George towards the 'business man in government' and detected in the Chesterfield speech an anticipation of Lloyd George's 'coalition idea'.[1] It would be fascinating to know whether either of the two politicians, so totally different in nearly all other respects, was aware of this connecting link. However, between Rosebery's hey-day and Lloyd George's emergence as a 'national' statesman, there was a period of renewed confidence in traditional liberal values and methods, in which the quest for national efficiency lost much of its political significance, and to this period we must now turn.

[1] E. T. Raymond, *The Man of Promise: Lord Rosebery* (1923), pp. 203–4, 210, 251.

CHAPTER V

THE LIBERAL REVIVAL 1902–1908

FROM THE SUMMER of 1902 onwards, talk about the possibilities of coalition largely faded away. Yet the ideology of national efficiency retained much of its appeal. The ending of the war in June failed to obliterate people's memories of the disturbing events of 'Black Week'; and although there was an easing of tension as the war drew to its close, the revival of confidence in Britain's international position proved short-lived, and foreign policy was conducted against a background of continuing tension and insecurity.[1]

In October 1902 a new note of alarm was sounded by the Admiralty: in a famous Cabinet memorandum, the First Lord, Selborne, warned his colleagues: 'The more the composition of the new German fleet is examined the clearer it becomes that it is designed for a possible conflict with the British fleet.'[2] British diplomacy did not as yet pivot around this consideration, but in April 1903 mounting Germanophobia was sufficiently strong to force the Cabinet to drop the Foreign Office's plans for co-operating with the Germans over the Baghdad railway project.[3] Anglo-German relations steadily deteriorated from this point. By the end of 1904 some violent articles in the right-wing press and the irresponsible and reckless talk of the First Sea Lord, Admiral Sir John Fisher, had convinced the German Government that the

[1] G. W. Monger, *The End of Isolation* (1963), p. 82.
[2] Arthur J. Marder, *From the Dreadnought to Scapa Flow*, Vol. I (1961), p. 107.
[3] G. W. Monger, op. cit., pp. 118–23.

British were about to execute a pre-emptive strike against their High Fleet in Kiel. Meanwhile, certain British newspapers were scrutinizing every movement of the German fleet and every action of the German Government for evidence of anti-British machinations.[1] The 'cold war' atmosphere thus generated prevented a return of self-assurance and complacency, and emphasized the pressing importance of carrying through reforms that would strengthen the 'scientific' basis of British society and administration and increase the Empire's readiness for a possible war.

Arthur Balfour, Prime Minister from July 1902 to December 1905, was sensitive to the dangers that threatened, even if he and his advisers on the Defence Committee spent more time brooding over the Russian advance towards India than making preparations for a future Anglo-German War. Yet Balfour lacked the 'earnestness' which contemporaries expected of their statesmen. In an article of June 1900, written in the aftermath of the regrettable Manchester speeches, the *Fortnightly Review* had criticized his 'lack of power and realism, of every sort of masculine energy and grasp' and 'the logic-chopping pettinesses and pedantic quiddities which have always been the weakness of Mr Balfour's habit.'[2] That was still a popular view of him in 1902. Although the new Prime Minister was heavily implicated in the failures of the Boer War, he did not try to conceal his own responsibility by calling for a national act of repentance; neither did he indulge in the melodramatic breast-beating, in which Rosebery specialized. Most of the people who rallied behind Rosebery in the 1900–1902 period must have seen Balfour as the personification of all that was decadent and flabby in English public life. Rosebery himself certainly had no faith in Balfour; and his contempt was heartily reciprocated.[3]

Yet there was another side to Balfour's complex character. His 'technological imagination' and his deep-seated interest in scientific research and higher education, which H. G. Wells so much

---

[1] See O. J. Hale, *Germany and the Diplomatic Revolution* (Philadelphia, 1931).

[2] *Fortnightly Review*, June 1900, Vol. LXVII, p. 1078; 'Lord Rosebery and a National Cabinet'.

[3] Hamilton Papers, Add. Mss. 48,679: Journals, 16.6.02: f. 108. Lady Frances Balfour, *Ne Obliviscaris*, Vol II (1930), p. 281. Blanche Dugdale, *Family Homespun* (1940), pp. 183–4.

admired,[1] may have lain hidden from the view of those who had no opportunity of observing the Prime Minister at close quarters. But these qualities made a strong appeal to certain members of the 'efficiency group'. Haldane and the Webbs were not alone in seeing Balfour in the years of his premiership as the one contemporary statesman who was both able and anxious to implement the kind of policy in which they believed.

Balfour was certainly no bigoted party man. Indeed, his intellectual curiosity and concern for *ideas*, rather than accepted party formulae, made him an object of some suspicion among the more conventionally-minded of his backbenchers. This disposition won him the confidence of many people who were not Conservatives at all. Nevertheless, he remained a true Cecil, conscious of his responsibilities as leader and determined, at all costs, to maintain the Conservatives as the 'natural governing party' of the country. The violent antagonism with which his Education Act had been greeted by all sections of the Opposition also accounts for the fact that Balfour was never in a position to assume the mantle of Rosebery and take up a position of 'independence', above the party fray.

Joseph Chamberlain, the other main figure in the Balfour Cabinet, operated from an altogether different power base. His behaviour during the Khaki Election had, as we have seen, caused deep resentment among nearly all Liberals; it was not only the radicals and Campbell-Bannerman who saw the Colonial Secretary as a dangerous and corrupting force in public life: Asquith, for example, could write in a private letter about Chamberlain having 'the manners of a cad and the tongue of a bargee'.[2] No amount of ideological agreement could induce Rosebery to overcome his aversion for the character and methods of 'pushful Joe'.

On the other hand, the wide-spread speculation in the press and among M.P.s during the 1900–1901 period about the possibilities of Chamberlain doing a deal with Rosebery, ill-informed though

---

[1] e.g. Balfour's letter to F. Herbert Stead, printed in *The Times*, 15.2.01, on the likely impact of the automobile upon the housing problem. Here is that 'glimpse of thought, of imagination, like the sight of a soaring eagle through a staircase skylight', which Wells wrote of in his admiring sketch of Balfour as 'Evesham' in *The New Machiavelli* (1911), p. 267 in the Penguin edition (1946).

[2] Herbert Gladstone Papers, Add. Mss. 45,989: Asquith to H. Gladstone, 7.10.00: f. 45.

they were in one respect, correctly recognized the Colonial Secretary's spiritual freedom from party ties. Chamberlain was no Conservative, and he had nothing in common with the Duke of Devonshire, the nominal leader of his organization, the Liberal Unionist Party. If he chose to collaborate, first with Salisbury, then with Balfour, this was because it suited his interests to do so. Once the bond of convenience had changed into an embarrassing restriction, it was easy to predict that he would break loose again.

By May 1903 Chamberlain had reached that point. The Education Act had sown discord between himself and his Nonconformist supporters in Birmingham and had stirred his own Dissenter's prejudices into life again. Consequently Chamberlain was still nursing a sense of grievance when he returned home from his South African tour in early 1903. Moreover, his political intuitions told him that the Balfour Cabinet was moving towards inevitable defeat at the next general election, and that the one way to arrest the decline in the fortunes of Unionism was to launch a positive programme and so regain the political initiative from the Liberals and Socialists.[1] On 15 May Chamberlain made his fateful move: in a speech at Birmingham he called for the abandonment of Free Trade and the adoption of a system of Imperial Preferences.

The story of Chamberlain's final abortive crusade for Tariff Reform, with all the attendant difficulties it made for the Unionist Party, has been often enough told.[2] Its significance to our theme is that it destroyed for the best part of a decade whatever lingering possibilities still remained of creating a new alignment reflecting the ideal of national efficiency. The controversy over the Education Acts had already made this an unlikely outcome. Chamberlain's Birmingham speech, however, did more than any other single event to disrupt the precarious alliance of Unionists, Liberal Imperialists and Fabians, which Rosebery had rallied behind him in 1901 and early 1902.

One may readily imagine the dilemma into which the Liberal

---

[1] See J. Amery, *Joseph Chamberlain and the Tariff Reform Campaign. The Life of Joseph Chamberlain*', Vol. 5 (1969).

[2] For the fullest and most authoritative account, see J. Amery, op. cit., Vols. 5 & 6.

Imperialists were plunged by the Tariff Reform Campaign. Chamberlain's proposals were designed to meet those very difficulties of which they had made so much in their public speeches. Thus, not only had Rosebery, in a sense, helped prepare the ground for Chamberlain; he could not now condemn Chamberlain's programme out of hand, without seeming to go back on all that he had previously stood for. Acceptance of Tariff Reform, on the other hand, would mean the final severance of all connections with the Liberal Party, to which he had drawn closer since the introduction of the Education Act, and a venture into a dangerous and unknown future. It would also involve him in a major political *volte face*, since his commitment to Free Trade had never before been in serious question.

There is, in fact, some evidence to suggest that soon after the Birmingham speech important members of the Liberal Imperialist group did actually make overtures to Chamberlain.[1] A full account of this incident was recorded by the Lady Edward Cecil, in a letter which she wrote to Milner on 24 June, after a conversation with Chamberlain himself:

Joe told me that scouts from the Liberal League had immediately after his Birmingham Speech been to him to offer him the leadership of their party if he would give them some hope on the Education Bill. 'I told them not to talk nonsense. I was as responsible for the Bill as my colleagues and that I did not mean to lead'. Then one of Rosebery's henchmen came in and said, 'do you want Rosebery to join you?', and Joe answered, 'If you mean, do I want him to make a speech as an outsider backing my idea up, of course I do, but not as a colleague'.[2]

This does not make it entirely clear whether Rosebery had authorized the approach from his 'henchmen'. However, there is the indication of the Burnley speech of 19 May, Rosebery's first public pronouncement on Chamberlain's proposals; on this occasion Rosebery recommended an 'independent enquiry', rather in the tone of a critical, but friendly, supporter of Tariff Reform.[3] A common press reaction was that Rosebery must be feeling his way towards an accommodation with Chamberlain. 'Is it possible',

[1] W. A. S. Hewins, *The Apologia of an Imperialist*, Vol I (1929), p. 67.
[2] Milner Papers, Vol. 41; Lady Edward Cecil to Milner, 24.6.03: f. 15.
[3] *The Times*, 20.5.03.

wrote the *Daily News*, 'that Lord Rosebery is looking to Mr Chamberlain, or that Mr Chamberlain is looking to Lord Rosebery, for assistance in pushing the new gospel?'[1]

Rosebery was soon obliged to explain away his equivocal pronouncement—but not before doubts had been sown in the minds of many of his supporters. Haldane found he had difficulty in keeping some prominent members of the Liberal League 'straight' on Tariff Reform, especially the wealthy business man element in Glasgow, which was giving him cause for concern even as late as August 1904.[2] A more immediate reaction came with the publication in *The Times* on 21 July 1903, of a letter from a number of Liberals who agreed with the outlines of the Birmingham policy. Although the letter was largely drafted by Amery, who could hardly be called a Liberal, the idea had originated with Saxon Mills, a former editor of the Liberal Imperialist newspaper, the *Daily Chronicle*, and the letter attracted the signatures of some well-known personalities in the Liberal world.[3] According to the Lady Edward Cecil: 'The rank and file of the Liberal Imps are very discontented with their leaders and want to follow Joe'.[4]

This statement must be viewed with some scepticism. Yet subsequently there *were* a few notable defectors from the Liberal League to the Unionist Party: the Duke of Sutherland, T. A. Brassey and Halford Mackinder among them. Many others, who had been keen for a policy of national efficiency wavered, undecided; and had Rosebery changed sides, he might well have taken a strong personal following with him. This accounts no doubt for Amery's hurt surprise when Grey, Asquith and Haldane refused to enlist in the Tariff Reform cause—'I am very annoyed with our Liberal Imperialist friends . . .'[5].

We have it on the testimony of Amery and Hewins that Edward Grey was initially tempted by Chamberlain's programme.[6] But

---

[1] *Daily News*, 20.5.03.

[2] Haldane Papers, Vol. 5906: Haldane to Rosebery, 18.8.04.

[3] L. S. Amery, *My Political Life*, Vol. I (1953), p. 238. The signatories included Asquith's father-in-law, Charles Tennant, T. A. Brassey, Halford Mackinder and the Duke of Sutherland.

[4] Milner Papers, Vol. 41; Lady Edward Cecil to Milner, 1.7.03: f. 19.

[5] ibid., Vol. 33; Amery to Milner, 20.6.03: f. 94.

[6] L. S. Amery, op. cit., p. 224. W. A. S. Hewins, op. cit., p. 69.

neither Haldane, still less Asquith, hesitated in attacking this proposed departure from Free Trade policy as both dangerous and impractical. Nevertheless, they were alive to the possibility that Chamberlain might run off with their old slogan of efficiency and identify it exclusively with Tariff Reform. Therefore, the Liberal Imperialist ploy was to counter Chamberlain by re-emphasizing that technical education alone provided the answer to the country's economic difficulties. A Liberal League pamphlet was published, entitled *Wanted—Efficiency not Tariffs.*

For the Liberal Imperialists, the announcement of the Charlottenburg scheme a mere month after the opening of the Tariff Reform Campaign came most opportunely. 'It really is a great scheme', wrote Haldane to his mother, 'and it is taking hold of the public mind as an alternative policy to Chamberlain'.[1] In July the *Daily Mail* printed an article from Haldane on the significance of the Wernher-Beit endowment and gave it the headline: 'Brains v. Tariffs: Mr. R. B. Haldane on Lord Rosebery's Scheme'.[2]

These tactics drove Chamberlain, who had hitherto been second to no-one in his enthusiasm for better industrial training, to denigrate technical education, now that it was being canvassed as a rival policy to his own. As he told a laughing and cheering audience at Leeds in December: 'When Mr. Haldane tells me that Charlottenburg schools are to be a cure for dumping, then I decline to learn business principles at the feet of this Gamaliel.'[3]

In this way, as in so many others, a polarizing of party attitudes followed the dramatic events of May 1903. There were many who, like Alfred Harmsworth, admired both Rosebery and Chamberlain, and were prepared to follow the statesman who took the bolder line.[4] Rosebery's equivocations in the summer of 1903 thus probably lost him much *independent* support, as well as alienating the majority of Unionists.

Especially significant is the reaction of the *Nineteenth Century*, since this periodical can almost be seen as the 'official' mouthpiece

[1] Haldane Papers, Vol. 5969; Haldane to Mother, 30.6.03.

[2] *Daily Mail*, 1.7.03.

[3] *The Times*, 17.12.03.

[4] See R. Pound and G. Harmsworth, *Northcliffe* (1959), p. 289. Wilson Harris, *J. A. Spender* (1946), pp. 137–8.

of the 'efficiency group' in the Boer War period. At first the regular contributors could not agree among themselves about the merits of Tariff Reform. One symptom of this division of opinion was that Wemyss Reid, a friend of Rosebery's, who had written a monthly survey of political events since November 1899, nominally, at least, from an impartial, non-party standpoint, was relieved of his sole responsibility in January 1904. 'Now that the country is engaged in a political controversy of exceptional acuteness, which is being waged on all sides with increasing vehemence', he explained, 'it becomes much more difficult to preserve that attitude of impartial detachment which I have hitherto striven to maintain.'[1] Thereafter, Wemyss Reid's article was coupled with one by Edward Dicey, putting the Unionist Party case.

Although the *Nineteenth Century* continued to be independent in the sense that its columns were open to people of all political convictions, after 1904 its tone was set by the type of Unionist who supported Tariff Reform and compulsory military service. Rosebery was virtually ignored. One reason for this was that, as we have already seen, several of the contributors were friends and admirers of Milner who, in Milner's absence, had put their money on Rosebery. But when Milner came out for Tariff Reform, they followed the lead of their hero. Of course, Milner could not declare himself publicly on such a contentious political issue while he was still South African High Commissioner, but no-one doubted where his sympathies lay. Nor did some of Milner's disciples need any guidance from their chief. Amery has described, in a famous passage in his autobiography, his own elation on first hearing of the Birmingham speech.[2] Lyttelton Gell and Birchenough were equally enthusiastic. Only Dawkins held back, uneasy at the inaccuracies and misleading statements in the speeches in which Chamberlain developed his case;[3] but from the

---

[1] *Nineteenth Century*, February 1904, Vol. LV, p. 336. It is perhaps significant that Wemyss Reid's first reactions to the Birmingham speech had been favourable (ibid, June 1903, Vol. LIII, pp. 1059–61), although his treatment of Chamberlain's campaign later became very hostile.

[2] L. S. Amery, op. cit., p. 236.

[3] e.g. 'Can (Chamberlain's) wild assertion that the Empire is threatened with disruption unless his programme is adopted, or his intimations that the Colonies might be asked to forego starting new industries, ever be forgiven or forgotten?'

start he approved of the general principle of Imperial Preferences, and in December 1903 he came off the fence and sent in a contribution to the Tariff Reform League.[1]

The tendency of Conservative imperialists to rally to Chamberlain's crusade brought virtual disintegration to a body which has recently aroused some interest among historians, the *Co-Efficient Club*. This was a small dining club founded by the Webbs in November 1902 to bring together some of the most eminent and intelligent advocates of a policy of national efficiency. To start with, the membership consisted of twelve men, each reputedly an 'expert' in his particular field. Here are their names, with the 'portfolio' they held: Sidney Webb (municipal affairs), Haldane (law), Grey (foreign affairs), Amery (the army), Dawkins (banking), Bertrand Russell (philosophy and science), Pember Reeves (colonial affairs), Hewins (economics), Leo Maxse (journalism), Mackinder (geography), Carlyon Bellairs (the navy) and H. G. Wells (literature). All these twelve original Co-Efficients can be classified as belonging to one of three main groups; Roseberyites, Milnerites and Fabians. So the club formed, socially and politically, a microcosm of that segment of the public which subscribed to ideas of national efficiency.[2]

According to Amery, however, this club was intended to be more than a forum of discussion for politicians and intellectuals sharing a similar outlook on the world. In his autobiography he explicitly states that the Webbs' objective in founding it was to engineer a new party, compromising both Liberal Imperialists and 'progressive' Unionists. 'The feud between Liberal Imperialists and Little Englanders,' he writes, 'seemed at the time hardly less bitter than that between Home Rulers and Unionists in Gladstone's day. That the Liberal Imperialist leaders could ever be

---

I fear it is 1886 and 1892 over again—the old man in a hurry! . . .' (Curzon Papers, Vol. 182: Dawkins to Curzon, 16.10.03: f. 263).

[1] Milner Papers, Vol. 41; Dawkins to Milner, 31.12.03: f. 70.

[2] For descriptions of the Co-Efficients: L. S. Amery, op. cit., pp. 223–30; W. A. S. Hewins, op. cit., pp. 65–6; Bertrand Russell, *Portraits From Memory and Other Essays* (1956), pp. 76–7; H. G. Wells, *The New Machiavelli* (1911), pp. 243–60 in the Penguin edition (1946); H. G. Wells, *Experiment in Autobiography*, Vol. II (1934), pp. 761–6; B. Semmel, *Imperialism and Social Reform* (1960), pp. 72–82.

induced to serve under Campbell-Bannerman would in 1902 have seemed a fantastic suggestion. A more natural outcome, many were inclined to think, would be some eventual coming together of Liberal Imperialists with the more progressive wing of the Unionist Party'. The Co-Efficients, Amery asserts, were meant to be 'a Brains Trust or General Staff', which would work out the details of a programme on which the new 'Party of Efficiency' might appeal to the country.[1]

It is not inconceivable that such lofty ambitions should have been entertained by the Webbs, since the possibility of which Amery writes formed a recurring theme in the journalistic speculation and political gossip of the day. But if the Webbs had indeed been thinking along these lines, they ought surely to have begun their operations in the course of 1901, not waited until November 1902; for by late 1902 the usual party animosities were coming to life once again. In fact, the practising politicians among the Co-Efficients never seem to have regarded the Club as anything more than yet another dining club where they could talk politics in congenial company. It was only the intellectuals on the periphery of the political scene, like Amery, Wells and Russell, who seem to have taken its deliberations with high seriousness.[2]

Therefore, the meetings of the Co-Efficient Club did not mark the beginning of any new political development, but rather the conclusion of one. There was a complex web of friendship and interest linking most of the twelve original 'members', long before the Webbs had organized them into a club. Indeed, the attempt to make these relationships more formal than they already were, merely drew attention to the differences which separated the men. Thus, whereas the Webbs must have hoped that the Club would discuss in a quiet, rational manner the technical problems involved in public administration, Chamberlain's proposals soon gave rise to passionate, ideological debates on the significance and function of the Empire. Irreconcilably divided on the question of preferential tariffs, the Club more or less disintegrated after May

---

[1] L. S. Amery, op. cit., pp. 222–3.

[2] Bernard Semmel asks: 'why did not the Co-efficients succeed in becoming the brains trust of a new social-imperial political party as the Webbs had hoped it would?' (op. cit., p. 81). The question is a somewhat unreal one.

L

1903, and although it maintained a shadowy existence until about 1909, it seems that meetings became sporadic and the membership fluctuating.[1]

The Tariff Reform Movement not only cut across the preoccupations of the Webbs, it even threatened their own household with a small schism. Beatrice Webb looked more sympathetically on Chamberlain's campaign than did her husband, since she thought that the introduction of import duties might contribute to the principle of the national minimum. On the other hand, she had little patience with Chamberlain's talk of 'driving trade into this or that channel' by means of a protective tariff. 'The urgent question nowadays,' she thought, 'is not maximum production or even equality of distribution, but the *character of consumption*—the vital problem of whether the use of a particular commodity does or does not increase efficiency'. Sidney did not see any relevance in this approach, so Beatrice kept these thoughts to her private journal.[2]

All along the Webbs' main concern was to avoid becoming too deeply embroiled in the Tariff Reform controversy. Possibly they may have originally underestimated its importance.[3] In any case, Beatrice did not rate very highly Chamberlain's chances of converting the country in the near future. Shaw, on the other hand, felt so convinced that Tariff Reform was a winning cause, that he was most anxious that the Fabian Society should not come out against it. In consequence, the pamphlet, *Fabianism and the Fiscal Question*, which he was mainly responsible for composing, gave somewhat the same impression as Rosebery's Burnley speech: that is to say, of providing a qualified, 'outside' support to Chamberlain's ideas, after an elaborate weighing up of the pros and cons.[4] Privately, Shaw had already written to Webb, urging him to throw over Free Trade as discredited nonsense: 'declare that if Chamberlain can form a government which will attack and

[1] Many members of the 'efficiency group', other than the twelve already mentioned, attended the club on occasions, among them Milner, Balfour, Birchenough, Garvin and Bernard Shaw.

[2] Passfield Papers, Vol. 24; Beatrice Webb's Journal, 5.10.03: f. 32.

[3] W. A. S. Hewins, op. cit., p. 66.

[4] *Fabianism and the Fiscal Question: An Alternative Policy:* Fabian Tract no. 116. The Fabian, Cecil Chesterton, followed this Shavian line in his *Gladstonian Ghosts* (1905?), pp. 66, 104.

reorganize the whole foreign trade of the country and burn all the laissez-faire phylacteries, you will do the Local Government part of the business as President of the L.G.B., while Hewins is doing the Board of Trade'.[1] 'A Protectionist right down to my boots' was how Shaw described himself to John Burns in September 1903.[2]

As for Hewins, he was now working very closely with Chamberlain, acting as his confidential adviser and engaging in propaganda in the Tariff Reform interest.[3] Since he still held the post of Director of the London School of Economics, the Webbs feared that they might become involved in Chamberlain's cause by a process of association. Sidney felt obliged to come out on the other side, if only to maintain the reputation of the School for impartiality.[4]

In November 1903 Hewins relieved the Webbs of their embarrassment by resigning his academic post in order to become Secretary of the Tariff Commission—not, however, before shrewdly warning Beatrice of the dangers of standing aloof in the fiscal controversy:

I am afraid you will find yourselves presently in very uncongenial economic company. The opposition to J. C. is sure to become more and more reactionary. . . You will be dragged into the controversy I am afraid whether you will or not, because your books are full of points favourable to Joe, and contain no important arguments on the other side. I am afraid the attitude of 'the convinced agnostic' can only be temporary. My advice is, make the most of existing conditions to settle everything educational, because some of the instruments on which you reckon at present may turn out worse than useless, and you yourselves may be isolated.[5]

In sensing the enormous difficulties of getting Tariff Reform with its unpopular food taxes, across to the electorate, the Webbs showed sounder judgement than Shaw or Hewins. Yet the danger that Rosebery and his supporters might be driven by their opposition to Chamberlain into mere negative obstructionism was a very

---

[1] Shaw to Webb, 17.11.03; cited in F. Bealey and H. Pelling, *Labour and Politics, 1900–1906* (1958), p. 171.
[2] Burns Papers, Add. Mss. 46,287: Shaw to Burns, 11.9.03: f. 327.
[3] W. A. S. Hewins, op. cit., Chapter III.
[4] Beatrice Webb, *Our Partnership* (1948), p. 267: 15.6.03.
[5] Passfield Papers, II 4 b: Hewins to B. Webb, 27.11.03; ff.299–300.

real one. It was, as it happened, a point-scoring speech of Rosebery's, in which Chamberlain was mocked at as a 'Jeremiah', that
finally convinced the Webbs in November 1903 that Rosebery
would never do anything 'constructive' in the social field. 'After a
sleepless night,' Beatrice wrote 'an angry little note to Haldane'.[1]
So ended, once and for all, the Webbs' political association with
Rosebery.

'If only Joe were to take up the "national minimum", he would
romp in after a few years' propaganda', Beatrice Webb had reflected at the moment of her breach with Rosebery.[2] On the Tariff
Reform side, there were some who realized that the Webbs were
far from being worshippers at the Free Trade shrine, and could be
drawn into Chamberlain's support, if given a little encouragement.
Professor Ashley, for example, wrote to Bonar Law, pointing out
the value which the Webbs and their friends would possess as
allies: 'I know', he said, 'that, though they are not yet with us and
indeed are rather on the other side so far as *merely protective* measures
are concerned, they have been very much disgusted by the way in
which the Liberal Party has fallen back into its old *Individualism*.
They are not opposed to *preference* in itself; and I think they could
be induced to be much more sympathetic to Mr. Chamberlain's
cause, if you on Mr. Chamberlain's side could see your way to
associate with it a policy of internal social reform'. Could Bonar
Law, Ashley politely hinted, press this consideration upon Chamberlain himself.[3]

Yet Chamberlain and the bulk of his supporters had no intention
of meeting people like the Webbs half-way. For after May 1903
Chamberlain was wedded to a one-idea programme. In theory the
Tariff Reformers were committed to an 'advanced' social policy,
but it was an article of faith with them that reforming legislation
could only be financed out of the revenue provided by a general
tariff; and that the principal social evils, unemployment, low
wages, dumped goods and sweated labour could be abolished only
by Tariff Reform and immigration controls. Any alternative social
policy which took no account of these remedies was dismissed as a

[1] ibid., Beatrice Webb's Journal, 26.11.03.
[2] ibid.
[3] Bonar Law Papers, Box 18, Folder 1; Ashley to Bonar Law, 21.12.04.

mere palliative which would probably lead to grave economic dislocation. Deeply concerned with the state of the 'national physique' though they claimed to be, the Tariff Reformers in practice presented a formidable obstacle to those who wished to improve it.

We have already seen how this obsession with a single idea dampened Chamberlain's former enthusiasm for the extension of technological instruction. True, the imminent publication of Haldane's Treasury Committee Report on the financing of university education did spur Chamberlain into writing Haldane a very remarkable letter in March 1905, suggesting that since few politicians cared about the subject, they should agree between themselves on a common policy and then press for its implementation.[1] Haldane responded eagerly to the overture.[2] Indeed, he became convinced in retrospect that only the sudden break-down in Chamberlain's health in 1906 had prevented their seeing a great deal more of one another politically.[3]

By and large, however, Chamberlain's energies after 1903 were focused on his tearing propaganda campaign, and he showed little interest in seeking for limited agreements with like-minded opponents. Though never a good party man, Chamberlain was always a fierce *partisan*. Moreover, as it became clear that his political gamble in going to the country was not paying off, and as his health began to deteriorate, Chamberlain grew increasingly reckless in argument and careless in his presentation of statistical material, often disconcerting even hard-core Tariff Reformers.[4] The result was that by 1905 Chamberlain had forfeited a good deal of the support that had once been his.

Starting off with an analysis of the country's economic and political difficulties that commanded a wide-spread acceptance or at least sympathy among people of various party loyalties, Chamberlain had ended up by subordinating all other considerations to

[1] Joseph Chamberlain Papers: J. Chamberlain to Haldane, 12.3.05.

[2] Haldane Papers, Vol. 5973: Haldane to Mother, 16.3.05: f. 102. Almeric Fitzroy, *Memoirs*, Vol. I (1925), p. 248: 28.3.05.

[3] Haldane Papers, Vol. 5923: Notes on Letters Contained in My Boxes (written in Autumn, 1926): f. 10.

[4] e.g. W. A. S. Hewins, op. cit., p. 163. Milner Papers, Vol. 41: Dawkins to Milner, 18.3.04: f. 64.

a fanatical crusade that not only threatened the Unionist Party with schism, but also, by introducing an element of violent factionalism into political life, undermined that 'national consensus' which he was theoretically anxious to maintain. In 1901 the cry for 'efficiency' had met with a response from members of both parties; that was because Rosebery and his followers, though sometimes scoring points off the Salisbury administration, had more often than not attributed Britain's lack of preparedness as revealed in the Boer War to decades of lethargy, complacency and neglect, for which the nation as a whole bore the responsibility. Chamberlain chose to single out one cause, Free Trade, and to prescribe a single remedy, fiscal reform: a stratagem that necessarily brought him into head-on conflict with the entire Liberal Party. Thus, to the extent that the slogan of efficiency was still being raised in the Tariff Reform camp, it acted as a partisan slogan, dividing the country on fairly simple party lines.

In October 1903 George Wyndham, the Irish Secretary, in a letter to his father, caught the atmosphere of the political conflict which the fiscal dispute had generated:

If anything were needed to expose the folly of those who cried 'efficiency' and cried for 'business methods', it is that they no longer cry for these things, but sit down in the stalls to enjoy a down-right rhetorical hammer-and-tongs set-to between the big wigs. That is what Englishmen enjoy. . . The huge blue-book of statistics; the speeches by manufacturers, all that is expert or informed, the rival theories of economic schools, are bundled aside to a general 'Ah' of relief and satisfaction, punctuated by 'go it, Joey', 'bravo, here's Rosebery in the ring!'[1]

Not everyone would have viewed this development in quite so complacent a light.

For friends and colleagues of Balfour, like Wyndham, the political prospects from 1903 onwards certainly held out little hope. It must be remembered that the largely favourable reputation that Balfour currently enjoys was not acquired until many years after he had

[1] J. W. Mackail and G. Wyndham, *Life and Letters of George Wyndham*, Vol. II (1934?), pp. 469–70.

left Downing Street. Seen from a narrowly political viewpoint, the Education Act of 1902 was a 'mistake': it angered the Opposition intensely, without giving corresponding satisfaction to the Government's supporters. Nor were there any votes to be won through reorganizing the Committee of Imperial Defence, Balfour's other main claim to fame.[1] From the moment that Chamberlain made his Birmingham speech, Balfour was to all intents and purposes a Prime Minister living on borrowed time. The amazing skill with which he clung to office for another two and a half years may have torpedoed Chamberlain's plan, which was to 'reconstruct' the Unionist Party along Tariff Reform lines after defeat in a general election he thought to be imminent;[2] but it did nothing to prevent Balfour's vacillating and accident-prone Cabinet from sliding down the slope to overwhelming defeat.

The common front formed between the various warring sections of the Opposition in attacking the 1902 Education Act, which Haldane alone supported, foreshadowed the eventual re-assimilation of the Liberal Imperialists into the mainstream of the Liberal movement. An even stronger impetus to re-union was provided by the Tariff Reform issue. But the effect of these developments was to strengthen the position of Campbell-Bannerman and to make it very probable that he would be the next Prime Minister. When in October 1903 Rosebery convinced his backers that he was no longer a contender for office in a future Liberal Cabinet,[3] this probability became a near certainty. The prospect of 'C-B' installed in number 10, Downing Street sent cold shivers down the spine of most members of the 'efficiency group', Liberals and Conservatives alike.

In despair at the operation of a party system that could propel a 'trifler'[4] like Campbell-Bannerman into the premiership, some people began to look outside the United Kingdom for salvation to the famous imperial proconsuls. Might not these men be

[1] For Balfour's work on education and imperial defence, see below, Chapter VI.

[2] e.g. Curzon Papers, Vol. 183: C. Dawkins to Curzon, 19.1.05: ff. 9–10.

[3] Roy Jenkins, *Asquith* (1964), pp. 143–4.

[4] As Milner called him in a moment of extreme exasperation: Haldane Papers, Vol. 5905: Milner to Haldane, 15.7.01: f. 86.

induced to return to London before the Empire disintegrated at
the centre, as the Roman Empire had done before it?

Ever since the middle of 1901 George Curzon had been under
pressure from his wife and certain of his friends to leave India and
restore the fortunes of the ailing Conservative Party.[1] Clinton
Dawkins was one of the most persistent of these friends. His
nagging drew from Curzon in November 1901 a particularly
interesting letter, which is worth quoting at some length, since it
illustrates the strengths and still more the limitations of the creed of
efficiency. In this letter Curzon speculated on what might occur,
should the Salisbury Government collapse and the Opposition fail
to form a Cabinet of their own. If he were holding a position at
home, declared Curzon, he might then have an opportunity of
accomplishing great things:

> I would not mind in the least forming a Concentration Cabinet of the
> strongest elements of both the Unionist and the Liberal Imperialist
> Parties. But I would run it on entirely new lines. I would be Prime
> Minister in reality, instead of in name. I would have my Cabinet meet
> once a week. . . I would take the big questions—Education, Temperance,
> etc., one a year. I would think them over carefully in advance: consult
> everybody, both parties, if you like: and then bring in a bold broad
> measure in each case that might be carried by the votes of the best men
> of each party. I would appoint to each post the particular man who was
> best suited to it, regardless of party howls. . . I would stir up each De-
> partment, until it realised that efficiency and business were the sole
> tests. . . In two years' time I should probably fall: but I should have set a
> standard that would probably affect English politics for years.[2]

Here is a superb statement of the 'administrator's fallacy': the
belief that politics can be put on ice, while a benevolent dictator or
the 'best men' carry quietly on with the task of providing the
country with strong, impartial government. These methods were
not altogether successful even in India. When the time finally came
for Curzon to leave the Viceroyalty, he looked back over his work
and summed it up a in single word: ' "Efficiency". That has been
our gospel, the keynote of our administration.'[3] But as one historian

[1] Earl of Ronaldshay, *Lord Curzon*, Vol. II (1928), pp. 173–4.

[2] Curzon Papers, Vol. 182: Curzon to Dawkins, 22.11.01: ff. 32–3.

[3] Curzon at dinner given by the United Service Club, Simla, 30.9.05:
quoted in T. Raleigh, *Lord Curzon in India* (1906) p. 564.

has commented, 'Efficient administration is not a fulfilment, but a process; and this was beyond the understanding of Curzon.'[1]

Curzon was at least realistic enough to end his letter of November 1901 with the recognition that the sort of government he had described was, in fact, 'utterly unlikely to occur, vastly incredible'.[2] In his reply to Curzon, Dawkins chose to pour cold water on the idea of a coalition government—which was not quite the line he was taking with his other proconsular friend, Milner. Nevertheless, Dawkins insisted that if Curzon rejoined the Unionist administration, he would soon emerge as *the man*, and the nation would eventually pick upon him to take overall control of policy.[3] Curzon demurred. As his breach with his old friends in the Cabinet widened, he felt increasingly reluctant to help the Conservative Party extricate itself from the mess which it had made. 'All the talkers,' he complained, 'seem to proceed upon the theory that I am willing to be shifted about to suit the exigencies of a somewhat sick and debilitated party, and still more that I am burning to become a Cabinet Minister in the present Administration. Strange as it may seem, I have no desire whatever in either direction . . .'[4]

In February 1904 Dawkins made his last serious attempt to cajole Curzon back to England. With great earnestness, he warned Curzon that, unless he soon returned to give the public a lead, he would develop such masterful and autocratic tendencies as Viceroy, that he would later find it impossible to serve with other Cabinet colleagues.[5] Good-humouredly, Curzon questioned his own qualifications for such a role and the assumption that the British public wanted to be 'led' by anyone.[6]

By 1904 Curzon knew himself to be politically isolated. He could never adopt Milner's ploy of pretending to stand above party. He was a committed member of the Conservative Party—but one who was out of sympathy with all its leaders. He was no longer on

---

[1] S. Gopal, *British Policy in India, 1858–1905* (Cambridge, 1965), p. 304.

[2] Curzon Papers, Vol. 182: Curzon to Dawkins, 22.11.01: ff. 32–3.

[3] ibid., Dawkins to Curzon, 26.12.01: ff. 54–5.

[4] ibid., Curzon to Dawkins, 12.3.03: f. 135.

[5] ibid., Dawkins to Curzon, 17.2.04: f. 285. Milner Papers, Vol. 41: Dawkins to Milner, 26.2.04: f. 60.

[6] Curzon Papers, Vol. 182: Curzon to Dawkins, 9.3.04: ff.191–2.

speaking terms with the Indian Secretary, Brodrick. Balfour had caused offence by not replying to one of his personal letters for over two years. On the other hand, Curzon equally disliked the Tariff Reformers, partly no doubt out of personal antipathy to Chamberlain,[1] but also because he failed to see how India was to benefit from Imperial Preference. He thus came to value the assistance given him by friendly Liberal Imperialists. In September 1904 Haldane, who supported the Viceroy's 'forward policy', actually wrote pressing him to return to the domestic political scene: 'The Conservative Party wants pulling into shape—nearly though not wholly, for that is hardly possible, as badly as the Opposition. There is any amount of work to be done—and it is in England that the necessity for it is greatest. . . . The Country is looking for new blood.'[2]

But while Haldane was exchanging pleasantries with Curzon, he and the other Liberal Imperialists were slipping further and further away from Milner. To Milner, the Chesterfield speech had shown up Rosebery as a political irresponsible; all the same, he still had enough confidence in the Asquith-Grey-Haldane set in early 1902 to advise Dawkins that his 'natural place' was with these men.[3] Then came the differences between Milner and his Liberal Party friends over Tariff Reform, and, on top of this, the Chinese Labour dispute, when Haldane alone took the High Commissioner's side against the attacks of the radicals.[4] The defection of Asquith and Grey was very significant. Although there seems to be no evidence for the assertion that it was only the promise of support from the Liberal Imperialist leaders which had encouraged Milner to press ahead with the importation of indentured Chinese labourers into

[1] Milner Papers, Vol. 41: Dawkins to Milner, 31.12.03: 'Curzon from letters seems to be moving in Joe's direction but I think is deterred a good deal by personal antipathy to Joe whom he bears very hard . . .': f. 70.

[2] Curzon Papers, Vol. 215: Haldane to Curzon, 21.9.04: item 153. Later, in June 1905 when the Viceroy's policy came under attack in the Commons, Haldane responded to Curzon's appeal for help and made a strong speech in his favour (Haldane Papers, Vol. 5906: Curzon to Haldane, 18.5.05: ff. 171–6: & Hansard, 4th Series, Vol. 147, cols. 1264–6: 21.6.05).

[3] Milner Papers, Vol. 28: Milner to Dawkins, 4.1.02: f. 5.

[4] Milner had introduced indentured Chinese labour into the gold mines of the Rand. This was attacked by the Opposition as a form of veiled slavery.

the Transvaal,[1] there is no doubt that the High Commissioner felt that he had been betrayed by his one-time allies. This incident, however, was merely one more indication that the period of confusion in party politics had ended. Just as Rosebery had been forced to descend from his pedestal and merge his identity in the Liberal Party, so Milner was drawn, albeit against his will, into closer co-operation with the Unionists.

All this while, Dawkins was busily accumulating as much money as he could as a director of Morgan's, in the hope that when Milner finally returned from South Africa he could finance his friend and go into partnership with him for the furtherance of those causes about which they both felt strongly, such as the reorganization of the machinery of the Empire and the adoption of some form of compulsory military service. Unfortunately, Dawkins had to inform Milner in May 1904 that Morgan had transacted some bad business in England, for which he was himself partly responsible, and that he feared the outcome would be to wound English suscep-tibilities and thus damage his own chances of 'being politically useful or employed'.[2] A year later Dawkins' health began to deteriorate rapidly. When Milner's time finally came to leave South Africa, his first concern was to nurse his sick friend. Together they visited the Italian lakes and consulted specialists in Paris.[3] In December 1905 Dawkins died of heart disease.

Despite the virtual failure of his South African policy, Milner found on his return to England that he still enjoyed enormous popularity with a certain type of Unionist. By turning down Balfour's offer of the post of Colonial Secretary in the autumn of 1903, a decision which had greatly annoyed the King,[4] Milner had at least escaped sharing responsibility for the blunders of the doomed Unionist Government. This gave him an advantage, which some of his admirers urged him to exploit. Typical of the appeals he received was this one from the editor of the *Morning Post*, Fabian Ware, written in June 1905:

[1] Cecil Headlam (ed), *The Milner Papers: South Africa, 1899–1905*, Vol. II (1933), p. 477.
[2] Milner Papers, Vol. 41: Dawkins to Milner, 5.5.04: ff. 61–2.
[3] Curzon Papers, Vol. 183: Dawkins to Curzon, 12.7.05: ff. 77–8.
[4] Philip Magnus, *King Edward the Seventh* (1964), p. 326.

To put my bottom thought first, we want you to come and lead us to put the country straight. 'We' is a large majority of the people who only want leading to do one of the biggest things this country has seen. . . Of course the country is getting so impatient that it will demand too much immediately definite from the man in whom it places its confidence. If he attaches himself to either party and plays the party game, compromising on vital matters, and sacrificing big principles to party exigencies the people will not follow him for long. But need a man in the House of Lords do this? Would he not by taking a more or less independent national line . . . make the party gather round him. *I am convinced the country would respond.* But the man who is to put things right—and if he doesn't come soon the country is done for—must start alone. The old parties do not correspond to the lines of thought in the country and are played out.[1]

There is something rather pathetic about this letter of Ware's, with its wild and quite unsupported generalizations about what 'the country' was demanding. Actually, the most obvious feature of the political scene in 1905 was the popularity of the Liberal Party, poised for a great electoral victory, once Balfour finally decided to resign. And Milner could expect nothing but kicks from the sort of radical government that seemed about to come to power.

For, as Beatrice Webb observed as early as March 1904, the decline of the Unionists was generating a great deal of negative radicalism within the ranks of the Opposition: 'Little Englandism crude democracy, economy, secularism, are all again to the front in the official Liberal Party—are, in fact, the only actively militant forces with a policy to push. The vacuum over which the "Limps" have zealously watched cannot be kept intact; and the old creed and the old cries are rushing in, in default of better stuff.'[2] This, of course, was an over-statement of the position. Having lost contact with the radicals over the Boer War and the Education Act, the Webbs persistently chose to ignore the ferment of political ideas that was going on within the Liberal Party. A new radicalism was taking root which differed considerably from old-fashioned Gladstonianism. But these developments had made a comparatively small impact, as yet, upon the party's leaders, who certainly

---

[1] Milner Papers, Vol. 40: Ware to Milner, 28.6.05: ff. 129–30.
[2] Beatrice Webb: op. cit., p. 283: 1.3.04.

lacked any strong incentive to spell out the details of a constructive programme, so long as they could defeat the Unionists by the simple expedient of pledging themselves to defend Free Trade and by brandishing the traditional slogans of Peace, Retrenchment and Reform.

The Liberal Imperialists were as liable to succumb to this temptation as the Campbell-Bannerman wing of the party. Writing in 1905, Cecil Chesterton, the Fabian, concluded that the Webbs had conceived their 'Houndsditch' article of September 1901 under the misapprehension that '"national efficiency" really meant something, and that "Liberal Imperialism" was a genuine attempt to form a party of progress free of Gladstonian tradition'. But subsequent events had demonstrated, wrote Chesterton, that 'the Liberal Imperialists were for the most part mere squeezable opportunists with all the effete prejudices of the Pro-Boers minus their sturdiness of conviction, men who . . . had not the slightest intention of abandoning a single Mid-Victorian nostrum, which could still be used to catch a few votes'.[1] Haldane alone continued to stand for ideas and proposals that were sharply distinguishable from those of the average radical M.P.: that was why he was so distrusted by most people in his party.

The collapse of Liberal Imperialism as a coherent creed removed the last obstacle in the way of Campbell-Bannerman's eventual succession to the premiership. In October 1905 Haldane made a last desperate effort to re-activate the Liberal Imperialist group when he met Asquith and Grey at Relugas, where a collective pact was made that they would none of them serve in a Liberal ministry, unless Campbell-Bannerman agreed to go up to the House of Lords. But this intrigue of Haldane's was almost bound to fail. When Balfour finally resigned office in December 1905, Asquith very quickly went back on his previous undertaking, and Campbell-Bannerman had things very much his own way. On 5 December the aged Liberal leader kissed hands. Haldane eventually accepted the War Office, Grey the Foreign Office, and Asquith became Chancellor of the Exchequer. In the following year the Liberals won a landslide victory at a general election from which extreme radicals were returned to the Commons in

[1] Cecil Chesterton, op. cit., pp. 12–13.

droves. Haldane, Grey and their hangers-on could count themselves lucky that Campbell-Bannerman had had to form a Cabinet *before* dissolving Parliament; otherwise they might have been left out of office altogether.[1]

In more ways than one, the 1906 election was a triumph for Campbell-Bannerman and the radical point of view he embodied. From the hustings countless Liberal candidates up and down the country put over the old radical catchcries. Even Haldane took a fairly traditional line, telling his constituents that 'the real issue at this election is between Free Trade and Protection'.[2] Bernard Shaw correctly concluded after the results had come in that the electorate had pronounced in favour of conservatism—conservatism with a small 'c'. It was the more novel aspects of the programme of the late Unionist Administration that had been most decisively rejected.[3]

The veteran Liberal M.P. and temperance reform fanatic, Sir Wilfrid Lawson, scented victory as early as December 1905. To a fellow spirit, Francis Channing, he wrote: 'to see the Sun rising at last "o'er the gloomy hills of darkness" ought to cheer us, irrespective entirely of what others think of us. Our motto should be, "This is the Lord's doing" (not the "House of Lords"). Let us rejoice and be glad in it.'[4] The conviction that a new moral epoch was dawning, in which the British nation, renouncing the twin idols of Efficiency and Empire, was about to return to the paths of godliness and righteousness, gave the Liberals their strong sense of religious purpose in the general election; and this almost apocalyptic mood buoyed up the enormous Liberal majority which assembled in the Commons for the first time in February 1906.

Initially, it seemed as though the wildest hopes of the radicals were going to be fulfilled. There was jubilation when Campbell-Bannerman succeeded in humiliating Balfour on the floor of the House, in his famous 'enough of this foolery' interjection: a trivial incident in itself, but possessing a wider symbolic significance. The

[1] See F. E. Hamer, *The Personal Papers of Lord Rendel* (1931), p. 171. A. Fitzroy, op. cit., p. 290: 4.4.06.
[2] copy in Haldane Papers, Vol. 5907: f. 12.
[3] cited in F. Bealey and H. Pelling, op. cit., pp. 265–6.
[4] G. W. E. Russell (ed.), *Sir Wilfrid Lawson: A Memoir* (1909), p. 316.

elderly Prime Minister only occasionally took the lead during Cabinet deliberations, but faced by a new Commons, where his own sturdy, sentimental brand of Scottish radicalism made a strong appeal to so many Liberal M.P.s, he quickly gained a personal ascendancy over his party and the House, which he was never really to lose. Those who remembered the ineffectual, fumbling politician of the previous Parliament—the somewhat pathetic figure whom Balfour had so easily out-manoeuvred, while Liberal backbenchers looked on, often with scarcely concealed exasperation—were amazed at the transformation.

Campbell-Bannerman, in short, was now 'the man on horse-back',[1] and the Liberal Imperialists, as a group, had to accept the situation with as good a grace as they could muster. In fact, there is no real evidence that after February 1906 they even tried to function *as a group*. Grey became immersed in his departmental work, while Asquith, always in spirit a party loyalist of middle-of-the-road opinions, prepared himself for the reversion of the leadership, becoming in the process the very personification of Liberal orthodoxy. Only Haldane continued to take the earlier talk about national efficiency seriously; but, conscious of his isolation, he largely withdrew from his ministerial colleagues and concentrated on his army reforms, seldom speaking in Cabinet[2]—though he was loquacious by nature—and taking little part, before 1909, at least in Parliamentary debates, except when War Office affairs were involved. He did, it is true, make an attempt in 1908 to reorganize the social services on more 'scientific' lines, but this venture ended in failure.[3] Beatrice Webb described Haldane's usual posture during this period when she met him in May 1907 and found him 'completely absorbed in his own department—and singularly aloof in his attitude both towards Parliament and towards his colleagues. "Not a good Parliament," he remarked, "no constructive ideas, merely objections to other people's ideas. I

---

[1] See Lord Shaw of Dunfermline, *Letters to Isabel* (1921), p. 263.

[2] D. Lloyd George, *War Memoirs*, Vol. I (1933), p. 603 in Odhams Press edition, n.d. Haldane wrote in retrospect: 'I was not really good in that Cabinet, partly from temperament, and partly because I found it difficult to get really interested in its work' (Haldane Papers, Vol. 5923: Notes Contained in My Boxes, written in autumn, 1926: f. 15).

[3] See below, Chapter VII, pp. 245–8, 255.

spend very little time there", he continued. (I thought he added, but I could not be quite sure, "Nor does the Cabinet interest me") . . . The only person he volunteered kindly interest in was the leader of the opposition! "I see a good deal of Balfour," he genially remarked . . .'[1]

Interestingly enough, Haldane also kept on friendly terms, for a while, with Milner. The two men had sat together in late 1905 on a small committee which was investigating the affairs of the Imperial Institute; and Haldane expected this to be the start of much common work.[2] However, the censure motion on Milner in 1906 imposed a further strain on the relations between the retired proconsul and his former Liberal supporters. Haldane assured his mother that he was 'looking after Milner' in the Cabinet, at the time when the Government's course of action on the censure motion was being decided.[3] But in the event, all the Liberal Imperialist leaders voted for the official Government amendment which, as introduced by Churchill, caused Milner and his Unionist friends so much offence.[4] Nor do they later seem to have regretted their action.[5]

As late as February 1907 Haldane remained on sufficiently good terms with Milner to have met him for a general political discussion. But Milner was not impressed by the other's views and wrote off irritably to Amery: 'I listened to Haldane for nearly 20 minutes the other night on the subject of "Imperial organisation"—a private conversation, so that he might have said something if he had a mind to. It was all *blather*. If that is *the best* we can expect from these fellows, Heaven help us.'[6]

---

[1] Beatrice Webb, op. cit., pp. 379–80: 3.5.07.

[2] Milner Papers: Haldane to Milner, 22.7.05. ibid., Milner to Haldane, 27.7.05.

[3] Haldane Papers, Vol. 5975: Haldane to Mother, 19.3.06: f. 125.

[4] Hansard, 4th Series, Vol. 154: Division List no. 23, cols. 505–12: 21.3.06. Perhaps Haldane regarded it as a triumph for his views that the Government did not decide to vote for the censure motion itself.

[5] By 1908 Grey concluded that he and Milner had never meant the same thing over South Africa: G. M. Trevelyan, *Grey of Fallodon* (1937), p. 79. In 1907 Haldane, in a letter to Bryce, picked upon South Africa as the 'highest spot' in the Liberal Government's record: Bryce Papers, Box E 28: Haldane to Bryce, 12.3.07.

[6] A. M. Gollin, *Proconsul in Politics* (1964), p. 133.

Disillusioned with the Liberal Imperialists ever since the censure debate, yet critical of the Unionist leadership, Milner was persuaded by Amery into launching out on his own;[1] and in December 1906 he delivered two big speeches in Manchester and Wolverhampton, which unfolded the programme to which he was to adhere for the rest of his life.[2] He stressed the inter-connection between imperialism and social reform, the need to organize the Empire's resources in the face of foreign competition and hostility, the dangers of *laissez-faire* and drift, the weakness of the existing machinery of government, and the over-riding importance of rearing a vigorous and efficient race of patriots capable of bearing the burdens of Empire.

At the same time Milner took great care to dissociate himself from either of the two major parties: 'I am a free lance, a sort of political Ishmaelite who has found hospitality in the Unionist camp,' he declared.[3] In his own view, Milner was a disinterested servant of the Crown who had got into the habit of looking at politics from a national, rather than a party, standpoint. Indeed, he claimed that there were no important issues which had not been gravely prejudiced by the intervention of party considerations. Therefore, said Milner, the only course for right-thinking people was to resolve to withdraw first one, then another, national problem from the arena of party strife and to tackle them from the 'national point of view'.

Of course, none of this was particularly original. We see here merely one more variation on the theme sung by Rosebery in the Boer War period. Yet, whereas Rosebery had captured considerable public interest in 1900 and 1901, Milner's campaign in December 1906 fell decidedly flat. One explanation is that Milner had chosen an inappropriate moment for delivering himself of these sentiments—only a few months after a general election. In addition Milner suffered by comparison with Rosebery, in being a poor public speaker, whose performances on the platform frequently embarrassed his warmest admirers.[4] The real weakness in Milner's

---

[1] L. S. Amery, op. cit., pp. 298–9.
[2] These two speeches are printed in Viscount Milner, *The Nation and the Empire* (1913), pp. 135–63.
[3] ibid., p. 153.   [4] e.g. L. S. Amery, op. cit., p. 299.

position, however, was his pretence to stand above party; however sincerely it was made, this claim was difficult to take seriously. Some of the Fabians, it is true, still kept in touch with him and viewed his ideals and achievements with a certain respect. H. G. Wells thought that the of 'Co-Efficients' group, which continued to meet sporadically, Milner was 'the most satisfactory intelligence among us'.[1] Yet Milner had become so associated with imperialism of an aggressive kind, that he was anathema to nearly all 'progressives', Liberals, Labour or Irish. His insistence upon Tariff Reform and compulsory military service was enough in itself to disqualify him from assuming a non-party role. The fact that Milner did not enjoy good relations with the opposition front bench did not make him seem any more 'impartial', any more of a 'national leader'. After the speech at Wolverhampton, the Liberal *Westminster Gazette* commented: 'For our part we do not see anything so very Ishmaelitish in Lord Milner's views. We are beginning to be accustomed to the mixture of Imperialism, Universal Military Training, Tariff Reform and Old Age Pensions. The Chamberlainites will rejoice greatly at the mixture . . .'[2]

To certain observers these speeches signalled a bid from Milner for the leadership of the Tariff Reform wing of the Unionist Party, left vacant since July 1906, when Joseph Chamberlain had had a stroke from which he had only partially recovered. Amery and Mackinder certainly nourished this ambition, and in 1908 Mackinder resigned as Director of the London School of Economics to help direct a new Tariff Reform campaign in association with Milner: a plan hampered, in the event, by a shortage of money.[3] But there was a coolness between Milner and the 'Highbury' group of Tariff Reformers, led by Austen Chamberlain.[4] And Hewins, the principal economic expert in the movement, viewed Milner with

[1] H. G. Wells, *Experiment in Autobiography*, Vol. II (1934), pp. 765–6. In his semi-autobiographical novel, *The New Machiavelli* (1911), Wells makes his hero fall under the influence of the Milner circle by 1908. Lord Gane represents Milner. The Webbs were more critical of Milner, but respected him nonetheless.

[2] *Westminster Gazette*, 18.12.06.

[3] L. S. Amery, op. cit., pp. 299–300. A. M. Gollin, *Proconsul in Politics* (1964), pp. 114–17.

[4] See Austen Chamberlain, *Politics From Inside* (1936), p. 368; A. Chamberlain to Mrs Chamberlain, 26.10.11.

something like contempt,[1] preferring at this time to 'work on' Balfour.[2] The result was that Milner lacked that firm basis of organized support which he would have needed to mount an effectual challenge for the place of either Balfour or Austen Chamberlain.[3] No-one realized this more clearly than Milner himself. So, in the 1906–1910 period he was content to limit his activities to the occasional speech in the House of Lords and the occasional public address: and to bide his time.

The main effect of these speeches of Milner's was probably to convince many Liberals that Germanic bureaucratic ideals of efficiency could not be engrafted on to British constitutional government or be reconciled with the practice of a liberal democracy. The same was even more true of articles which appeared in papers like the *Morning Post* and the *Nineteenth Century* and, at a more vulgar level, some of the Harmsworth Press publications. In the warnings they contained of the dangers confronting the Empire, these articles showed such a bias against the Liberal Party, that their appeal must have been largely confined to virulent opponents of the Government. Indeed, it was all too easy to see in these warnings merely the frenzied hysteria of wild and unreasoning men who would never admit that a Liberal administration had a right to exist.

In the middle of 1909 Massingham of *The Nation* felt able to look back complacently on the old outcry about efficiency as though on a distasteful episode that had now become history:

When Lord Rosebery first introduced into this country the game called National Efficiency, made, like other political and philosophic toys, in Germany, he can have had little notion of the vogue it was destined to achieve, or of the fine tinge of ironic humour conveyed by his personal introduction. . . It first became a serious pastime among journalists,

---

[1] W. A. S. Hewins, op. cit., pp. 39–40.
[2] Austen Chamberlain, op. cit., p. 80: A. Chamberlain to Mrs Chamberlain, 4.5.07.
[3] I cannot, therefore, accept the proposition that Milner's emergence made Balfour fear for his own position as leader of the Unionist Party (See A. M. Gollin, op. cit., pp. 109–14).

platform politicians and unsuccessful merchants at Chambers of Commerce. They would speculate or dogmatise, according to the mood, upon the questions what in particular this National Efficiency might mean, and how to get it, and whether we or Germany, or later on Japan, had most of it. . .[1]

But Massingham was being a little hasty in thus using the past tense; for even while these caustic lines were being penned, 'the game called National Efficiency' was reappearing on the political scene and the ideas once associated with Rosebery's name were enjoying a new lease of life. The heady atmosphere of 1906, when the ultimate triumph of the Liberal ideal had been taken for granted by the party faithful, had long ago given way to a mood of doubt and pessimism, especially at Cabinet level. Several Ministers, conscious that the Government had been blown off course by unforeseen difficulties, were re-examining their fundamental beliefs and looking for new policies better attuned to the circumstances of the hour. In this context, the creed of national efficiency, modified in certain particulars, suddenly seemed highly relevant again. By the autumn of 1910 even the prospect of a 'national government' was being discussed once more. The wheel had indeed turned full circle.

[1] *The Nation*, 1.5.09: p. 153.

CHAPTER VI

LLOYD GEORGE'S ATTEMPTED NATIONAL SETTLEMENT OF 1910

WHEN LORD RIPON resigned from the Cabinet in October 1908, the elderly Lord Chancellor, Loreburn, wrote to express his regrets: 'I was very downcast about it,' he explained, 'for C-B and Bryce and you were on the foundation of the Government the men I most agreed with and relied upon.' But in January 1907 Bryce had been appointed British Ambassador at Washington, and in April 1908 Campbell-Bannerman had died. The only other surviving member of the older group of radicals, John Morley, had weakened his position by accepting a peerage when Asquith became Prime Minister. 'It is a different Government today from what it was three years ago,' Loreburn sadly noted.[1]

The shift of power within the Cabinet which these changes of personnel had produced did not, however, benefit the Liberal imperialist group as such; and when Morley and Loreburn dwelt obsessively on the 'Liberal Imperialist take-over of the Government', which they thought to have followed Campbell-Bannerman's departure,[2] they were really living in the past. For by this time the old dividing line between the 'imperialist' and 'radical' wings of the party had been replaced by new factional groupings. Lloyd George and Churchill were the two ministers who grew most appreciably in authority and stature in 1908. Both men thought of themselves as radicals, but their radicalism had little in

---

[1] Ripon Papers, Add. Mss., 43,543: Loreburn to Ripon, 30.10.08: f. 155.
[2] J. H. Morgan, *John, Viscount Morley: An Appreciation and Some Reminiscences* (1924), p. 48. J. L. Hammond, *C. P. Scott of the Manchester Guardian* (1934), p. 153: Journal entry of 20.7.11.

common with the beliefs of Campbell-Bannerman, Morley or Bryce.

The sudden and remarkable rise of Lloyd George and Churchill to dominating positions within the Cabinet took place at a time when the Liberals were passing through a major crisis. As Campbell-Bannerman lay dying at 10 Downing Street, the object of almost universal affection, the ideals which had guided him during his long political career were being increasingly called into question by many of his ministers.

The arrival in Britain in late 1907 of a trade depression, 'the Rich Man's Panic', had pushed up the total of unemployed and produced a series of Government defeats at by-elections. The Liberal ministers, if they were to ward off the long-term challenge of socialism and the more immediate danger of a Tariff Reform break-through, had to show that a Free Trade administration of the traditional kind could still control the economy and contain social unrest. Their difficulty was that the programme on which they had been confirmed in office in 1906 was irrelevant to the problems they faced; for not only did their sectarian policies, like Welsh Disestablishment, now seem side-issues, but so did what little perfunctory thinking had been devoted to social and economic problems in the years of opposition. Campbell-Bannerman's own belief that retrenchment and reform could be combined by cutting back on wasteful expenditure and unnecessary foreign 'adventures' may have seemed reasonable in 1906 and 1907; but by 1908 Ministers knew that further social legislation would strain the country's fiscal resources. Again, the old conviction that land reform provided the key to the social problem had not survived two and a half years of ministerial experience. It would be too harsh a judgement to say that the Liberal Government's reform programme had proved a failure, since the obstruction of the House of Lords had prevented their most important legislative measures from reaching the statute book. Nevertheless, ministers were looking around for new policies and new ideas. The Webbs enjoyed a short-lived period of influence over the Liberal Administration in the spring of 1908 because of this situation. That Asquith should have asked Beatrice Webb's advice about what he should say in his Budget speech is simply one indication among many of the desperate condition to which the Liberals had been reduced.[1]

At the same time as the Government began to grope towards a 'new departure' in social policy, events were forcing it to make a reappraisal of Britain's world role. Edward Grey and his Foreign Office advisers may have been consistency itself; not for one moment did they waver in their belief that German hostility was the principal factor to be taken into account in the formulation and execution of Britain's foreign policy. Campbell-Bannerman and the radicals, however, had held high hopes of the 1907 Hague Conference, believing that an arms reduction agreement would produce a relaxation of international tension. In the event, the Hague Conference proved to be a fiasco. Soon afterwards, the Army and Navy Estimates, which had been cut for two successive years, began to rise steeply again. The accelerating tempo of the Anglo-German naval arms race, which reached a hysterical climax with the 'scare' of early 1909 and the popular clamour for eight new Dreadnoughts, were manifestations of the renewed fears about the security of the Empire in a hostile world.[2] In this situation, Campbell-Bannerman's kind of radicalism was of limited usefulness, since it did not deal in the harsh realities of power.[3]

Thus, by the spring of 1908, the foundations of the Liberal edifice had collapsed, leaving ministers looking for a new shelter in which to take refuge from their domestic and international difficulties. More than any of their colleagues, Lloyd George and Churchill seemed fitted to rise to this emergency. Admittedly, in 1908 and 1909 they were concentrating their energies on social reform, to the extent of begrudging the service departments the increased sums of money which international developments had rendered necessary. In August 1908, Churchill told his audience at

[1] See below, Chapter VII, p. 246.

[2] See Arthur J. Marder, *From the Dreadnought to Scapa Flow*, Vol. I (1961).

[3] Campbell-Bannerman's disregard for the realities of international power comes through in this letter of January 1901: '. . . instead of blustering about reinforcements and Army reform, or, shall we say, platitudinizing about commercial education, it would be well if our eminent ones applied themselves to this problem—How to make those love us who now hate us.' The recipient of this letter, Thomas Shaw, a Liberal M.P., could twenty years later describe these sentiments as 'the pure gold of statesmanship'. (Lord Shaw of Dunfermline, *Letters to Isabel* (1921), p. 241).

Swansea that talk of a probable war between Britain and Germany was 'all nonsense'. 'There was no collision of primary interests—big, important interests—between Great Britain and Germany in any quarter of the globe', he asserted.[1] But neither Churchill nor Lloyd George saw foreign affairs throught the eyes of the true 'economists' and 'Little Englanders' within the Cabinet, like Morley, Burns or Loreburn. During the crisis over the Naval Estimates in February 1909, Esher shrewdly noted: 'Lloyd George, in his heart, does not care a bit for economy, and is quite ready to face parliament with any amount of deficit, and to "go" for a big Navy. He is plucky and an Imperialist at heart, if he is anything. Besides, he despises the "stalwarts" on his own side.'[2] Much the same was true of Churchill, with his martial temperament and instincts.

Even at the height of his radical enthusiasm, there was always something of the 'aboriginal and unchangeable Tory' about Churchill, as Mrs. Masterman put it.[3] This did not endear him to the Opposition, who had never forgiven his remarks about Milner during the Censure Debate of March 1906 nor his obstructive behaviour at the 1907 Colonial Conference.[4] The Conservatives long continued to see Churchill as a turn-coat and traitor to his class.

Lloyd George, however, was more highly regarded by his opponents. When Asquith's government was formed, *The Times* commented: 'Mr. Winston Churchill, though possessed of many striking qualities, has not done anything to command the confidence of men of business, which is so largely given to Mr. Lloyd George.'[5] The reputation that Lloyd George had acquired at the Board of Trade as a 'practical man of business' was never alto-

[1] Randolph S. Churchill, *Winston S. Churchill: Young Statesman, 1901–1914* (1967), p. 282.

[2] M. V. Brett (ed.), *Journals and Letters of Reginald Viscount Esher*, Vol. II (1934), p. 370: Journals, 12.2.09.

[3] Lucy Masterman, *C. F. G. Masterman: A Biography* (1939), p. 165.

[4] During the 1907 Colonial Conference, Churchill, then Under-Secretary at the Colonial Office, had brusquely and publicly declared the Government's total opposition to all schemes of Imperial Preference. This was widely construed as a snub on the Colonial Premiers who were advocating this idea at the London conference.

[5] *The Times*, 13.4.08.

gether to be effaced by his subsequent fame as a demagogic social reformer and unorthodox financier. For example, at the height of the constitutional crisis in 1910 Garvin was able to remind his Conservative readership of Lloyd George's work at the Board of Trade and the high praise he had earned there 'by showing something like a genius for conciliation'.[1]

From a relatively early stage, the shrewder Conservatives realized that Lloyd George's adherence to Liberal principles was more lip-service than the result of conviction, especially in the matter of Free Trade: 'Of course you disagree with us,' McKenna had told Balfour at a City dinner in May 1907, 'but you *can* understand our principles. Lloyd George doesn't understand them and we can't make him.'[2] In short, the Opposition sensed that Lloyd George was, potentially, a second Joe Chamberlain: that other 'outsider' who first entered politics as spokesman for sectional radicalism and nonconformity against the 'establishment', only to end his career as an imperialist statesman working for an accommodation between the classes in the cause of national unity.[3]

As a person, too, Lloyd George rather attracted the Unionist leaders. From the days of their long drawn-out struggle over the 1902 Education Act, a strong bond of interest and respect seems to have been formed between Balfour and Lloyd George. Talking to his friend, Riddell, in October 1908, Lloyd George said: 'I could work with B[alfour], but his underlying sense of class superiority is the trouble with him.'[4] A shrewd observer of the political scene, Lucy Masterman, wrote in her Journal in August 1909: 'On the whole the Opposition are very fond of George. He amuses Arthur Balfour by his quickness and acuteness, and he has a kind of magnetism over the whole House possessed by very few others . . .'[5]

[1] *Observer*, 15.5.10.

[2] Austen Chamberlain, *Politics From Inside* (1936), p. 87: A. Chamberlain to Mrs Chamberlain, 14.5.07.

[3] Lloyd George himself was rather intrigued by parallels between his own career and that of Chamberlain. Lord Riddell, *More Pages From My Diary, 1908–1914* (1934), p. 64: 27.5.12.

[4] Lord Riddell, op. cit., p. 5: 31.10.08.

[5] Lucy Masterman, op. cit., p. 142.

It may seem strange that this attitude should have survived the
introduction of the 'People's Budget'. The violence and class
bitterness of Lloyd George's platform oratory at this time was not
simply put on for effect. In private, the Chancellor was alarming
Churchill with his jesting talk about setting up a guillotine in
Trafalgar Square.[1] Churchill had some cause for alarm; behind
the joke, he sensed Lloyd George's grim determination to force
through a social revolution in which the power of 'the classes'
would be destroyed and 'political democracy' reign in its stead.

Yet at the same time Lloyd George was watching the consequences of his actions with considerable misgiving. The crisis with
the House of Lords, which he had done much to provoke, threatened to paralyse the machinery of government, delay important
measures of social reform to which he was committed, and weaken
the nation at a time of international tension. No sooner had he
whipped up party feeling to fever pitch, than the Chancellor was
looking for a way out of the impasse.

As he returned from the general election of January 1910, Lloyd
George was in a very perplexed mood. For a while he wavered
undecided between the alternative policies of 'reforming' the
Lords and abolishing its veto.[2] Mrs. Masterman describes him in
March as playing about with the possibility of setting up a government, of which he would be premier, with business men, like Sir
Christopher Furness and Alfred Mond as his Ministers; such a
Government, he mused, would carry enormous weight in the
country.[3] Consciously or unconsciously, Lloyd George was returning to the ideas which Rosebery had aired in his Edinburgh
speech of November 1901.[4] This was not entirely accidental,
perhaps, and reflects a certain similarity between the situation in
1910 and the situation in which Rosebery had flourished at the end
of the Boer War. The important difference was that then the case
for a non-party government had rested on a belief that the party
system was disintegrating: in early 1910 it rested on the fear that
party strife was *too* fierce and unrelenting, so that national energies

---

[1] ibid., p. 139.
[2] ibid., p. 154: Journal entry, February 1910.
[3] ibid., p. 160: Journal entry, March or early April, 1910.
[4] see above, Chapter III, p. 87.

were being dissipated, to the benefit of Britain's enemies and rivals.

When King Edward VII died suddenly in May, Garvin in the *Observer* and Milner's friend, F. S. Oliver, in letters to *The Times* under the pseudonym of 'Pacificus', appealed for a 'Truce of God', in which the party leaders could meet and try to de-fuse the constitutional crises. Their propaganda helped prepare the way for the formal Constitutional Conference which first assembled in June and, against a background of anxiety and wild speculation, dragged on until November.[1]

One consequence of this was that Lloyd George and Balfour were brought into close contact with one another. A few months later Mrs. Masterman found Lloyd George 'absolutely hypnotized by Arthur Balfour, by his charm, his quickness, and his undeniably very clever intellect'.[2] In the Conference Chamber itself, Lloyd George took a less flexible line than his other colleagues, Asquith, Crewe and Birrell; on 28 July he came near to breaking it up altogether by his intransigence.[3] All the while, however, the Chancellor was revolving in his mind the grandiose project of a 'national government', which could tackle all the outstanding problems of the day and guarantee Britain's internal stability and external security, in a way that the Liberals, unaided, seemed powerless to do.

The sequence of events, in brief outline, was as follows. While the Constitutional Conference was in recess, Lloyd George went home to Criccieth and there composed a memorandum, dated 17 August in which he stated the case for a coalition and itemized some of the policies which such a government might carry.[4] The first politician he took into his confidence was probably Churchill, who, initially

[1] See Roy Jenkins, *Mr. Balfour's Poodle* (1954). For convening of the conference, see A. M. Gollin, *The Observer and J. L. Garvin* (1960), Chapter VI.

[2] Lucy Masterman, op. cit, p. 164: Journal entry, 12.10.10.

[3] Corinne Comstock Weston, 'The Liberal Leadership and the Lords' Veto, 1907–1910' (*Historical Journal*, 1968, Vol, XI, no. 3, pp. 527–8). On July 28th Birrell associated himself with Lloyd George's 'ultimatum' to the Opposition delegates.

[4] This memorandum is reproduced in Sir Charles Petrie, *The Life and Letters of the Right Hon. Sir Austen Chamberlain*, Vol. I (1939), pp. 381–8.

hesitant, soon took up the idea with the greatest enthusiasm.[1] The
Liberal Chief Whip, the Master of Elibank, was also involved at an
early stage.[2] Not until October, however, did Lloyd George begin
negotiating in a serious spirit. Then, probably in the first week of
that month, Churchill wrote a letter to his friend, the Conservative
backbench M.P., F. E. Smith. When Churchill's letter brought no
response, Lloyd George himself wrote to Smith, inviting him round
to Downing Street. Lloyd George there showed Smith the
memorandum and talked to him about his plans for a 'national
settlement'.[3] Greatly excited, Smith informed Balfour of what was
in Lloyd George's mind, and a preliminary discussion took place
between Balfour and Lloyd George soon afterwards, probably on
11 October, the day the Constitutional Conference reconvened.[4]
After about a week Balfour asked leave to consult his colleagues at
the conference, Austen Chamberlain, Lansdowne and Cawdor.
Lloyd George gave permission.[5] At about the same time he authorized Smith to bring Bonar Law into the picture, too, and Bonar
Law quickly got in touch with Austen Chamberlain and joined the
inner circle of Conservatives who were 'in the know'.[6]

[1] M. Thomson, *David Lloyd George* (n.d.), p. 195. Balfour Papers, Add.
Mss. 49,767: undated aide-memoire written by Balfour's secretary, Jack San-
dars. According to Mrs Masterman, Churchill did not initially approve of
Lloyd George's scheme, especially when it was suggested to him that he might
be left out of the national coalition; later he became passionately in favour of it
(Lucy Masterman, op. cit., pp. 164–5).

[2] A. M. Gollin, *Garvin*, p. 207.

[3] Balfour Papers, Add. Mss. 49,767: Sandars' undated aide-memoire.
A. Chamberlain to Lord Cawdor, 21.10.10: printed in A. Chamberlain, op.
cit., p. 286; A. Chamberlain to Landsowne, 26.8.12: printed in A. Chamberlain, op. cit., p. 291.

[4] 'I have some informal suggestions which I should like to put to you. You
thought tomorrow at 4 would suit you. Don't you think dinner or lunch would
be a more convivial opportunity for discussing things? If you agree, it would
give me great pleasure if you could dine with me tomorrow evening, or failing
that lunch with me after the Conference. The servants are Welsh and could
not follow the conversation and the only other person present would be my
little daughter of eight summers'. (Balfour Papers, Add. Mss. 49,692: Lloyd
George to Balfour, 11.10.10). Clearly, Lloyd George had already broached his
coalition plans before writing this letter, so October 11th is that *latest* date we
can fix on for their preliminary meeting; it could have been a day or two earlier.

[5] A. Chamberlain to Lansdowne, 26.8.12: printed in A. Chamberlain, op.
cit., p. 291.

[6] A. Chamberlain to Cawdor, 21.10.10: ibid., p. 286.

Meanwhile, some time in the middle of October, *after* the approach to Balfour had been made, Lloyd George told Asquith of his plans, though precisely what account he gave of them is anyone's guess.[1] In any case, Asquith agreed to his Chancellor of the Exchequer trying for a settlement with the Conservatives outside the Conference, if one was obtainable. Other Liberals were then contacted. On 20 October Lloyd George posted the memorandum to Crewe[2] and on 25 October he had a long talk with Edward Grey;[3] Birrell and Haldane, it appears, were also approached and expressed their general approval.[4] A junior minister, C. F. G. Masterman, also knew about the memorandum, possibly in early October, because he was on friendly terms with both Lloyd George and Churchill, his departmental chief, and might well have been present at some of their original discussions.[5] All this while, Balfour was bringing a few more of his party colleagues into consultation. Another important figure to be let into the secret was J. L. Garvin, the editor of the *Observer*, whom Lloyd George entrusted with the task of creating a press atmosphere favourable to the idea of a coalition.[6] In all, then, some twenty people must have been aware of Lloyd George's plans for a 'grand settlement'.

[1] This is stated clearly in the Sandars aide-memoire (Balfour Papers, Add. Mss. 49,767). See also A. Chamberlain to Lansdowne, 26.8.12: op. cit., p. 291. In a letter to Crewe of 20th October, Lloyd George says that he had no opportunity of showing his memorandum to the P.M. 'until last week' (J. Pope-Hennessy, *Lord Crewe* (1955), p. 119). That does not altogether clarify the point, however, since 'last week' could include any date between the 9th and the 15th October. A piece of evidence on the other side is contained in a memo. which Chamberlain drew up on 27.11.13 after meeting Churchill. According to this, Churchill said 'that Asquith had been fully informed of the conversations from the first but, until Crewe and Birrell were informed, had maintained an attitude of strict reserve and aloofness' (A. Chamberlain, op. cit., p. 577). The bulk of the evidence, however, is opposed to Churchill's recorded opinion.

[2] Lloyd George to Crewe, 20.10.10: printed in Pope-Hennessy, op. cit., p. 119.

[3] Edward Grey to Asquith, 26.10.10: printed in Roy Jenkins, *Asquith* (1964), p. 217.

[4] F. E. Smith to A. Chamberlain, 21.10.10: printed in Lord Birkenhead, *Frederick Edwin Earl of Birkenhead*, Vol. I (1933), pp. 207–8 in the Keystone Library 1936 edition.

[5] See L. Masterman, op. cit., Ch. 7. However, this account must be read with caution. What purports to be taken from a journal entry of October 12th must partly have been written at a much later date.

[6] A. M. Gollin, *Garvin*, Ch. VII.

However, all the negotiating was entirely left to Lloyd George and Balfour; the others did no more than offer suggestions and comments from the wings.[1]

The greatest flurry of activity was concentrated into the third week of October. Thereafter, discussion somewhat sagged. On 29 October Lloyd George produced a second and briefer memorandum of sixteen paragraphs, summarizing the reforms he wanted his 'national government' to sponsor.[2] At this point, Balfour's understanding of the situation was, briefly, that Lloyd George was offering him an instalment of Tariff Reform, the adoption of compulsory military service and a 'big navy' policy, in return for an acceptance by the Unionists of some scheme of devolution or 'Home Rule All Round' as a final resolution of the Irish problem. But Balfour, on whom rested the sole responsibility for continuing or breaking off these discussions, finally reached the conclusion that he could not enter a coalition on such terms. By the end of the month, nearly all hope for a settlement was lost. The crucial interview between Balfour and Lloyd George took place on 2 November. Next day Smith learned that the 'big scheme' had failed.[3] The formal Constitutional Conference collapsed soon afterwards, and on 10 November an official communique informed the public that the party leaders had dispersed, without reaching any agreement.

The informal talks on the possibility of coalition were, of course, conducted in circumstances of complete secrecy. Even the affairs of the Constitutional Conference were shrouded in mystery. On 22 October the *Westminster Gazette* wrote irritably: 'There have been many moments in recent weeks when the political journalist has felt like the captain of a tramp steamer who has lost his compass overboard and is trying to steer by the Pole star on a foggy night.'[4] Readers of Garvin's editorials in the *Observer*[5] and of a

---

[1] A. Chamberlain to Lansdowne, 26.8.12: printed in A. Chamberlain, op. cit., p. 293.

[2] Elibank Papers, Ms. 8802: ff. 123–7. There are also a number of drafts in the Lloyd George Papers, Series C/Box 16/Folder 9/item C.

[3] A. M. Gollin, *Garvin*, pp. 228–31.

[4] *Westminster Gazette*, 22.10.10: editorial.

[5] *Observer*, 16.10.10, 23.10.10.

second series of letters in *The Times* from 'Pacificus'[1] would have suspected that the leaders at the Constitutional Conference were broadening their discussions in a search for a compromise solution of the Irish Question. Indeed, the merits of 'Home Rule All Round' had been expounded by Birrell way back in July, and Elibank commended this arrangement in a number of his speeches.[2]

The nearest Lloyd George himself came to 'flying a kite' was on 17 October, when he delivered an address at the City Temple to the Liberal Christian League. In this address he emphasized the common ground between the two parties over matters of social reform and went on to pay a tribute to Joseph Chamberlain, whose 'historic agitation', he said, had rendered an 'outstanding service to the cause of the masses' by drawing attention to the 'great number of real crying evils festering among us.'[3] Extraordinary utterance attracted a certain amount of comment in the newspapers. The point holds good, all the same, that the wider public was never informed of the plans that were on foot to foist a coalition on them. And for many years afterwards the participants, by a sort of 'gentlemen's agreement', preserved a discreet silence on the subject.

The first public disclosure was made in July 1919, when Lloyd George and Churchill were working for 'fusion' between the coalition Liberals and the Conservatives, and Churchill, presumably with Lloyd George's consent, spoke about 'the coalition that nearly was'.[4] Nothing further leaked out until 1930, when the writer of *The Times* obituary article on Balfour went into a little detail. But it was largely left to Lloyd George to provide the world with the first full account of the coalition talks in his *War Memoirs*, published in 1933.[5] Ever since then, additional information, in the form of letters, memoranda and reminiscences, has come to light;

---

[1] *The Times*, 20.10.10, 22.10.10, 24.10.10, 26.10.10, 28.10.10, 31.10.10, 2.11.10. 'Pacificus' was Milner's friend, F. S. Oliver, the biographer of Alexander Hamilton.

[2] A. M. Gollin, *Garvin*, pp. 200–1. Also, Elibank's speeches at Belfast and Edinburgh (*The Times*, 19.10.10, 20.10.10).

[3] *The Times*, 18.10.10.

[4] Trevor Wilson, *The Downfall of the Liberal Party, 1914–1935* (1966), p. 193.

[5] David Lloyd George, *War Memoirs*, Vol. I (1933), pp. 20–4 in Odhams edition.

yet this has, in many ways, made the story more, not less, difficult to piece together.

The major problem is to discover Lloyd George's true motives. Lucy Masterman derived the impression that what first impelled Lloyd George to make his coalition overtures was his anxiety to carry through a state-sponsored scheme of insurance against death: a scheme that no party dared introduce alone, for fear of the electoral consequences.[1] It seems that Lucy Masterman is here muddling together *funeral* benefits, to which Lloyd George never attached much importance, and *widows and orphans* benefits, which were central to the measure of social insurance on which he had been working since 1908.[2] We certainly know that in early August 1910 the Chancellor had had an ominous meeting with the industrial insurance agents, from which he learned, for the first time, the strength of their opposition to competition from the state in this field.[3] Insurance problems must, therefore, have been at the front of his mind when, soon afterwards, he retired to Criccieth and wrote his coalition memorandum. Significantly, the longest and most detailed paragraph in this document is the one in which Lloyd George attacks the great industrial insurance companies and argues that the state could provide widows and orphans benefits much more economically. Lucy Masterman's assessment of Lloyd George's motives in penning the August memorandum is thus highly plausible.

Astonishingly enough, though, Lloyd George makes no specific reference to National Insurance in his *War Memoirs* account. Instead, one finds a somewhat melodramatic description of how he had been haunted in 1910 by the prospect of a European war: 'There were ominous clouds gathering over the Continent of Europe and perceptibly thickening and darkening. . . . Great nations were arming feverishly for an apprehended struggle into which we might be drawn by some visible or invisible ties, interests

[1] L. Masterman, op. cit., pp. 163–4.
[2] Bentley B. Gilbert, *The Evolution of National Insurance in Great Britain* (1966), pp. 328–30.
[3] ibid., p. 326.

or sympathies.' This vast external danger, he writes, had coincided with an arrest in the expansion of Britain's foreign trade, social unrest at home, a great constitutional struggle over the House of Lords threatening revolution in England, another threatening civil war in Ireland.[1]

The obvious wisdom of hindsight displayed in these remarks immediately arouses one's suspicions. In one passage Lloyd George actually writes as though he had foreseen the important part soon to be played by German Zeppelins and submarines, and had grasped the dangers to national survival involved in Britain's dependence on overseas sources of food supplies. In fact, few people in 1910 had this prescient understanding of the nature of the coming war, least of all Lloyd George. In any case, the August memorandum makes mention of none of these things. True, there is a suggestion that Britain should adopt military training on the model of the Swiss militia system. Otherwise, questions of defence take a very subordinate place, and in the one short paragraph devoted to the subject Lloyd George seems to be as much con-cerned with the possibility of *saving* money by a review of arma-ments expenditure as he is with preparations for an inevitable war.

Yet Lloyd George clearly wishes people to suppose that the account of the coalition talks contained in his *War Memoirs* is based upon the text of the August memorandum. But we have seen that this is by no means the case. There are a few factual discrepancies between the two documents, while the emphasis is entirely different. When he came to write his *War Memoirs*, Lloyd George certainly had two copies of the August memorandum in his possession;[2] the inaccuracy of his observations cannot therefore be explained as forgetfulness or as an unconscious projection back into 1910 of emotions and calculations which he was only to feel once the war had broken out. It is very tempting to conclude that Lloyd George was trying in 1933 to present himself as the far-sighted statesman, who could have reduced the sufferings of his countrymen and achieved a speedier victory, had his 1910 project not been

---

[1] D. Lloyd George, op. cit., p. 21.

[2] These, plus early drafts, survive in the Lloyd George Papers, Series C/ Box 16/Folder 9.

N

wrecked by small-minded opponents. To put over this interpretation, Lloyd George might have to falsify the record slightly, but then he was not the man to shrink from such a course of action when there were political advantages to be reaped. Besides, who was in a position to throw doubt on the accuracy of the *War Memoirs*? It so happened that in January 1915 Lloyd George had handed over a copy of his August memorandum to Austen Chamberlain,[1] but by 1933 he may have forgotten that fact; or perhaps he was counting on the unlikelihood of Chamberlain coming forward to correct his statements. These are the first cynical reflections that come to mind.

But further examination of the evidence makes one hesitate to dismiss the *War Memoirs* account in so summary a fashion. Later in the 1930s Austen Chamberlain did, in fact, set down his own version of the 1910 coalition talks.[2] Yet although he possessed a copy of the August memorandum, Chamberlain nevertheless quoted extensively from the *War Memoirs* without comment—as though accepting the truth of all Lloyd George's claims. He seems to be quite unaware that there are considerable dissimilarities between this description and the actual contents of the August memorandum.

Some light is thrown on this mystery by the survival of several of the letters, which passed between the Opposition leaders in October 1910.[3] These letters, many of them long and carefully drafted, make it clear that at the time *all* the Conservatives understood Lloyd George's proposals and motives to be what the *War Memoirs* claims that they were. For example, Lloyd George somehow managed to leave Balfour, Chamberlain and Smith with the firm impression that putting the Navy on to a satisfactory footing was one of the principal, perhaps *the* principal, plank in the proposed 'grand settlement', with a sympathetic review of the Tariff Reform programme coming a close second.[4] Yet, oddly

---

[1] Austen Chamberlain's Memorandum of 29.1.15: Austen Chamberlain Papers: AC 13/2/2.

[2] A. Chamberlain, op. cit., pp. 191–3.

[3] ibid., pp. 283–9. Lord Birkenhead, op. cit., pp. 205–8.

[4] e.g. Smith to A. Chamberlain, 20.10.10 in Lord Birkenhead, op. cit., p. 205.

enough, the August memorandum makes no specific mention of the navy. Still less does it suggest that Lloyd George was prepared to make a substantial move towards the Conservatives over Tariff Reform. The one paragraph touching on the fiscal issue is vague in the extreme:

The various problems connected with State assistance to trade and commerce could be enquired into with some approach to intelligent and judicial impartiality if Party rivalries were eliminated. We have not merely problems connected with tariffs, but we have the question of inland transport that ought to be thoroughly overhauled.

Moreover, although the Conservatives soon became aware that in return for these concessions, they were being asked to commit themselves to a federal solution of the Irish problem (and it was this issue that finally broke up the attempts to negotiate a coalition), the August memorandum itself merely refers in passing, in a paragraph devoted to imperial organization, to the desirability of a 'non-Party treatment of this vexed problem'. Yet neither the meticulous Chamberlain nor the quick-witted Balfour seems to have grasped that Lloyd George was importing into the negotiations ideas and proposals that had been virtually ignored in his original memorandum.

The obvious deduction to draw is that, while the negotiations were in progress, Lloyd George never actually handed the August memorandum over to the Opposition leaders. Chamberlain has explicitly stated that he, for one, was never shown the document at the time, and that his colleagues, Lansdowne and Cawdor, had been similarly treated.[1] However, Chamberlain and Lansdowne certainly believed that *Balfour* had been given the document to study and had retained a copy of it among his papers.[2] When in January 1915, for reasons that can readily be guessed, Lloyd George chose to remind Austen Chamberlain about the events of 1910, he encouraged him in this belief. Lloyd George said that his intention at the time had been that Balfour should show the memorandum to his three colleagues at the Constitutional

---

[1] A. Chamberlain, op. cit., p. 192.
[2] Lansdowne to A. Chamberlain, 30.11.13: ibid., p. 578.

Conference and to Joseph Chamberlain; indeed, he 'appeared much surprised' when told that this had not been done.[1]

But did Balfour ever possess a copy of this document at all? If so, it has disappeared from his voluminous papers. What has survived is an undated aide-memoire, written by Balfour's secretary, Jack Sandars, which seems to be a record of the verbal report that Smith had sent to Balfour after his dramatic interview at Downing Street. This aide-memoire purports to summarize the contents of the August memorandum, but as such it is highly inaccurate. This unsatisfactory document must have been all that Balfour ever possessed *in writing* about Lloyd George's actual proposals.[2] At least, that is the conclusion one is forced to draw, unless one assumes that Balfour was given the memorandum to read, but *misunderstood* its sense: surely, a most far-fetched supposition. Yet why in that case should all the Opposition leaders have attached such importance to the August memorandum, in the belief that it had played a highly important part in the Balfour-Lloyd George negotiations?

The most plausible way of resolving this mystery is to deduce from the evidence that something of the following kind occurred. In mid-August Lloyd George came away from his meeting with the industrial insurance company representatives, convinced that against their hostility he could never carry through an insurance scheme that included widows and orphans benefits. He then drew up a reasoned plea for a coalition government that could settle this and other problems on 'national lines'. Later, however, his attention was distracted by a different set of issues, and the memorandum was put to one side until the first week of October. At this point, it became evident that the Constitutional Conference had reached deadlock. Lloyd George then concluded that the only way to avert a return to sterile party conflict was to confront the Opposition members of the Conference with a proposal for coalition. Once he had made this resolve, Lloyd George found the August memorandum a most serviceable document. Quite clearly,

---

[1] Austen Chamberlain's memorandum of 29.1.15: AC 13/2/2.
[2] Balfour Papers, Add. Mss. 49, 767.

he waved it in the face of, first Smith, and then Balfour, when he had his meetings with them. Possibly he read out the opening paragraphs, with their measured condemnation of party warfare, and referred to the document from time to time, with the intention of demonstrating how well thought out his proposals were. Equally clearly, however, when he came to debate the specific items of policy on which the coalition was to agree, he began to extemporize at some length, adopting arguments and making suggestions likely to appeal to his Conservative audience, regardless of whether or not mention was made of these things in the August memorandum from which he pretended to be talking. Subsequently, through the medium of Smith and Bonar Law, he brought forward further new ideas: ideas even more favourable to the Opposition.[1] By comparison with these verbal assurances the August memorandum, with its emphasis on 'progressive' social legislation, would have been a far less attractive proposition to any Conservative politician.

Lloyd George was able by this manoeuvre to capture the interest of his political opponents. F. E. Smith, for one, was convinced that Lloyd George had abandoned his followers and colleagues: 'I am tempted to say of him, *quem Deus vult perdere prius dementat*. It seems to me that he is done for ever unless he gradually inclines to our side in all the things that permanently count.'[2] Austen Chamberlain, too, was impressed. 'I know that when Balfour first told us of the overtures,' he later recalled, 'we were astonished at George's concessions and someone asked, "But how can he justify such a volte face! What will his people say of him?"'[3] Although Balfour was never very optimistic about his chances of success, he naturally felt that Lloyd George's proposals were worth examining in an accommodating spirit.

While winning over the Unionists in this way, Lloyd George was working upon certain members of the Liberal Cabinet. With them, however, his approach was different. He most definitely *posted* the

[1] A. Chamberlain to Cawdor, 21.10.10: printed in A. Chamberlain, op. cit., pp. 286–7.

[2] Smith to A. Chamberlain, 21.10.10: printed in Lord Birkenhead: op. cit., p. 208.

[3] Chamberlain to Lansdowne, 26.8.12: printed in A. Chamberlain, op. cit., p. 293.

memorandum to Crewe and left a copy with Grey, so that they could read it at their leisure, and the likelihood must be that Asquith was shown it too.[1] Moreover, when informing orthodox Liberals of his plans, Lloyd George was careful to put a 'liberal' gloss on his memorandum; for example, he assured Crewe that 'an agreement as to the lines of settlement of the Education and Welsh Church questions was a necessary preliminary to any Coalition. The Nonconformists could not come in on any other terms.'[2] It is highly unlikely that he made this equally clear in conversation with the Conservatives. Since the August memorandum makes no mention of the Welsh Church issue, the assurance that something would be done about it satisfactory to the nonconformist point of view must have convinced Crewe that Lloyd George was at heart *more* solicitous of Liberal interests than his memorandum indicated.

Presented in this kind of way, Lloyd George's coalition proposals did not seem that alarming to the Liberal Ministers who were consulted. Crewe and Grey both responded favourably, and Asquith unconcernedly let the talks go on. After his fall from power, Asquith let it be understood that 'he had known all about (these) proposals from the first' and that, confident that they would fail, he had just sat back with amused detachment.[3] From motives of pride, Asquith was bound to claim in the inter-war period that he had been well in charge of the situation and of his intriguing Chancellor. On the other hand, the one piece of evidence surviving about Asquith's attitude in October 1910, a letter to Crewe dated 27 October, rather substantiates his later claims.[4]

Yet what exactly did Asquith (or Grey or Crewe) understand Lloyd George to be up to? Asquith may in 1923 have sincerely

---

[1] Lloyd George to Crewe, 20.10.10: printed in J. Pope-Hennessy, op. cit., p. 119. 'Ll. G. has given me a copy of his Memo. . .' (Grey to Asquith, 26.10.10: Asquith Papers, Vol. 12: f. 214.)

[2] Pope-Hennessy, op. cit., p. 119. An early draft of this letter in the Lloyd George Papers (series C/Box/4/Folder 1) went into a little detail about the Swiss militia system. This sentence was omitted, and a reference to the education question and the necessity of satisfying the Nonconformists inserted instead. Lloyd George clearly was at some pains to sugar the pill for Crewe's benefit.

[3] A. Chamberlain, op. cit., p. 291, n. 2. Also, Lucy Masterman, op. cit., p. 172.

[4] Asquith to Crewe, 27.10.10: printed in Roy Jenkins, *Asquith*, p. 217.

believed that he had 'known all about' the coalition talks from the start. In this belief, however, he was almost certainly deceived. Did Asquith ever really understand that Lloyd George had begun to negotiate with Balfour *before* obtaining his permission? Moreover, did he realize that Lloyd George had actually gone into the composition of the proposed coalition government and promised Balfour the leadership of the Commons, in place of Asquith, who was to be 'promoted' to the House of Lords?[1] It may be difficult to understand how anyone could have seriously entertained the idea of Asquith, who was still at the height of his powers in 1910, agreeing to be 'kicked upstairs' in this way. The important point, however, is that Lloyd George should have made the suggestion at all, and should have done so behind his leader's back—for the amused self-satisfied attitude evinced by the Prime Minister throughout October shows fairly conclusively that he was blissfully ignorant of the fate Lloyd George had in store for him.

An inquiry into the history of the elusive memorandum of 29 October provides additional confirmation for the theory that Lloyd George hoped to bring the two parties together by writing in a liberal sense to his colleagues and talking in a conservative sense to his opponents. Admittedly, little is known about this second memorandum. We are told of the Mastermans having supper with Lloyd George in late October and working through the document with him, altering a word here and a word there.[2] What then happened to the memorandum is less clear. A copy exists in the Elibank Papers, so presumably Lloyd George intended the Liberal Chief Whip to show it to a few chosen Liberal notables. Yet no Conservative seems to have been aware of the existence of this document, although they all wrote copiously about the first one. Lloyd George cannot have told them about it.

A closer examination of the 29 October memorandum suggests that Lloyd George would certainly have been wise to keep it from Conservative scrutiny. For this was a production designed to appeal to a Liberal reader. Its largest paragraph, for example, is

---

[1] A. Chamberlain to Lansdowne, 26.8.12: printed in A. Chamberlain, op. cit., p. 293. See also Blanche Dugdale, *Arthur James Balfour*, Vol. II (1936), pp. 75–6

[2] Lucy Masterman, op. cit., pp. 170–2.

devoted to the regeneration of agriculture; Welsh Disestablishment (not mentioned in the August document) is also discussed; and there are references to housing, the Poor Law, educational reform on the lines of the Liberal Bill of 1906, reduction of the number of public houses, insurance against unemployment and sickness, and widows and orphans pensions: a strong radical programme.

At the same time, the major concessions held out to the Opposition in Lloyd George's talks with them in the middle of October have nearly all been withdrawn. Thus, although the memorandum recommends an enquiry into the tariff question and immediate remission of existing colonial duties, there is no suggestion that this committee of inquiry should report *within six months*: a concession that had greatly excited Austen Chamberlain when he first heard of it through Bonar Law on 19 October.[1] Again, in the section on national defence the 29 October memorandum offers the Conservatives very little—less, in fact, than the earlier document. Nothing whatever is said about compulsory military service. Instead, Lloyd George writes of a careful investigation to be undertaken by the Cabinet, aided by the Committee of Imperial Defence, to enable the Government to take 'all necessary steps . . . for the defence of the Empire at home and abroad'. The Conservatives could hardly have been expected to enthuse over this paragraph, and they would have been positively dismayed by the one that followed it: 'Every effort [ought] to be made by Diplomatic means to secure an International understanding which will, if not effect a reduction in the cost of Armaments, at least arrest the alarming growth in expenditure on preparations for war.' The Conservatives did not believe that such an agreement was obtainable and they felt little alarm at the growth of arms expenditure.

The most controversial paragraph is the one devoted to Ireland. Lloyd George here recommends provincial assemblies on the lines sketched out by Joseph Chamberlain in his speech on the first reading of the 1886 Home Rule Bill, with the suggestion that such a plan of devolution would ease the 'congestion in the House of Commons' and pave the way for 'the Federation of the Empire at some future date'.

[1] A. Chamberlain to Cawdor, 21.10.10: printed in A. Chamberlain: op. cit., p. 286.

Incidentally, it is amusing to note that when working through this document with the Mastermans, who rather disapproved of it. Lloyd George observed, 'with a comic face', that he hoped the 'Home Rule' section would prove unacceptable to the Opposition leaders. And he insinuated that the retreat from official Liberal Party policies contained in his memorandum had been encouraged by his *'dear* colleagues'. 'The P.M.', he added, 'would rejoice at an arrangement which refers all the most contentious questions of the day to a Royal Commission'[1]—a clear case of Lloyd George transferring on to an 'innocent' party his own somewhat discreditable designs.

The duplicity of Lloyd George's behaviour in October 1910 is sufficiently clear. What the Chancellor was obviously trying to do was to reconcile the irreconcilable by telling one set of politicians one thing, their opponents something rather different, in the hope that before these misunderstandings had been cleared up, a mood of goodwill would have been generated in which all the difficulties would seem insignificant and a compromise agreement emerge. This cunning stratagem, however, would obviously misfire, should Asquith and Balfour meet for the comparing of notes; then the deviousness of Lloyd George would stand revealed.

Possibly Balfour had his suspicions on this score, for we find him writing to Chamberlain on 24 October that he wished to motor over to the Prime Minister's Scottish home and have 'a "fishing" talk' with him to try 'to find out where he stands in all this business'.[2] This meeting can never have taken place. But perhaps Balfour persisted in his attempt to draw Asquith out. On 2 November Lloyd George wrote him the following note: 'I have just seen the P.M. as to your suggestion. For the reasons I gave to you he thinks it undesirable *at this stage* to take part in the negotiations. But he asked me to say that all I did was with his full concurrence.'[3] This letter is somewhat difficult to interpret. By 2 November the Constitutional Conference was on the point of collapse, so Asquith's unwillingness to negotiate with Balfour 'at this stage' is unintelligible, unless he was deliberately trying to sabotage any prospect of

[1] Lucy Masterman, op. cit., p. 171.
[2] Balfour Papers, Add. Mss. 49,736: Balfour to Austen Chamberlain, 24.10.10.
[3] ibid., Add. Mss. 49,692: Lloyd George to Balfour, 2.11.10.

coalition: and there were plenty of more effective ways he could have accomplished this, such as by raising the matter at a meeting of the full Cabinet.[1] Knowing Lloyd George's character and methods, one is led to wonder whether he may not simply have invented this message to prevent an Asquith-Balfour interview from materializing. The last sentence of the letter certainly raises one's suspicions: Lloyd George seems to be protesting too much.

However, as so often happened, Lloyd George's deviousness ultimately proved self-defeating. The man who held the key to the situation was Balfour, and Lloyd George should have done everything to win Balfour's confidence. He did nothing of the sort. For a start, he picked upon F. E. Smith to act as his intermediary with the Conservative leader, and Smith was a politician for whom Balfour had no great trust or liking.[2] Then, for no good reason that one can discover, Lloyd George seemed to be trying to sow discord between Smith and the official Conservative leadership by confusing the negotiations at the Constitutional Conference (of which Smith, of course, was not a member) with the Coalition talks he was having with Balfour. No sooner had Balfour and Chamberlain caught him out over this, than they began to move much more warily.[3]

Moreover, Lloyd George probably did his cause no good by holding back from the Conservatives all those items in his proposed deal that they would find difficulty in swallowing. In fact, only in the third week of October did Austen Chamberlain and his colleagues realize the extent of the counter-concessions that Lloyd George was asking them to make.[4] The effect was discouraging on a man like Balfour, who, as a conscientious party leader,

[1] Churchill informed A. Chamberlain in 1913: 'The Cabinet as a whole were never informed. "How could we tell them? Some of them would have had to go!". . .' (A. Chamberlain, op. cit., p. 577).
[2] In 1911 Balfour tried to prevent Asquith conferring a Privy Councillorship on Smith (R. Jenkins, *Asquith*, p. 224. n. 1).
[3] A. Chamberlain to Smith, 21.10.10: printed in A. Chamberlain, op. cit., pp. 284–5; Balfour to A. Chamberlain, 22.10.10: ibid., pp. 287–8; A. Chamberlain to Cawdor, 21.10.10: ibid., pp. 286–7.
[4] ibid., p. 193.

was highly nervous about taking any decision that his followers might construe as a 'betrayal'. In his *War Memoirs* Lloyd George confidently asserts that Balfour finally broke off the negotiations on the advice of a former Conservative Party Whip, Akers-Douglas.[1] This assertion will not stand a moment's serious consideration. An autocratic party leader like Balfour was not in the habit of having his mind made up for him by anyone of the stature of Akers-Douglas;[2] and in subsequently seeking to lay the blame for the failure of his 'grand settlement' on to the obscure and prejudiced 'backwoods' Tory M.P.s, whom Akers-Douglas represented, Lloyd George was probably trying to draw a parallel in his readers' minds between the events of 1910 and the Conservative backbench rebellion that later put him out of office for good and all in 1922.

Yet, of course, Balfour did feel bound to take the sentiments of his rank-and-file followers into account. It was all very well for Smith to dismiss the Irish question as 'a dead quarrel for which neither the country nor the party cares a damn outside of Ulster and Liverpool.'[3] Smith was an unblushing opportunist, without convictions of any kind. Lloyd George differed in having plenty of convictions, most of them radical ones; but, like Smith, he had no real sense of obligation to the party organization through which he had risen to political prominence; and he held his Irish allies in contempt, being prepared, if need be, to leave the nationalists 'to stew in their own juice'.[4] But Balfour always identified himself closely with the Conservative Party machine and his position was thus altogether different; indeed, it was a fear of appearing as 'another Robert Peel' in Conservative eyes that finally turned him against Lloyd George's attempt to hustle through a compromise on Ireland.[5]

[1] D. Lloyd George, op. cit., p. 23 in Odhams edition.

[2] It would seem that Balfour finally broke off these talks entirely on his own initiative; Austen Chamberlain could only speculate about his precise reasons for doing so: A. Chamberlain to Lansdowne, 26.8.12: printed in A. Chamberlain, op. cit., p. 293. See also, Third Viscount Chilston, *The Political Life and Times of Akers-Douglas, First Viscount Chilston* (1961), pp. 344–7.

[3] Smith to A. Chamberlain, 20.10.10: printed in Lord Birkenhead, op. cit., p. 205.

[4] A. Chamberlain to Lord Cawdor, 21.10.10: printed in A. Chamberlain, op. cit., p. 287.

[5] At least this part of Lloyd George's account carries conviction: D. Lloyd

Lloyd George had hoped to get round the Irish difficulty by converting the Unionists to some form of 'Home Rule All Round', such as Joseph Chamberlain had favoured in his radical days; and he was encouraged to pursue this line of approach by a growing body of evidence that many Unionists had begun of their own accord to move towards acceptance of 'federalism' and were bringing pressure on Balfour to sponsor a 'new departure' in the Party's Irish policy.[1] This helped Garvin, working now as Lloyd George's man, when he tried to persuade the Conservative leader that 'Home Rule All Round' was politically and administratively feasible. But Garvin failed to make any real impression. Balfour did not believe that he could unite his Party behind any such scheme, and his cross-questioning of Garvin about how in practice the new federalized constitution was to work showed only too clearly that Lloyd George and his allies, in their enthusiasm to secure some kind of agreement, *any* kind of agreement, had not really thought through the implications of their proposals.[2] Balfour could only have been convinced by precise and constructive reasoning; and this Lloyd George, Smith and Garvin were incapable of producing.

Underlying this difficulty lay a more fundamental one. Basically, Lloyd George and Balfour were approaching their discussions about Coalition from entirely different positions. Lloyd George saw that the formal negotiations at the Constitutional Conference were likely to prove abortive. He hoped to break the deadlock by making agreement over the House of Lords part of a wider settlement. In other words, he argued that since party

George, op. cit., p. 23 in the Odhams edition. Chamberlain thought Balfour turned down the project because 'his whole history forbade his being a party to any form of Home Rule, though younger men less involved in the controversies of '86 and '93 might be free to contemplate what he could not accept' (A. Chamberlain to Lansdowne, 26.8.12: printed in A. Chamberlain, op. cit., p. 293).

[1] See Ronan Fanning, 'The Unionist Party and Ireland, 1906–1910' in *Irish Historical Studies*, 1966, Vol. XV, esp. pp. 165–8. For the views of Milner's circle on the subject, see J. E. Kendle, 'The Round Table Movement and "Home Rule All Round" ' in *Historical Journal*, 1968, Vol. 11, no. 2).

[2] Balfour's sceptical reply to Garvin in a letter dated 22.10.10 is largely reproduced in A. M. Gollin, *Garvin*, pp. 215–18.

feeling ran too high for the leaders to reach a compromise agreement on any single contentious issue, like the Lords, a settlement could only be produced if he dramatically confronted his political opponents with a comprehensive 'package deal'. In fact, inside the formal Constitutional Conference itself, Lloyd George was not really an influence for peace; if the Liberal position were to be compromised, Lloyd George intended to hold out for a larger prize than was ever likely to emerge from these restricted negotiations. It was the 'big settlement' or nothing, as far as he was concerned.

The very ambitiousness of Lloyd George led him into vagueness and imprecision. Of course, the opportunistic shuffling around from week to week, which characterized his dealings with the Opposition politicans, was sometimes the result of a conscious desire to deceive and confuse. But it also reflected his basic conviction that acceptance of the *idea* of Coalition was so over-ridingly important that it should not be prejudiced by dwelling too long on differences of policy. Once the coalition was formed, these differences would resolve themselves.

Balfour, however, wished to proceed in the opposite direction, and make a conference settlement the first stage in a gradual elimination of party differences, leading eventually to coalition. He therefore thought that Lloyd George was being premature in his advancing of detailed proposals. As he put it to Chamberlain, 'I saw no object in a detailed discussion about the pattern of the wall-papers which are to adorn this new political structure when the foundations have not been laid!'[1] On this issue, Balfour's attitude seems to have been the more realistic one. At least, it proved decisive in wrecking any further substantial progress. Moreover, it seems clear that, far from being swept off his feet by Lloyd George's enthusiasms, Balfour was still thinking in terms of party advantage. He told Chamberlain that 'in many respects it would be far easier to promise our support to the Government if they were prepared to defy the Irish and their own extremists than to offer to form a

[1] Balfour to A. Chamberlain, 22.10.10; printed in A. Chamberlain, op. cit., p. 289. See also, A. Chamberlain to Lansdowne, 26.8.12: ibid., p. 293. And letter from Garvin to Northcliffe, dated 6.11.10, reproduced in A. M. Gollin, *Garvin*, pp. 230–1.

Coalition'.[1] Lloyd George would have been very naïve to have bought that idea!

What, then, was the significance of the whole episode? Perhaps its most interesting feature is the recrudescence of an approach to politics that had been widely held in the Boer War period but had then lost much of its appeal. The parallels between passages of the August memorandum and Rosebery's speeches during 1900 and 1901 are particularly striking. Like Rosebery, Lloyd George makes great play with analogies between the state and business corporations; the August memorandum recommends that the two parties bring their resources 'into joint stock in order to liquidate arrears which, if much longer neglected, may end in national improverishment, if not insolvency'. Assuming that the ends of government are agreed upon by all men of patriotism and goodwill, Lloyd George then proceeds to discuss politics solely in terms of management, grading politicians into 'first-rate' and 'second- or third-rate' men. The normal interplay of party rivalry stands condemned because it enables 'partisans' and faddists' to deflect the 'first-rate' men from pursuing the 'national interest:' a 'national interest' which is assumed to transcend the demands of sectional groups within the community. It is this emphasis on good administration and national cohesion which makes the August memorandum read like the production of a Conservative, disillusioned with the whole process of parliamentary government.

Notwithstanding its inclusion of certain 'advanced', though mostly woolly, items of social policy as subjects for the proposed coalition to tackle,[2] the memorandum is, in one sense, an absolute repudiation of all that Liberalism had ever stood for. This makes it all the more surprising to find 'middle of the road' Liberal ministers responding to the memorandum with sympathetic interest. Nothing better illustrates the feeling of hopeless defeatism or the

---

[1] Balfour Papers, Add. Mss. 49,736: Balfour to A. Chamberlain, 24.10.10.

[2] Except for the paragraph on insurance, the recommendations are vague in the extreme: e.g. '*The Poor Law*. This requires overhauling and re-casting, and I can see nothing in the principles of either Party which are irreconcilable in this matter.'

ideological bankruptcy which had overcome the Liberal Party only four years after its 1906 landslide victory than Crewe's view that 'we have got pretty nearly to the end of our tether as regards great reforms on party lines'.[1] Grey even foresaw 'the break-up of the Liberal Party and a time of political instability, perhaps of chaos', if the Government allowed itself to be pushed forward by the 'explosive and violent forces' at its back.[2]

September 1910 was certainly a bad month for labour disputes, and signs were multiplying that the long 'industrial peace' was drawing to a close.[3] The defeatism of some Liberal ministers may partly be connected with this development. Lloyd George himself was well aware of it, and in his City Temple address of 17 October he spoke at length about 'the great unrest among the people' which was sweeping like a disease throughout the civilized world, leaving a vast area of disturbance in its trail.[4]

Fearful of the political excitement generated by the Budget agitation, deeply distrustful of the Labour, Irish Nationalist and extreme radical M.P.s, and apprehensive about the mounting industrial tension, several ministers started to look longingly at the possibility of 'fusion' with their political opponents. Of course, the actual terms that Lloyd George was offering the Conservatives in mid-October would, if accepted, have smashed organized Liberalism for a decade, as Smith gleefully foresaw. True, also, that these terms were probably never made clear to Ministers, like Crewe and Grey. Yet, by accepting the *idea* of a 'national government', with all that this implied, they too were turning their backs on traditional Liberal beliefs, just as much as Lloyd George and Churchill.

The unsettled international scene, as well as domestic difficulties, made it seem important to suspend the party struggle Even though the August memorandum does not, as Lloyd George suggests in his *War Memoirs*, look forward to an imminent war, the

[1] Crewe to Lloyd George, 21.10.10: printed in M. Thomson, op. cit., p. 197.
[2] Grey to Asquith, 26.10.10: printed in R. Jenkins, *Asquith*, p. 217.
[3] 'Evidence of the unrest of labour is furnished by the fact that the Board of Trade records 45 disputes started in September, as compared with 26 in August and nineteen in September 1909. The duration of the disputes was 864,200 days, or 723,700 more than in August' (*Westminster Gazette*, 17.10.10).
[4] *The Times*, 18.10.10.

section about compulsory military service is evidence that he was unmindful of its possibility. Moreover, this document contains an apprehensive reference to the continental nations having developed their industrial and commercial equipment to an extent that menaced Britain's supremacy. And running through it is a note of unease and insecurity. Ten years earlier Rosebery had questioned Britain's capacity to hold her own in a world where rival states were daily increasing their power at her expense. By 1910 such alarmism had much greater justification.

Lloyd George's coalition project came, in short, as the climax of a decade of efforts to increase national efficiency. His actual proposals combined the demands of Tariff Reformers, Liberal Imperialists, Milnerites and Fabian collectivists. Each group was offered something of what it wanted, in return for making certain concessions. Admittedly, there is a difficulty in this interpretation, in that Lloyd George's approach to social reform did not, on the whole, accord with the views of the 'efficiency group', as we shall see in the next chapter.[1] For the moment, however, the radical Chancellor, with his mercurial temperament, grasped the essential ideas of this political philosophy and used them as the basis of his programme of action. What is more, the very metaphors and turns of phrase employed in the August memorandum echo the speeches of Rosebery ten years earlier, and make one speculate about how far Lloyd George was conscious of the ancestry of his ideas.

Symbolic of the link between the two phases of the agitation for a coalition of national efficiency is the part played by Garvin. It will be recalled that, in an article in the *Fortnightly Review* in January 1902, he had advocated a government of efficiency which would include Rosebery.[2] In May 1903 he threw himself enthusiastically behind Joseph Chamberlain and became a leading propagandist for Tariff Reform in the Unionist press. Now, in October 1910 Garvin decided that Lloyd George was 'the man' destined to provide that vigorous national leadership for which he had long been looking.[3]

*

[1] See below, Ch. VII, pp. 252–3.   [2] See above, Ch. IV, p. 134.
[3] A. M. Gollin, *Garvin*, pp. 204–5.

So far we have concentrated our attention on the secret coalition negotiations themselves. But all this while a parallel debate was being conducted in the press about the possibility of a compromise settlement of the Irish dispute, and this debate has an interest of its own, for the light which it throws on contemporary political attitudes. Garvin had less to do with this development than Milner's friend, F. S. Oliver, who had long been convinced of the merits of 'Home Rule All Round'. Oliver was also a great believer in the method of 'settlement by conference'. As he argued for Balfour's benefit in a memorandum of September 28, 'This method seems to be the natural safety valve of popular government in the circumstances in which popular government now finds itself. If you are ever going to make an attempt at Imperial union this is the only possible method. And also in national affairs; for how is such a matter as the Poor Laws, for example, to be dealt with satisfactorily by party tactics and parliamentary debates?' 'The method of conference or convention', Oliver added, 'stands in excellent credit at present (1) owing to the South African settlement and (2) owing to the present Conference having been undertaken.'[1]

Oliver developed these ideas in a series of seven letters, under his old pseudonym, 'Pacificus', which appeared in *The Times* between 19 October and 2 November, right in the thick of the secret coalition talks. His message, in brief, was that the electorate was tiring of prolonged party warfare—'the plain man who reads his daily newspaper is not so determined a partisan as the practical politicians are apt to imagine': that the situation in Ireland had changed since the 'bloody eighties': and that some federal arrangement could be devised, if a representative convention was first summoned.[2] These letters became more than the expression of a single man's opinions, when *The Times* gave them a guarded welcome in its leader columns.[3] This created something of a political sensation.

Now, neither Oliver nor the editor of *The Times* can have known

---

[1] Balfour Papers, Add. Mss. 49,861: Memorandum of 28.9.10.

[2] *The Times*, 20.10.10, 24.10.10, 22.10.10. Oliver suggested that the Constitutional Conference might formally summon this convention.

[3] ibid., 22.10.10, 28.10.10.

O

about the bolder plan for a 'national coalition' which was currently being discussed in high places.[1] For the expedient they were recommending, had it been successfully adopted, would have made such a coalition largely unnecessary. Oddly enough, though, Garvin also took Oliver's line, giving the readers of the *Observer* to understand that the Irish problem was about to be settled by the *conference method*.[2] Perhaps he was trying in this way to sound out public opinion on the subject.

Mild though the proposals of Oliver and Garvin were, in comparison with the ambitious schemes of Lloyd George, they nevertheless drew excited opposition from the party stalwarts. Already these people were nervous and apprehensive, because of the secrecy of the Constitutional Conference sessions and the suspension of normal political warfare which this had entailed. Austen Chamberlain was warning Balfour on September 23 that 'the keenest and most active politicans' on the Unionist side harboured the suspicion that the conference was 'a "put up job" between the leaders to silence their followers and damp down all activity.'[3]

The alarm was even greater in the Liberal camp, as a scrutiny of a newspaper like the *Westminster Gazette* shows. When the Constitutional Conference finally broke up, the paper breathed an audible sigh of relief: 'The withdrawal of great affairs from the public in order that they might be settled by secret conferences between the parties might easily, if it became the practice, confuse the boundaries of politics and increase the personal power of a few eminent people.'[4] The previous month had certainly provided the worthies of the *Westminster Gazette* with some very nasty moments. There had, for example, been the warm response given to Lloyd George's City Temple address by the Tariff Reform press, which the *Westminster Gazette* had been obliged to treat as an 'amusing'

---

[1] This is a reasonable deduction from the evidence. Garvin certainly kept the proprietor of the *Observer*, Northcliffe, informed of the high politics in which he was involved (see A. M. Gollin, *Garvin*, Ch. VII). And Northcliffe was also the proprietor of *The Times*. But there is no evidence which suggests that Northcliffe tried to influence the editorial policy of *The Times*.

[2] e.g. *Observer*, 23.10.10, where Garvin urges a settlement of the Irish problem 'whether by this Conference or another'.

[3] Balfour Papers, Add. Mss. 49,736: A. Chamberlain to Balfour, 23.9.10.

[4] *Westminster Gazette*, 11.11.10.

misunderstanding.[1] The editor's sense of unease then deepened, as rumours spread of a compromise over Ireland being in the offing; we do not like the prospect of 'Mr. Balfour melting into Mr. Lloyd George or Lord Cawdor into Mr. Birrell', he commented.[2] That same day, 28 October, sensing treachery in high places, the *Westminster Gazette* coupled a reaffirmation of its basic faith with a veiled warning to the Liberal leaders:

There are people who talk glibly of the existing parties having done their work and seen their day, and dream of a great 'national party'. This idea will never prevail as long as there is life and strength in Parliamentary institutions and a wholesome interest in public affairs among the mass of the people. That interest must always issue in parties and political contention. In our opinion, there never was a time when a strong Liberal Party was more important to the well-being of the country, and we look confidently to the Liberal leaders to bring their party out of the Conference as they took it in—a Liberal Party standing on a Liberal foundation, and not a coalition or a group of opportunists.[3]

Meanwhile, similar movements of opinion were taking place amongst the Unionist rank-and-file. Amery, predictably, welcomed the prospect of a convention to discuss the Irish problem, and believed that a federal arrangement, together with a solution of the constitutional conflict, would result 'in a real increase in our national efficiency';[4] in a letter to *The Times* of 8 November, he even broached the question of a grand national settlement, embracing Imperial Preference and compulsory military service, arguing that such great measures could not be carried through on orthodox party lines.[5] But at the same time as Amery and other 'federal Unionists' were rallying their forces, the staunch party

[1] ibid., 19.10.10.
[2] ibid., 28.10.10. The great cartoonist, Gould, provided the appropriate illustration on 31.10.10.
[3] ibid., 28.10.10.   [4] *The Times*, 1.11.10.
[5] ibid., 8.11.10. But *The Times* commented that same day in its editorial: 'We cannot follow Mr Amery when he confuses and nullifies his good counsel by going on to insist that a number of questions, which however important are not constitutional, should be dragged in to complicate constitutional questions already sufficiently difficult'. It seems unlikely, in view of this comment, that the editor of *The Times* had been informed by Northcliffe or by anybody else of Lloyd George's Coalition plan.

men were organizing their counter-attack. Lord Hugh Cecil referred to 'reckless schemes to divide this kingdom', Walter Long joined in the hue and cry[1] and on the very day that the newspapers announced the break-down of the Constitutional Conference, *The Times* printed a joint letter of protest from a group of Unionist M.P.s and Peers, mostly Ulstermen and diehards, damning 'Home Rule All Round' in no uncertain terms.[2] Undoubtedly, Balfour had been right in his judgement that the situation was not yet ripe for his party to adopt a new approach towards the Irish question.

Perhaps, we can leave Masterman to provide the epitaph to this whole curious episode in British politics. On 10 November, with the parties about to resume their normal warfare, Masterman told his constituents that the leaders had failed to reach agreement, not because individuals had shown any obduracy, but 'because Liberalism was Liberalism, and Conservatism was Conservatism. If both parties conceded as many points as they possible could, there was still an unbridgeable gulf between them.'[3] The time for the formation of a 'national government' had not yet come.

In the years that followed, Churchill was the politican most inclined to look back wistfully to the coalition talks of 1910. When in November 1913 he met Austen Chamberlain for an exchange of views on Ulster, he tried to broaden the discussions by alluding to the attempted settlement of 1910, indicating that he would like to see these negotiations re-opened. But Chamberlain pointedly refused to pursue the matter.[4]

Unlike Churchill, Lloyd George, always the realist, was content to leave well alone; and soon he was plunging vigorously into the party political fray. But the development of his political career was to be profoundly affected by the line he had taken in 1910. By September 1911, if not earlier, an indignant Loreburn had learned about Lloyd George's secret manoeuvres during the Constitutional

---

[1] ibid., 4.11.10, 29.10.10.

[2] ibid., 11.11.10. The signatories include Long, Willoughby de Broke, Carson and Craig.

[3] ibid., 10.11.10.

[4] A. Chamberlain, op. cit., pp. 576–7.

Conference.[1] No doubt he passed on the information to his fellow radicals in the Cabinet. These Ministers—Morley, Burns, Harcourt—had always had their doubts about Lloyd George, but henceforward they were even more suspicious of his intentions. Even when the Chancellor of the Exchequer took a course of action of which they approved, as when he threatened resignation over the high naval estimates of 1913–14, they hesitated to accept his leadership.

Nor, in fact, did Lloyd George now make any very serious attempt to put himself at the head of the radical faction inside the Cabinet. During the Agadir crisis of 1911 and the ensuing Cabinet 'revolt' against Grey's exclusive control of foreign policy, Lloyd George sided unequivocally with Grey, Haldane and Asquith, the old Liberal Imperialist trio, against their radical critics. So too did Churchill.[2] Moreover, later in the year Churchill went to the Admiralty, where he rapidly developed into a 'big navy man', a change of posture which involved him in a decisive and final breach with his former radical allies.

Thus, in foreign affairs and imperial defence, Lloyd George and Churchill had, in effect, 'crossed sides' by the end of 1911. This pulled the Liberal Cabinet somewhat closer to the standpoint of the Opposition; but it did not, of course, lead to more harmonious relations between the two political parties. On the contrary, party strife reached an all-time peak of bitterness and violence during the passing of the Parliament Act and the Home Rule dispute which followed it. In this connection, it is interesting to identify among the more virulent partisans F. E. Smith, the former advocate of a 'national settlement'. Much had been said during the 1910 Coalition talks about the dangers which the party system posed to national cohesion and good government. It was as though certain politicians, like Smith, were deliberately behaving during the following four years to show that their warnings had not been mere idle words.

This widespread defiance of the conventions that normally confined party political differences within tolerable bounds, made

---

[1] C. P. Scott Papers: Add. Mss. 50,901: Journal entry, 17.9.11: f. 40. See also, ibid., Journal entry, 7.1.12: f. 58.

[2] ibid., Journal entry, 7.1.12.: f. 58.

the case for a coalition stronger than it had been in 1910—yet also put formidable difficulties in the way of its attainment, as Chamberlain pointed out to Churchill when they had their meeting in November 1913. In one sense, therefore, the outbreak of the First World War, which forced a party truce upon Liberal ministers and their opponents, came as a blessing in disguise to leading politicians of both sides. For now exploratory talks about coalition could begin once again: but this time in a situation of such menace to Britain's survival as a Great Power that the issues which had previously kept the two parties apart necessarily faded into comparative insignificance.

In May 1915 the First Coalition Government was formed by a fusion of the two Front Benches, the Liberals retaining most of the important posts. This 'all-party' government gave way in December 1916 to the Lloyd George Administration, which was a genuinely *non-party* affair: members were selected on the ground of their personal abilities, rather than for their party status or usefulness; Milner, for example, was made one of the small War Cabinet of five, although his political position was still that of an 'Ishmaelite'.[1] Outside the War Cabinet several Ministers owed no allegiance to any party organization. A 'national government' of the sort that the 'efficiency group' had long advocated was at last in being. There was a certain appropriateness in the fact that Lloyd George was its Prime Minister.

[1] A. M. Gollin, *Pronconsul in Politics* (1964), *passim*.

CHAPTER VII

THREE CASE STUDIES

THUS, THE 'NATIONAL GOVERNMENT' which might have been formed in the years of peace to prepare the country for the ordeal of war did not come until war was actually raging; and this government then had to improvise many measures, which could have been established in a more orderly and systematic fashion during the previous decade. Yet the fact that the various attempts to form a 'government of efficiency' all ultimately failed should not divert attention from the important work which the 'efficiency group' successfully accomplished during this very period.

'It seems impossible to get rid of the party system altogether,' Sidney Low once observed, 'but we might at least render it a little more logical and coherent.'[1] Across the barrier of party, those people concerned to promote national efficiency were often able to effect a limited co-operation in pushing through much-needed reforms. A list of some of the more important measures that were carried between the Boer War and the First World War shows the magnitude of this achievement. In this period of little more than twelve years the National Physical Laboratory was developed, higher education facilities extended by the founding of new 'civic universities', elementary and secondary schooling was co-ordinated through the machinery of Local Education Authorities; the affairs of both army and navy were completely overhauled, and the Committee of Imperial Defence became an important instrument of government; the state assumed responsibility for a School

[1] *Nineteenth Century*, Oct. 1902, Vol. LII, p. 688: Sidney Low: 'A Conservative Reform Programme'.

Medical Service, and by adopting Trade Boards, Labour Exchanges and Social Insurance, Britain largely caught up with Germany in the field of organized social welfare.

Admittedly, it would be difficult to demonstrate that all these measures were *conscious attempts* to apply ideas of national efficiency to the external world, and to present the issue in such a way would betray a considerable naïvety. Reforming legislation and administrative growth seldom follow so simple an ideological purpose. Political pressures and counter-pressures and the sheer logic of necessity are usually equally instrumental in directing social and administrative changes; the Edwardian period was no exception. Yet even if one believes that 'inexorable necessity' compelled pre-war governments to adopt or accept most of these reforms, it remains true that the 'efficiency group' had at an early stage recognized these 'circumstances' and had attempted, in their different ways, to come to terms with them. Moreover, it is surely no coincidence that prominent members of the 'efficiency group', Haldane, Balfour, the Webbs, Morant included, were closely involved in these developments in an active and creative role.

Success was most likely to attend their efforts, when they operated quietly, away from the blare of publicity. But once their activities became a matter of party controversy or caught the attention of the press, the result, as often as not, was frustration and obstruction. For the national efficiency ideology was, so uncongenial both to traditional radicals and to certain old-fashioned Tories that any measure which seemed to be imbued with it would usually meet a spirited and determined opposition. This will become apparent if we put the spotlight on the designs of the 'efficiency group' in three different areas of public concern: education, imperial defence and social welfare.

Over the Education Act of 1902 the 'efficiency group' largely got their way, though they had to pay a heavy price for their success. The founding of the Committee of Imperial Defence also ranks as a substantial achievement, even if it did not produce all the benefits that had been expected from it. But the attempt to reorganize the public welfare services along the lines laid down in the Webbs' Poor Law Minority Report was a failure, which simply demonstrated the continuing strength of the opposing radical school of thought. Each of these three issues will now be examined in turn.

THE EDUCATION ACT OF 1902

Balfour's Education Act achieved fame, or notoriety, in its day, because of its provisions for rate-aid to church schools. The Non-conformists and their Liberal Party allies could unite in denouncing this as an affront to religious liberty and an insult to the consciences of millions of law-abiding citizens. This bitter sectarian dispute does not concern us here; neither did it greatly concern those members of the 'efficiency group', like Haldane and the Webbs, who came forward to give the Conservative Prime Minister a general support. To them the main importance of this Act was its abolition of the old School Boards and the creation of a Local Education Authority, a committee of the county or county borough council, to organize all grades of public instruction.

When the Liberals came to power, they attempted to reverse the bargain which the Unionists had driven with the Anglican Church. Yet they otherwise left completely unchanged the administrative structure which Balfour had established. This was by no means a foregone conclusion, however. Liberal Party stalwarts were a long time in accepting the finality of Balfour's abolition of the School Boards; as late as July 1907 a deputation from the London Liberal Federation was pressing upon Campbell-Bannerman the desirability of including in the Government's next Education Bill provisions for restoring a metropolitan educational authority elected on an *ad hoc* basis.[1] But Campbell-Bannerman never tried to do this—which was in its way a triumphant vindication of Balfour's efforts in 1902, and one in which the Conservative Leader took an understandable pride.[2]

We have already seen how much the 'efficiency group' disliked all *ad hoc* bodies.[3] The School Boards had given particular cause for offence by moving into the field of secondary education, where in certain localities they had come into conflict with the municipalities and county councils, the authorities responsible for promoting

[1] *Daily Telegraph*, 18.7.07.
[2] Hansard, 4th Series, Vol. 156, col. 1592: 10.5.06.
[3] See above, Ch. III, p. 68.

technical instruction. The result was the existence of two public bodies competing against one another: precisely the kind of thing that made the English educational system the laughing-stock of Europe. This absurd situation was only terminated by a legal judgement, the Cockerton Judgement, which declared that the School Boards which were providing education for older children had acted *ultra vires*. It was this decision which forced the Government into reorganizing the whole educational system.[1] Hence, the 1902 Education Act, which finally ended the overlapping by setting up a single authority in each locality. In this way the state gave formal recognition to the 'organic unity' of the educational process.

This feature of the 1902 Act particularly recommended it to the 'efficiency group'. Sidney Webb, for example, claimed that the 'excellence' of the measure lay in the fact that 'for the first time we have education made a public function, simply as education, without definition or limit, and without restriction of age, or sex, or class, or subject, or grade'.[2] Now that there was a single L.E.A., Webb claimed, it would be possible to plan courses of education extending from nursery school to university level.

In the Commons the Liberals could not really agree among themselves about whether or not they approved of this arrangement. James Bryce, whom Campbell-Bannerman had designated as the Party's 'educational pundit',[3] actually went to the lengths of denouncing the idea of a unified educational administration: elementary and secondary instruction, he argued, were different in their character, and this difference should be expressed by the existence of two separate authorities.[4]

The Liberals who rushed to the defence of the School Boards, and many of them did, were undoubtedly affected by a variety of considerations. It must, first of all, be remembered that most of the School Boards in the urban areas were in the hands of radical groups, whereas the majority of the County Councils in England

---

[1] On the Cockerton Judgement and the background to the 1902 Education Act, see E. Eaglesham, *From School Board to Local Authority* (1956).

[2] *Nineteenth Century*, Oct. 1902, Vol. LII, p. 605: 'Symposium on the Education Bill'.

[3] Herbert Gladstone Papers, Add. Mss. 45,988: Campbell-Bannerman to H. Gladstone, 4.5.02: f. 13.   [4] Hansard, 4th Series, Vol. 107, col. 641: 5.5.02.

(though not, of course, the Welsh ones) were Conservative controlled. The biggest exception to this rule, the London County Council, had, perhaps significantly, been excluded from the scope of the 1902 measure. The Liberals had some cause, therefore, for doubting whether the abolition of the School Boards was really inspired by the high motives of administrative rationalization and educational efficiency to which Balfour and other ministers laid claim.

But apart from such calculations of party advantage, many radicals had even darker suspicions about the purposes of those who had sponsored and who supported the Education Act. Balfour's boast was that, by sweeping away some 2,500 School Boards and transferring their responsibilities to a body subordinated to the general rating authority, the provision of education would be brought into much closer relation with the other social services organized by the municipalities and county councils. Sidney Webb took up this point and went on to predict that the effect of the Government's Act would be to 'raise the status and improve the composition of town and county councils, and simplify local government.'[1]

In so far as administrative rationalization held out the hope of saving public money, most radicals welcomed it. But what alarmed them was that 'efficient local government', as Balfour and the Webbs understood the term, apparently entailed a reduction of popular control and a watering down of 'democracy'. Although the Liberal Imperialists were careful not to associate their names with this complaint, many of their party associates obviously felt uneasy about the creation of an educational authority responsible only at two removes to the local electorate.[2] They were scarcely

[1] *Nineteenth Century*, Oct. 1902, Vol. LII, p. 607: 'Symposium on the Education Bill'.

[2] In October 1902 the Archbishop of Canterbury found Rosebery 'in a position of great difficulty on the question—from his own belief in Municipal bodies and the maintenance or increase of their responsibilities (G. K. A. Bell, *Randall Davidson: Archbishop of Canterbury* (Oxford, 1935), Vol. I, pp. 376–7). Grey publicly conceded that there would be advantages in having one educational authority and that this meant transferring powers from the school boards to the County and County Borough Councils. Asquith, on the other hand, wanted the school boards in the large towns to be preserved for the time being (Hansard, 4th Series, Vol. 107, cols. 825, 1133–4: 6.5.02, 8.5.02).

reassured when Sir John Gorst, the Vice-President of the Council, told the Commons that the Government's reforms would shield educational administrators from the kind of irrelevant political and sectarian controversies around which School Board elections had usually been fought in the past.[1] Behind this sort of talk, radicals rightly detected an assumption that the average elector was not capable of making an intelligent assessment of the educational requirements of his locality.

Certainly, both Morant, the civil servant largely responsible for drafting the Act, and Balfour distrusted popular judgements on matters of this kind. From his study of continental educational systems, Morant had come to realize the danger posed by his countrymen's disregard of specialized intelligence and by the absence in Britain of what he called 'directive brain centres'. 'Without this "control by knowledge" in the sphere of public education *of all grades* . . .', declared this dedicated bureaucrat, 'a democratic State must inevitably be beaten in the international struggle for existence, conquered from without by the force of the concentrated directing brain power of competing nations, and shattered from within by the centrifugal forces of her own people's unrestrained individualism.'[2]

This consideration underlay those clauses of the Act which provided for the co-option of so-called 'educational experts' on to the new L.E.A.s. Equipped with this 'expert' element, these bodies could act as what Morant had called 'directive brain centres': valuable antidotes to the excesses of crude democracy. A similar argument was deployed by Balfour when he defended his Bill in the Commons:

Under our plan all the best educational elements in the country will be turned on the work of education. They will not have to go through (the) elaborate electoral process, or not necessarily; and we shall be able for our educational needs to reach strata of experts not now accessible—representatives of Universities, of higher education in all its

[1] Hansard, 4th Series, Vol. 107, col. 679: 5.5.02.
[2] R. L. Morant, *The Complete Organisation of National Education of All Grades as Practised in Switzerland* (1898): Special Reports on Educational Subjects, Vol. 3: c. 8988, p. 24.

forms, who now cannot, from the nature of the case, submit themselves to the laborious tests of a School Board election.[1]

It was reasoning like this which attracted Haldane and the Webbs. But the radicals were correspondingly shocked by it. Campbell-Bannerman, in a hit at Haldane, wrote bitterly in August 1903 about 'certain philosophic gentlemen who are, *au fond*, thoroughly anti-democratic, but who speak very glibly and plausibly, and pose as the highest authorities' on educational matters.[2] Campbell-Bannerman's strong feelings found outlet the following year, when the Government introduced an Education Bill extending the main provisions of the 1902 measure to London. His violent outburst took place, after the new Vice-President of the Board of Education, that mildest of donnish figures, Sir William Anson, had observed that no direct system of representation could provide an educational authority with all the 'experts' it required. At this the Liberal leader flew into a great rage, or pretended to do so. The Government, he said, had treated the House to 'a homily against representative government, more sweeping, more trenchant, more uncompromising, than anything that we have heard since the days of the Reform Bill'. All the Government's objections to School Boards applied equally to the House of Commons itself: clearly, he said, the Unionists intended to 'de-democratize' everything they could lay their hands on.[3]

During the second reading of the 1903 Bill, a number of Opposition spokesmen defended the School Board organization. Indeed, so extravagantly did a number of them pursue this line, that Balfour was able to make a devastating reply. What would happen to Parliament, he asked, if these Liberals were to have their way:

We have got to decide matters connected with the Army, the Navy, Education, Foreign Policy, and every species of domestic legislation, and every kind of problem. I suppose the democratic principle of the future is that there must be a classification of all the questions on which the electors are interested, and that there should be in each case a separate

[1] Hansard, 4th Series, Vol. 105, col. 865: 24.3.02.
[2] Campbell-Bannerman Papers, Add. Mss. 41,237: Campbell-Bannerman to Professor A. J. Paterson, 13.8.03: ff. 147–8.
[3] Hansard, 4th Series, Vol. 120, cols. 1273–4, 1277: 7.4.03.

election of an *ad hoc* body, and a separate election of experts to deal
with each. . .[1]

This was turning the tables on the Opposition with a vengeance.
But it did not stop Campbell-Bannerman fighting to the last to
preserve the London School Board and the principle of an *ad hoc*
authority—to Haldane's intense disgust.

Here, in fact, was a central problem, to which political debate
kept returning in the Edwardian period. There may seem something quaint in retrospect about Campbell-Bannerman's fears that
abolishing the School Boards and handing over their functions to a
committee of the local rating authority portended some dreadful
repudiation of the democratic ideal. But the Liberal leader was not
simply casting around, as opposition politicians often do, for any
argument with which to belabour the government of the day. He
correctly perceived that the Conservative Education Acts would
do something to make educational policy less amenable to popular
control. Indeed, such was the avowed intention of the Government.
If the British educational system of the present day has much in
common with that of France or Germany, but has diverged from
the American pattern, this is largely the consequence of the 1902
Education Act. Many radicals foresaw this development and tried
to arrest it.

Balfour, Morant, Haldane and the Webbs did not, of course,
think in terms of 'de-democratizing' local administration. What
they were searching for, in education as in other fields, was a
system that preserved the representative character of local government, yet guaranteed a certain continuity of policy and brought
well-informed intelligence to bear upon it. These were the necessary preconditions, they believed, of educational advance, and
hence an important contribution to industrial prosperity and the
national well-being in its widest sense.

There is a genuine note of urgency in Balfour's vindication of his
Bill, which suggests that Rosebery's insistence upon the inter-
connection between educational reform and national efficiency
had not gone disregarded. On introducing the measure into the
Commons in April 1902, he referred to the dangerously wide gap

[1] ibid., Vol. 121, col. 694: 28.4.03.

that had opened up between the educational standards of England and those of rival states. 'Reasoning either from theory or from the example of America, or Germany, or France, or any other country which devotes itself to educational problems,' said Balfour, 'I am forced to the conclusion that ours is the most antiquated, the most ineffectual and the most wasteful method yet invented for providing a national education.' He presented his Bill as a way of remedying many of these deficiencies, especially those in the sphere of higher education. By putting secondary education onto an organized basis for the first time, he claimed, students would in future be enabled to take proper advantage of the facilities that were being provided in the newly founded university colleges and technological institutions.[1] There was evidence to show that many students were not then profiting as they might have done from their technological training, because they lacked the background of a sound general secondary education.

Now, this sort of talk displeased some radicals, like Bryce, since it seemed to ignore all those aspects of education that did not directly promote economic success.[2] Other Liberal M.P.s, including Asquith, chose to counter Balfour's arguments by challenging the Government on its own grounds. They admitted that the prosperity of British trade depended upon an improvement in the quality of secondary and higher education. But, they asked, were the County Councils, with their passion for keeping down the rates, the bodies best equipped to expand the nation's secondary education to the required point, especially in view of the fact that, with only limited funds, they would be saddled with the costly task of raising the level of the church schools in their area to that of the old board schools. This objection was made the more weighty by Balfour's refusal to help out the new educational authorities with grants-in-aid for secondary education and by his imposition of a rate limit on the provision that the L.E.A.s could make towards 'education other than elementary'.[3]

[1] ibid., Vol. 105, cols. 854, 868: 24.3.02. English education prior to 1902 was a 'by-word', as Balfour often put it: see Balfour Papers, Add. Mss. 49,854: Balfour to the Rev. Arnold Thomas, 22.4.02.

[2] Hansard, 4th Series, cols. 661–2: 5.5.02.

[3] ibid., Vol. 107, cols. 1131–2: 8.5.02. Eventually the 2d rate limit on 'higher education' was abolished for the county boroughs (ibid, Vol. 110, cols. 337–41:

Yet it is noticeable that for the rest of his period as Prime Minister, Balfour did all he could to promote technological education and stimulate the 'civic universities' movement. No doubt he was anxious that some of the prophecies he had made during the Education Bill debates should be fulfilled. But one must, in fairness, add that he took a genuine interest in educational problems. This was the bond that drew Haldane and the Webbs so closely to the Conservative leader in the 1902–1905 period.[1]

Was the controversy over the subsidizing of the church schools out of public funds therefore a mere side-issue, as far as the 'efficiency group' were concerned? Not entirely. Balfour, as Leader of the Conservative party, the traditional defender of Anglican interests and of the idea of a 'religious education', was bound by his position to favour the church party. And it may be significant that Morant, although he had lost his faith many years before, had once intended to enter Holy Orders and perhaps retained a residual reverence for the Anglican Church.[2] But Haldane and the Webbs were 'religious-minded agnostics', without fixed loyalty to any denominational sect, indeed not orthodox Christians at all. Haldane, in fact, seems to have regretted the excessive favour shown to the church, but to have been still more disgusted by the narrow bigotry of the militant dissenters, whose unconcern for education as such was only too apparent.[3] In any case, he was shrewd enough to see that in the long run the church schools, by receiving rate-aid and coming under the general supervision of the L.E.A.s, would lose their separate identity and become swallowed up in a 'national' system of education.[4]

The Webbs took a slightly different line. There is, incidentally,

---

30.6.02), but not for the county councils. Balfour was obviously under pressure from backbench Conservatives, representing agricultural constituencies, to exercise extreme frugality.

[1] When he later entered the Liberal Cabinet, Haldane discovered that he enjoyed less influence in educational matters than he had done while Balfour was in power (Sir Almeric Fitzroy, *Memoirs* (1925), Vol. I, p. 291: 25.4.06).

[2] See B. Allen, *Sir Robert Morant* (1934) for an extremely friendly assessment of Morant's character and ideals.

[3] See A. Fitzroy, op. cit., Vol. I, p. 291: 25.4.06.

[4] Haldane Papers, Vol. 5967: Haldane to Mother, 10.6.02: ff. 192–3. He also took this line in public: e.g. his letter to the *Daily News*, 1.7.02.

no truth in the view that has found its way into certain reputable history books, that the Fabians had a share in the formulation of the Education Act.[1] In November and December 1901, when the crucial struggle was taking place inside the Board of Education, they were, like Haldane, largely absorbed with Rosebery and the political prospects of the Liberal Imperialists.[2] Again like Haldane, they had been prepared in 1901 to settle for a measure of educational reform that fell far short of the radical Bill which the Government finally sponsored; and only slowly did they awaken to the possibilities which this Bill offered.[3] The major policy contribution made by the Fabian leaders was their successful campaign to alter the London Education Bill of 1903, so that it gave the L.C.C.'s representatives a majority on the new metropolitan authority. Their anxiety over the composition of the L.E.A. for London was bound up with their fear that Sidney Webb might lose his important position in London education at the very moment when the 'Charlottenburg scheme' was nearing fruition.[4]

But the Webbs were happy to justify the Government's two Education Acts on more general political grounds, and in the course of doing so, they did not shrink from discussing the denominational issue. In an article in the *Nineteenth Century*, Sidney defended rate-aid to church schools with the argument that this maintained the *status quo* and guaranteed *diversity*: a consideration to which he

[1] e. g. A. Tropp, *The Schoolteachers* (1957), p. 173, note 22. E. Halévy, *Imperialism and the Rise of Labour* (1926: Ernest Benn, 2d revised ed., 1951), pp. 199–200, 207.

[2] See above, Ch. IV, pp. 122–7.

[3] For Haldane's views in late 1901, see the address printed in R. B. Haldane, *Education and Empire* (1902), pp. 78–82. The Fabians had produced their solution in the form of a tract, *The Education Muddle and the Way Out* (Jan 1901). Pease, the secretary of the society, has claimed that 'the authorities at Whitehall' asked to see this pamplet when it was in proof, and that when it was later published, it was 'greedily devoured by perplexed M.P.s' (E. R. Pease, *The History of the Fabian Society* (1918) p. 144). Interestingly enough, however, this pamphlet took a much more cautious line than the Government Bill. It envisaged the survival of the school boards in the larger towns, and nothing was said about rate-aid to church schools.

[4] G. R. Searle, 'The Development of the Concept of "National Efficiency" and its Relation to Politics and Government, 1900–1910' (Cambridge doctoral dissertation, 1965), pp. 135–40.

P

attached much importance. Even if all schools were made unde-
nominational or even secular, he argued, it would still be impossible to frame a code of belief which commanded general assent.
And, of course, Webb dismissed as a principle of anarchy the claim
that people had a right to withhold payment of rates and taxes
whenever they happened to disapprove of some of the objects for
which this money was being spent.[1]

Bernard Shaw was more cynically opportunistic in the defence
he made of the 1902 Act. 'The situation must be accepted as
representing, on the whole, the balance of power in the constitution', he told a correspondent, adding, 'we shall not do so badly as
the Free Churchmen fear. Those who pay the piper generally call
the tune in the long run . . .'.[2] But then the 'efficiency group' as a
whole prided itself on this sort of 'realism'. They had comparatively
little patience with popular agitations to secure reforms that were
not, in fact, immediately obtainable, and preferred instead to
strike the best possible bargain with the 'power-that-be'. And the
Education Acts of 1902 and 1903 seemed to justify their belief that,
given the right circumstances, important measures of 'national
reconstruction' could come out of a traditional party administration, even out of a Unionist Administration.[3] The Webbs and
Haldane were encouraged by this to intensify their tactics of
'permeation'.

THE COMMITTEE OF IMPERIAL DEFENCE

From the standpoint of the 'efficiency group', the Education Act
had been welcomed, because it seemed to provide for a situation in
which the local authorities could pursue a systematic educational
policy, aided by the informed 'expert' element which co-option
would secure. In the sphere of imperial defence, similar reforms

[1] *Nineteenth Century*, Oct. 1903, Vol. LIV, pp. 575–80: S. Webb, 'London
Education'.

[2] Shaw Papers, Add. Mss. 50,514: Shaw to Mr Whitaker, 23.2.04.

[3] It is remarkable how deferentially the Conservative Press was treating the
Webbs in 1902–3: e.g. the *Morning Post* called Sidney Webb 'that indefatigable
worker for the benefit of the six millions who inhabit the vast maze which is
called London . . .' (29.9.02).

were even more urgently required. The principal 'lesson of the Boer War' seemed to be that civilian control of the service departments, as it then operated, was incompatible with military efficiency. Even the Prime Minister had openly confessed that the British Constitution 'was unsuitable as an instrument of war'.[1] Had the party system and Parliamentary control, therefore, demonstrated their complete incapacity to handle the affairs of War Office and Admiralty, or could minor modifications be made to the *status quo*, which would reconcile military requirements with political expediency?

The main threads in this controversy can be traced back to 1890, the year when the Hartington Commission submitted its famous report. The commissioners had tentatively suggested the formation of 'a naval and military council, which should probably be presided over by the Prime Minister, and consist of the Parliamentary Heads of the two services and their principal professional advisers'.[2] But in a minority note appended to this report, Lord Randolph Churchill had proposed an alternative solution: he wanted the Commander-in-Chief of the army and a Lord High Admiral to be appointed for five years, with the rank of privy councillors, and 'summoned to all Cabinet councils when military and navy questions (were) under consideration', though they would have no voice when other issues were being debated.[3]

Both proposals were intended to achieve the same purpose: that of co-ordinating military and naval policy at the highest level, while at the same time bridging the gap between ministerial responsibility and professional knowledge. The difference lay in the means by which this objective was to be reached. The Hartington Commission wanted an association of politicians and 'experts', presided over by the Prime Minister, which could come under the control of a Cabinet that was in turn responsible through

[1] Hansard, 4th Series, Vol. 78, col. 30: 30.1.00.

[2] *Report of Royal Commission into Civil and Professional Administration of the Naval and Military Departments and the Relation of Those Departments to Each Other and to the Treasury* (1890): C. 5979, par. 20.

[3] ibid. Lord Randolph's memorandum is also printed in W. S. Churchill, *Lord Randolph Churchill* (1906), Vol. II, pp. 517–23.

Parliament to the electorate. Lord Randolph Churchill, however, favoured a 'continental' style solution: after all, the men whom he proposed to put in charge of the armed services would have been professional service ministers, in all but name.

A slight refinement on Churchill's idea was made by Charles Dilke and his friend, the military correspondent, Spenser Wilkinson, who campaigned tirelessly throughout the 1890s for the appointment in each service of a 'single responsible adviser'. They wanted extensive power to be conferred on the Admiral and General in whom the Cabinet had most confidence; these two officers would represent their particular branch of the armed services and be responsible for supplying the Government with advice, tendered personally over their own signature; in the event of a difference of opinion between ministers and their naval and military advisers, the latter would resign, leaving the Government to explain to the public what reasons they had for over-ruling the 'experts'.[1]

This proposal ran so counter to British constitutional theory and practice that it won no support on either Front Bench. And in 1895 the Rosebery Administration, with Balfour's encouragement, moved cautiously in the direction of the Hartington Commission's suggestion, by setting up a Defence Committee of the Cabinet: a Committee which the Unionists reorganized under the chairmanship of the Duke of Devonshire, when they returned to office later that year. Yet although service chiefs could be invited to attend the Defence Committee's meetings, in a consultative capacity, they were not members of it, and did not enjoy an equal status with the civilian ministers, as the Hartington Commission had wanted. For this reason and because of the lack of urgent interest shown in the Committee's affairs by Devonshire and Salisbury, this addition to the British machinery of government achieved little in practice, and the Boer War fiascos destroyed what little prestige it possessed.[2]

[1] H. Spenser Wilkinson, *Thirty Five Years: 1874–1909* (1933), pp. 182–5, 189–94. S. Gwynne and G. Tuckwell, *The Life of Sir Charles W. Dilke* (1917), Vol. II, Ch. LVI; J. Luvaas, *The Education of an Army: British Military Thought, 1815–1940* (Chicago, 1964: Cassell ed., 1965), pp. 260–7.

[2] See J. Ehrman, *Cabinet Government and War, 1890–1940* (Cambridge, 1958). F. A. Johnson, *Defence by Committee: the British Committee of Imperial Defence, 1885–1959* (Oxford, 1960).

Arnold-Forster was summing up a wide-spread feeling in 1900 when he dismissed the Defence Committee out of hand as 'a joke and a very bad one'.[1]

Professional soldiers and sailors, ever impatient of civilian control, exploited the mood of the hour to press for extreme solutions. Lord Wolseley, the retired Commander-in-Chief, actually proposed to the Elgin Commission that the British should have a Military Minister of War, as all the other great nations of the world did—'they are not fools, remember,' said Wolseley, 'England does not contain all the wisdom of the earth...'[2] Many newspapers and periodicals joined in the cry. Lord Charles Beresford was saluted as the strong man who ought to be put at the head of the Admiralty, while War Office reform was a task which, according to certain journalists, could only be tackled effectively by a distinguished soldier.[3]

The 'single responsible adviser' solution, though somewhat more moderate than these proposals, would similarly have had the effect of encroaching on the powers of Parliament and weakening the control which civilian ministers exercised over questions of imperial defence. That, however, did not deter certain prominent parliamentarians in the Boer War period from advocating it; and of such people none spoke out so frequently or so forcefully as Lord Rosebery, who by 1900 had obviously despaired of the Cabinet Defence Committee he had himself created five years earlier. In July 1900 he told the House of Lords that he found it quite extraordinary that the War Secretary should not be an 'expert', that is to say, a professional soldier.[4] The excessive interference from politicians which the British system produced must inevitably impair efficiency, he argued. At this time Rosebery's answer to the dilemma was that the Commander-in-Chief should be asked to

---

[1] H. O. Arnold-Forster, *The War Office, the Army and the Empire* (1900), p. 75.

[2] *Report of Royal Commission of Inquiry into the South African War* (1903): Cd. 1789, par. 267. See also, for similar complaint from a professional soldier: Cpt. C. Ross, *Representative Government and War* (1903), *passim*.

[3] e.g. *National Review*, Dec. 1902, Vol. XL, p. 509. Beresford himself urged Balfour in 1900 to put a soldier and a sailor with the necessary qualifications into the Cabinet: see Balfour Papers, Add. Mss. 49,713: Beresford to Balfour, 8.4.00.

[4] Hansard, 4th Series, Vol. 86, col. 1470: 27.7.00.

give Parliament a personal assurance at periodic intervals that the defences of the Crown really *were* on a satisfactory footing; in this way there would be a check on the evasions and mendacities of ministers and politicians.[1]

By 1902 Rosebery had convinced himself that, since no civilian could be entrusted with the pressing task of War Office reform, Kitchener should be brought into the Cabinet for this purpose, on the understanding that he would be absolved from responsibility for Cabinet decisions on non-military matters:[2] a return to the ideas contained in Randolph Churchill's memorandum. When it was pointed out that it would be 'unconstitutional' to make the War Secretaryship a 'non-political' appointment in this way, Rosebery contemptuously brushed the objection aside as a pedantic quibble.

It so happened that Kitchener had no intention of undertaking War Office work of any kind whatever. Neither did he often correspond with Rosebery or try to attach himself to Rosebery's group.[3] But others were not to know this. Late into 1905, for example, Arnold-Forster, then War Secretary, believed that Kitchener might well be his successor, when the Liberals came into power.[4] It is interesting to see how, when Curzon and Kitchener fell out in India, Curzon's friends tended to blame the Liberal Imperialists for the Government's eventual decision to back Kitchener. 'But note this,' wrote Goschen to Curzon, 'Rosebery has publicly recommended Kitchener to be made Secretary of State for War, or at least Dictator, free to reform the War Office and reorganize the Army, with full powers. The knowledge of this has doubtless added fuel to Kitchener's despotic tendencies.'[5] The

---

[1] e.g. ibid., Vol. 90, cols. 537–43: 5.3.01. ibid., Vol. 91, cols. 32–7: 15.3.01. This proposal was made by Rosebery in the course of his defence of the former Commander-in-Chief, Wolseley, who had become involved in a public altercation with the ex-War Secretary, Lansdowne, over the reasons for Britain's inadequate preparations before the outbreak of war. Rosebery's espousal of Wolseley's cause must be seen as an expression of his belief in the superiority of 'the expert' over the 'amateur' politician.

[2] Hansard, 4th Series, Vol. 120, cols. 7–9: 24.3.03.

[3] See P. Magnus, *Kitchener: Portrait of an Imperialist* (1958), pp. 228–9.

[4] Arnold-Forster Papers, Add. Mss. 50,345: Arnold-Forster to Kitchener, 16.3.05: f. 79. ibid., Add. Mss. 50,350: Journals, 5.8.05: f. 17.

[5] Curzon Papers, Vol. 183: Goschen to Curzon, 25.10.05: f. 183.

consequences of this idolatry of Kitchener extended well beyond 1905, of course.

In retrospect, it is easy to understand why the 'single responsible adviser' proposal finally fell by the wayside. A strengthened and reorganized Cabinet Committee not only had the advantage of being more in accordance with British constitutional practice, it was also more flexible and better suited to the complex requirements of a naval and imperial power. Balfour, in particular, realized that an advisory committee could call to its councils visiting statesmen and service chiefs from the British self-governing colonies. The advisory character of the Committee of Imperial Defence and the theoretical equality of its members, which Balfour so carefully stressed, served to remove colonial fears that, by participating in its affairs, they would become entangled in European power politics and suffer dictation from London. Yet another advantage of keeping the membership of the committee fluid was that the Prime Minister could then, whenever necessary, call into council the head of any of the departments that might be concerned in a particular issue. For Balfour understood that national strategy ought not to be kept in a separate compartment from considerations of internal policy. By contrast, the 'single responsible adviser' idea, if implemented, would surely have isolated the service departments still further from the activities of the 'domestic' ministries.

The forcefulness of this logic was widely conceded. In fact, when in 1904 Balfour completed his reorganization of the Defence Committee, several politicians who had once called for a 'single responsible adviser' came out in the Prime Minister's support. Arnold-Forster, the new War Secretary, performed this *volte-face*, and so, in a way, did Rosebery himself.[1]

But the Committee of Imperial Defence (hereafter called the C.I.D.) might never have developed as it did, but for the influence on Balfour exercised by Lord Esher. The reports of the War Office

---

[1] Though Rosebery seems to have misunderstood the functions of the new Defence Committee, judging from his inane remark that he did not 'admire the transformation of the Commander-in-Chief into the Prime Minister, nor the Prime Minister into the Commander-in-Chief' (Liberal League pamphlet, no. 144: speech of 10.6.04).

(Reconstitution) Committee, which Esher had chaired, provided the Prime Minister with the very justification he needed in pressing ahead with his plans for imperial defence.[1] It was Esher's strong conviction that army reform, to which the Unionist Government was firmly committed, could not be embarked upon with any profit, until a 'thinking department' had been set up to assess the military requirements of the Empire as a whole, within the context of a coherent strategic plan.[2] Like so many reformers of his day, he admired the 'scientific spirit' which the Germans had brought to the study of war, as exemplified in their General Staff organization. Yet though Esher wanted the British War Office to have its General Staff, too, he realized, as Balfour did, that a slavish imitation of the German model was to be avoided. Britain differed from Germany in being a predominantly naval power, with a large transmarine Empire; therefore, the work which was carried out in Germany by a General Staff had in Britain to be entrusted to a co-ordinating body which could harmonize the policies of both armed services: and this was one of the main *raisons d'etre* of the C.I.D.[3]

Its other function was to achieve what Professor Johnson, in his excellent book on the subject, has called 'a free association of the amateur and the expert'.[4] The Prime Minister, as the President and only *ex officio* member of the Committee, could call to its councils whomever he wished. This ensured that professional soldiers and sailors who received invitations would be on an equal footing with the ministers present, and so would probably feel less inhibited in expressing their opinions. In the kind of atmosphere created by such meetings, politicians and service chiefs could learn to co-operate and to understand each other's point of view. At the same time, Balfour was careful to observe the consititutional proprieties by insisting on the *advisory* nature of the C.I.D. The service chiefs could share in the formulation of reports and memoranda, which would inevitably carry enormous weight if

[1] *Report of the War Office (Reconstitution) Committee* (1904): Part I, Cd. 1932.

[2] Esher's memorandum of 27.3.04, entitled *National Strategy*: copy in Balfour Papers, Add. Mss. 49, 718.

[3] e.g. M. V. Brett (ed.), *Journals and Letters of Reginald Viscount Esher* (1934), Vol. II, pp. 144–5: Esher to Sir George Clarke, 18.2.06.

[4] F. A. Johnson, op. cit., p. 81.

and when they were submitted to the Cabinet as recommendations for particular actions. But the Cabinet would retain the ultimate say, and so 'responsible government' would in no way be imperilled.

But Esher's most important contribution to the evolving machinery of the C.I.D. was undoubtedly his 'conversion' of Balfour to the idea of attaching a 'permanent element' or secretariat to the committee. The purpose of this innovation was twofold: it would help minimize the dangers of sudden changes in defence policy, following a change of party administration; and it would offset the equal danger of the advent to the premiership of a politician ignorant of or indifferent to military and naval problems. Esher had every confidence that under his friend, Balfour, all defence questions would be competently handled, but he argued that the country would be unwise to count upon all future Prime Ministers possessing Balfour's abilities and interests. Although they did not spell this out in brutal detail, Esher and his associates were clearly appalled at the prospect of Campbell-Bannerman at 10, Downing Street.

Campbell-Bannerman was no less appalled by the manner in which Balfour and Esher were reorganizing the Defence Committee and he was not a politician to leave his opinions unexpressed. He objected, for a start, to what he considered the hysteria and alarmism of Esher's language. But his objections went deeper than this. Campbell-Bannerman had once served as Cardwell's Financial Secretary, and for the rest of his life he did his best to prevent any basic changes being made to the principles of organization which Gladstone's great War Secretary had established.[1] When the Esher Committee Report was being debated in the Commons in March 1904, Balfour was able, with some justification, to taunt him with taking 'a fine crusted old Tory view of army reform': no change could be made slowly enough for him.[2]

Because he had been the War Secretary from 1892–1895, Campbell-Bannerman was held by many to be indirectly responsible for the state of affairs that had produced the fiascos of the South African campaigns. Thus, he must probably have felt that

[1] See J. A. Spender, *Sir Henry Campbell-Bannerman* (1923), Vol. I, pp. 125, 141.
[2] Hansard, 4th Series, Vol. 131, col. 619: 9.3.04.

an admission on his part of the need for drastic reform would be interpreted by his enemies as a confession of past failure. Moreover, the Liberal leader, since going out of office, had kept on friendly terms with some of the older civilian officials at the War Office, whom the 'reformers' were concerned to displace; this too made him incline to the *status quo*.[1]

We have already seen how Campbell-Bannerman's dislike of 'militarism' had induced him to attack the idea of a General Staff, as proposed by the Hartington Commission. The famous dissenting memorandum, in which he had expressed his objections, probably did more than anything else to discredit Campbell-Bannerman in the eyes of the 'efficiency group'.[2] But nothing that had transpired during the Boer War caused him to change his views one jot. He remained convinced that ministers should insist on the old consti-tutional, civilian control of the war machine: military 'experts' made good servants, but dangerous masters.

It was on just such an issue of principle that Campbell-Banner-man felt compelled to speak out against the creation of the C.I.D.; he disliked the constitutional implications of making professional soldiers and sailors members of Cabinet committees. In an earlier debate, in February 1903, the Opposition leader had criticized Balfour's first hesitant attempt to strengthen the Defence Commit-tee. Describing himself as a man who was 'old fashioned' enough to believe that governments should determine policy and that their subordinates should merely advise them, Campbell-Bannerman had argued that putting members of the armed services on to the Committee would lead to extravagance and weaken Cabinet control.[3] When Balfour arranged a special debate on this issue

[1] See Campbell-Bannerman's correspondence with Sir Ralph Knox, Per-manent Under-Sec. at War Office, 1897–1901 in Campbell-Bannerman Papers, Add. Mss. 41,221. Sir George Clarke, one of the members of the 'Esher Com-mittee', commented: '. . . I do not rate C-B very high; but I confess, I should have thought he would hardly have sought inspiration from the prophets of a system which made the Elgin Report possible . . .' (Balfour Papers, Add. Mss. 49, 719: Clarke to Esher, 11.10.05).

[2] see above, Ch. I, pp. 23–4. Amery wrote of Campbell-Bannerman's 'extraordinarily fatuous minute of dissent'. 'The man who gave vent to these silly opinions shortly afterwards became Secretary of State for War.' (L. S. Amery, *The Problem of the Army* (1903), p. 130).

[3] Hansard, 4th Series, Vol. 118, cols, 713–14: 24.2.03.

soon afterwards, the Liberal leader had tried to move the adjourn-
ment in protest—but so misjudged the mood of the House, that his
backbench supporters had had to extricate him from an impossible
situation.[1]

This minor fiasco did not lead Campbell-Bannerman to modify
his attitude when, twelve months later, the Esher Committee
Report came up for debate. This time his main objection was to the
power which the reorganized Defence Committee concentrated in
the hands of the Prime Minister and its tendency to shroud defence
policy in secrecy. 'The House knows nothing of the Committee of
Defence,' he complained. 'Even the Cabinet does not know much
about it. At least I suspect it does not . . .'[2] Campbell-Bannerman
wanted military, naval and defence matters generally to be determined openly on the floor of the Commons: a point of view,
incidentally, which Esher publicly dismissed as 'antediluvian'.[3]

The Opposition leader's suspicions about the C.I.D. were
sharpened by his dislike of the circumstances in which the Esher
Committee had set about its work. These circumstances *were*,
admittedly, very odd. Esher had persuaded Balfour as early as
September 1903 to appoint him chairman of a small committee
which would 'take the War Office Administration right through,
from top to bottom, and endeavour to make it a first-class business
machine'. Esher had already, in his personal notes to the Elgin
Commission Report, formulated the principles on which reorganization should take place. Indeed, helped by Amery, he was sketch-
ing out the details of his scheme two months before his committee
was formally constituted.[4] Sir John Fisher, a friend of Esher's, who
joined the committee as the Admiralty representative, expressed
the spirit which governed its proceedings when he observed that 'a
committee, if it is to be of any practical use, must be unanimous
before it begins to sit'. That was why Esher and Fisher went to
such lengths to get Sir George Clarke made the third member of

---

[1] ibid., Vol. 118, cols. 1578–1649: 5.3.03.

[2] ibid., Vol. 132, cols. 998–1000: 29.3.04.

[3] In an interview with W. T. Stead: Stead, *Coming Men on Coming Questions*
(1905?), p. 475.

[4] M. V. Brett (ed.): op. cit., Vol. II, pp. 23, 10: Esher to Knollys, 27.9.03 and
Esher to M. V. B., 7.9.03. L. S. Amery, *My Political Life*, Vol. I (1953),
p. 205.

their committee; they knew Clarke agreed with them on all the basic points.[1]

Throughout this period Arnold-Forster, the recently appointed War Secretary, was settling into his office, and he was excluded, not only from actual membership of the committee, but even from sitting on it while evidence was being taken.[2] The Esher Committee then set down to work at such a speed that part two of its report appeared in the newspapers before ministers had had time to read it.[3] Not content with this piece of high-handed behaviour, Esher and his colleagues then 'ran their own men' for the vacant places on the new Army Board, and for a time usurped the authority of Arnold-Forster completely, for example, sounding out senior officers about appointments entirely on their own initiative.[4] Esher could only act in this way, because he was confident of the Prime Minister's approval and support. Other ministers, however, naturally objected to being rushed into decisions, and wondered on what authority the Esher Committee was basing its executive actions.[5]

A stickler for correct constitutional procedure like Campbell-Bannerman was bound to disapprove of the goings-on of the 'damned, dictatorial, domineering trio', as he called the Committee. And, basing his argument on a memorandum prepared for him by that other Liberal veteran, Sir William Harcourt, the Opposition leader made a forthright speech in the Commons: 'What is this Committee?', he asked. 'We know what a Royal Commission is, and we know what a Departmental Committee is. But this Committee was appointed, so far as we know, not by the King, not by the Cabinet. It seems to have been a personal affair of the Prime Minister's. . . It is like a revolutionary committee

[1] M. V. Brett (ed.), op. cit., Vol. II, p. 72: Esher to Sandars, 14.1.05. G. R. Searle, op. cit., pp. 166–71.

[2] M. V. Brett (ed.), op. cit., Vol. II, p. 22: Esher to Knollys, 27.9.03.

[3] Balfour Papers, Add. Mss, 49, 721: Brodrick to Balfour, 29.2.04.

[4] A. J. Marder, *Fear God and Dread Nought: the Correspondence of Admiral Fisher*, Vol. I (1952), pp. 295–7: Fisher to Esher, Jan. 1904. Arnold-Forster Papers, Add. Mss. 50, 336: Arnold-Forster to Esher, 13.2.04: ff. 128–9 (copy). C. E. Callwell, *Field Marshal Sir Henry Wilson: His Life and Diaries* (1927), Vol. I, pp. 55–6: 3.2.04, 10.2.04, 11.2.04 and 12.2.04.

[5] St. John Brodrick, the former War Secretary, was particularly incensed about this: see Balfour Papers, Add. Mss. 49,721: Brodrick to Balfour, 29.2.04.

of public safety—appointed and prepared to overturn anything and to guillotine anybody.' Campbell-Bannerman concluded by damning the committee's operations as 'an infringement in some respects of constitutional practice, and certainly of the decent conduct of public affairs . . .'[1] No-one doubted after this that the Liberal leader disapproved most violently of the recent reorganization of the War Office, and that he still entertained the objections to the Defence Committee, which he had voiced in May 1903.[2]

Subsequent events were to show that Campbell-Bannerman's uneasiness at the implications of Balfour's reforms was certainly not a baseless fear. Although the new War Secretary, Arnold-Forster, had largely himself to blame for his failure to convince his Army Council and the Cabinet of the viability of his proposed army reforms, his task was made harder than it would otherwise have been by the existence of the C.I.D. For both Sir George Clarke, who had been made the Committee's first Secretary, and Esher, who took part in most of its investigations, had come by the middle of 1904 to view Arnold-Forster with considerable distrust.[3] And through their connection with the C.I.D., they were in a position to obstruct the War Secretary's work with impunity. In February 1905, when Arnold-Forster was seen to have failed to reduce the estimates significantly, his Scheme was sent for examination to a sub-committee of the C.I.D., composed of Esher, Clarke and a Treasury official. In the absence of the Prime Minister, Esher presided over this small sub-committee, of whose proceedings Arnold-Forster was kept largely unaware. This body also had before it an entirely different scheme, which was later printed on War Office stationery and dignified by the name of the 'Blue Paper'; in fact, it was the work of Clarke himself, who, with Esher's support, had fathered it on to Balfour. In formulating his

[1] Campbell-Bannerman Papers, Add. Mss. 41,220: Harcourt to Campbell-Bannerman, 7.3.04: ff. 162–4. Hansard, 4th Series, Vol. 131, cols, 350–4: 7.3.04.

[2] Spender has written in his biography of the Liberal leader: Campbell-Bannerman 'heartily consented to (the Esher Report's) principal proposals—the Army Council, the General Staff, and the Committee of Defence . . .' (J. A. Spender, op. cit., Vol. II, p. 150). Nothing could be further from the truth.

[3] See A. Tucker, 'The Issue of Army Reform in the Unionist Government, 1903–5' (*Historical Journal*, 1966, Vol. 9, no. 1).

scheme, Clarke, helped by Esher, had freely used his position on
the Defence Committee to 'commandeer' War Office papers,
without going through the formality of asking the Secretary of
State's permission.[1] Although the influence of Esher and Clarke
rested ultimately on the confidence they inspired in the Prime
Minister, their position was greatly strengthened by the roles they
were playing on the C.I.D. Thus, Campbell-Bannerman's fears
that this Committee might have the effect of encroaching on the
responsibility of the civilian ministers turned out to be by no means
unfounded.

Another radical fear was that the operation of the party system
would be thwarted, and a spurious 'bi-partisan' defence policy be
thrust upon the country as the result of the machinations of this
new 'secretive and irresponsible' body. Again, some colour is
lent to these violent allegations by a study of the events of 1905,
when Balfour was preparing for his imminent departure from
office.

It must be remembered that Balfour himself, and the men who
formed the nucleus of the Defence Committee, had a strong fore-
boding that Campbell-Bannerman would disband the Committee
altogether, when he came to power. The public and private
utterances of the Liberal leader all suggested that this was likely.
Clarke, a fussy man at the best of times, worked himself up into
something of a panic at the thought of a change of administration,
and spoke of resigning as Secretary forthwith; Esher had to restrain
him by pointing out that his enemies in the Liberal Party would be
only too delighted to have their chance of making their own
nomination to the vacant post.[2]

The one cheering element in the situation was that Campbell-
Bannerman clearly did not speak for all members of his party.
When the Esher Committee Report was being discussed in March
1904, Sir Edward Grey had been silent on the subject of the
Defence Committee, while Haldane, on a later occasion, was

---

[1] M. V. Brett (ed.), op. cit., Vol. II, p. 78: Journals, 7.3.05. Arnold-Forster
Papers, Add. Mss. 50,344: Journals, 1.2.05: ff. 2–3. ibid.; Arnold-Forster to
Esher, 5.2.05: ff.21–3 (copy). ibid, Add. Mss. 50,346: Journals, 14.4.05: ff.
49–50.

[2] Balfour Papers, Add. Mss. 49,719: Esher to Clarke, 10.10.05.

positively effusive in congratulating Balfour on his achievement.[1] What Balfour eventually attempted to do, therefore, was to draw Haldane into informal consultations with the Defence Committee group before going out of office, in order to secure some continuity of policy.

It so happened that Haldane had spent the previous five years on a small research committee concerned with the manufacture of high explosives,[2] and this work had brought him into frequent contact with Fisher at the Admiralty[3] and with Esher and Clarke as well. As early as February 1905 we find Asquith and Haldane dining with Clarke to talk over army matters.[4] It is a complete myth that Haldane entered the War Office in December 1905 in total ignorance of the problems he was about to encounter— though Haldane himself wanted other people to believe that this was so.[5] In fact, for an Opposition M.P., Haldane was very familiar in these years with the functioning of the War Office and with defence problems generally. It was this experience, combined with his openly expressed approval of the C.I.D., which made him the obvious Liberal for Balfour to summon to the important conference that was held at Buckingham Palace at the beginning of October, 1905.

The other men present at this conference were the King, Esher and Lord Knollys, the King's Private Secretary. The main decision they reached was that the permanent element on the C.I.D. should be strengthened while Balfour was still in office. This was to be effected by the creation of two sub-committees to pursue investigations, which it was known that the next government could not

[1] Hansard, 4th Series, Vol. 131, cols, 641–2: 9.3.04. ibid., Vol. 139, cols. 633–4: 2.8.04.

[2] R. B. Haldane, *An Autobiography* (1929), pp. 164–5. A. Fitzroy, op. cit., Vol. I, pp. 274–5: 13.12.05. Haldane Papers, Vol. 5963: Haldane to Mother, 28.4.00: ff.120–1. ibid., Vol. 5905: Lansdowne to Haldane, 1.4.00, 10.4.00, 15.4.00: ff. 24–9.

[3] In Jan. 1903 he was 'in full correspondence with the breezy Fisher' (ibid., Vol. 5906: Haldane to Thursfield, 5.1.03: f. 1). By mid-1905 he was receiving confidential Admiralty papers (e.g. ibid., Vol. 5906: Fisher to Haldane, 25.5.05: f. 178). In return, Haldane tried to get his Liberal Party colleagues to appreciate the work that Fisher was doing.

[4] ibid., Vol. 5973: Haldane to Mother, 1.2.05: f. 33.

[5] See the letter of General Sir James E. Edmonds, printed in F. A. Johnson, op. cit., p. 82, note 3.

suddenly terminate. The hope was that this would ensure the survival of the Committee itself. In addition, Esher was made one of its 'permanent members'. 'It is splendid, and I am so glad,' he wrote to Sandars. 'Please thank the beloved P.M., and say that I will hold the fort for him as best I can.'[1]

Of all this Haldane had approved. Moreover, he had given comfort to the other people present by pledging the imperialist wing of his party to fight for the interests of the C.I.D. Indeed, he went on to say that the Liberal Imperialists intended, if anything, to reinforce the 'permanent' element still further and give the Committee a more 'scientific' and less 'political' complexion. So strongly did he insist on this last point that an agitated Clarke derived the mistaken impression that Haldane wished the Committee to be constituted *entirely* of 'experts'.[2]

Haldane's contribution to the development of the C.I.D. proved to be invaluable. He 'begged the life' of the Defence Committee, when Campbell-Bannerman became Prime Minister;[3] and then used its machinery and the informed conclusions it had reached during Balfour's Premiership as a basis for his own schemes of army reform. We have seen how one of the nagging fears in the minds of the 'efficiency group' was that imperial interests might be jeopardized when one party replaced another in government. The authors of the C.I.D. were especially anxious to place defence issues above the level of party strife; and this much was very largely achieved through the part played by the C.I.D. in smoothing the transition from Unionist to Liberal rule in December 1905.

At this stage the question naturally arises of why Campbell-Bannerman failed to stick to the line he had adopted during the years of opposition and did not attempt to disband the Defence Committee or to modify its powers. In December 1905 he hinted to Esher that a lot of what he had said over the past few years should not be taken too literally: these criticisms had served a party

---

[1] Balfour Papers, Add. Mss. 49,719: Esher to Sandars, 7.10.05. M. V. Brett (ed.), op. cit., Vol. II, pp. 114–15: Esher to Balfour, 5.10.05. ibid., p. 122: Esher to Sandars,7.10.05.

[2] Balfour Papers, Add. Mss. 49,719: Clarke to Esher, 9.10.05.

[3] Lord Hankey, *The Supreme Command, 1914–1918* (1961), Vol. I, p. 51.

purpose and could now be forgotten.[1] Such an explanation, how-ever, scarcely seems adequate. Campbell-Bannerman's disapproval of Balfour's work on imperial defence had been real enough in 1904. One possible factor in his subsequent climb-down may have been a desire to conciliate the powerful imperialist faction in his party and government. It seems more likely, however, that a certain listlessness descended on the elderly Liberal leader when he finally became Prime Minister. Many of his close radical friends and colleagues continued to view the Defence Committee with considerable aversion, particularly when they detected signs of the Committee developing into a sort of 'inner Cabinet' that could commit the Liberal Government as a whole to measures that had never been properly thrashed out by Cabinet or Party.[2] Campbell-Bannerman must have sympathized with these doubts and an-xieties; but he showed his dislike of the C.I.D., only through the way he neglected its affairs. During his Premiership the Committee met a mere fifteen times.

In fact, through their lethargy and indifference, Campbell-Bannerman and Asquith between them allowed the two service departments to develop diametrically opposed strategic plans; and it took the Agadir Crisis of 1911 to force the Government into resolving the damaging inter-departmental dispute.[3] Of course, this was precisely the sort of problem the C.I.D. had been intended to iron out. That it did not do so must also in part be blamed on the Secretary, Sir George Clarke, whose meddling in the purely internal affairs of War Office and Admiralty[4] led to his super-session in the summer of 1907—but not before he had implanted in Fisher's mind a secretive and hostile attitude towards the Commit-tee, which Fisher never shook off, despite the energetic remon-

[1] M. V. Brett (ed.), op. cit., Vol. II, pp. 127–8: Journals, 13.12.05.

[2] e.g. Campbell-Bannerman Papers, Add. Mss. 41,230: Sinclair to Campbell-Bannerman, 8.1.07: f. 143.

[3] See R. B. Haldane, *An Autobiography* (1929), pp. 225–232. W. S. Churchill, *The World Crisis, 1911–1914* (1923), pp. 56–9; Roy Jenkins, *Asquith* (1964), pp. 240–2.

[4] For his attempts to prevent Haldane's plans for reconstituting the militia as a special reserve and to upset Fisher's Dreadnought programme, see Lord Sydenham, *My Working Life* (1927), pp. 192–3, 208–10, and letters from Clarke to Campbell-Bannerman in Campbell-Bannerman Papers, Add. Mss. 41,213.

Q

strances of Esher.[1] Fisher's refusal to co-operate with the C.I.D. gravely prejudiced the success of its work.

As a device for effecting strategic unity, then, the C.I.D. disappointed the hopes of its founders. On the other hand, it proved much more successful in lifting defence questions out of the arena of party controversy. But for this, Haldane could never have carried through his army reforms. Faced by a sceptical Premier and an indifferent and sometimes hostile party,[2] Haldane was reliant on the quiet, unobtrusive help he was receiving from Balfour.[3] The importance of the Defence Committee in this situation was that it served as one of the channels through which information passed from the Cabinet and the service departments to the Opposition Front Bench.

Esher, who had now ingratiated himself with Haldane, proved to be an especially invaluable intermediary. Esher was continuously trying to secure a bi-partisan approach to problems of imperial defence.[4] He records in his journal a luncheon party he gave at the Carlton Club in July 1908 for Asquith, Balfour, General French, Knollys, and the new Secretary of the C.I.D., Ottley. His aim was to carry 'a step further the plan of bringing the Leaders of the Government and the Opposition together upon the highest questions of Peace Strategy'. 'I think it had some success,' he added.[5] Later in the same year Asquith and Haldane employed Esher to 'explain' confidential defence papers to Balfour, after the latter had turned down the offer to read the papers for himself.[6] As this incident shows, Balfour did not wish to be too much in the

---

[1] e.g. M. V. Brett (ed.), op. cit., Vol. II, p. 199: Esher to Fisher, 21.10.06. ibid., pp. 219–20: Esher to Fisher, 4.2.07.

[2] His critics included Loreburn, Morley and, most bitter of them all, Sinclair. Campbell-Bannerman's own position was equivocal. Haldane thought that the Prime Minister had slowly come to appreciate his work (R. B. Haldane, *An Autobiography* (1929), p. 182), but there is a good deal of evidence for the view that Campbell-Bannerman never forgave Haldane's past intrigues and disliked the drift of his War Secretary's army reforms.

[3] G. R. Searle, op. cit., pp. 199–201.

[4] This did not preclude his priming Balfour with material for attacks on the Government, when he felt that this would serve a good purpose. See Balfour Papers, Add. Mss. 49, 719: Sandars' Memo. of 15.3.09.

[5] M. V. Brett (ed.), op. cit., Vol. II, p. 326: Journals, 3.7.08.

[6] ibid., p. 364: Journals, 28.12.08.

secrets of the Government, for fear that he would thereby lose his freedom to oppose, when conscience or expediency dictated.

For the same reason Balfour had brusquely rejected the suggestion made by Colonel Seely in the Commons in August 1906 that the leaders of the Opposition should sit regularly on the Defence Committee.[1] However, he welcomed the opportunity to give evidence before the Committee on *specific issues of policy*, about which he felt he had some authority to pronounce. Accordingly, in May 1908, at Asquith's request, Balfour attended a sub-committee investigation into invasions and raids, where he made a closely reasoned statement of his own views upon the general strategy of national defence, to the admiration and stunned astonishment of Asquith, Grey, Haldane, Crewe and Lloyd George. Esher, who was present, was delighted with Balfour's speech, and even more with the sight of the leaders of the two parties taking counsel together upon vital issues of national policy and defence. 'It is a novel departure full of interest and good omen,' he wrote to the King.[2] Later, in 1912, Haldane invited Balfour to join the C.I.D. Balfour refused, but agreed at Asquith's request to sit as a member of the sub-committee, which between January 1913 and May 1914 once more examined the possibility of invasion.[3]

In this way, the C.I.D. brought together those politicians from both parties who realized the gravity of the German danger, and were planning to meet it by fashioning a small, highly professional, thoroughly equipped and mechanized force, which would simultaneously satisfy the requirements of efficiency and economy. The result was that a moderate, middle-of-the-road, 'bi-partisan' defence policy began to develop—much to the annoyance of extremists of both wings. Near-pacifist radicals and socialists who wanted drastic reductions in the service estimates, almost regardless of the consequences, and fire-eating Tories who felt that the best way to defend the Empire was to launch a violent campaign for ever more lavish expenditure on war preparations, now found

[1] Hansard, 4th Series, Vol. 162, cols. 1389–97: 2.8.06.
[2] M. V. Brett (ed.), op. cit., Vol. II, pp. 317–18: Esher to Balfour, 29.5.08. ibid., p. 318: Journals, 29.5.08. ibid., pp. 316–17: Esher to the King, 29.5.08.
[3] See K. Young, *Arthur James Balfour* (1963), pp. 341–2. By this time Balfour was no longer leader of the Unionist Party, which probably accounts for his greater readiness to associate himself with the regular work of the Committee.

themselves equally isolated. Thus, the effect of the C.I.D. was to help counter-balance the swings of the electoral pendulum and to produce a basic continuity of policy through successive changes of party government.

The natural annoyance of those politicians who stood outside this 'national consensus' found expression in personal attacks upon Esher, the distinguished backstairs operator, whose influence had survived Balfour's fall from power into the period of Liberal rule. Radical Liberals understandably disliked a man they saw as an emissary of the Conservative Party leader. But when in March 1907 Arnold-Forster—moved, one assumes, by personal pique— attacked Esher's position on the C.I.D. as 'unconstitutional', it was extreme Conservative journals, like the *National Review*, the *Morning Post* and the *Standard*, which took up the charge.[1] The diehard Tories were as anxious to revert to a 'no holds barred' political fight with the Government as the radicals were to break with the defence policies of the former Balfour administration. Neither set of politicians had much success.

Of course, those who had helped create the C.I.D. and who believed in it as a force for good positively welcomed those very constitutional changes of which radicals and extreme Tories alike complained. In 1903 Amery had gathered together a series of articles he had written for *The Times* in a volume entitled, *The Problem of the Army*. In this book Amery warmly praised the Defence Committee, not least because he saw the possibility of its evolving into 'an Imperial Advisory Council—as it were, a political General Staff of the Empire'. Amery wrote:

Just as the German General Staff directs the policy of the army without interfering in the absolute decentralised autonomy of the army corps, so this political General Staff might guide the policy of the Empire as a whole, without interfering in the practical independence of every part. . . After all, direct government by representative assemblies is not the last word in politics, and it may well be that the secret whereby Prussia reconciled administration with forethought and decentralization with unity in military matters can be turned to account by us for all the great business of an Empire. . .[2]

[1] See M. V. Brett (ed.), op. cit., Vol. II, pp. 225–7; Esher to Knollys, 19.3.07.
[2] L. S. Amery, *The Problem of the Army* (1903), pp. 134–5.

Approaching the problem from a slightly different vantage-point, Haldane expressed his belief that the C.I.D., as reorganized by Balfour, constituted an important model 'in respect of the scientific organization of Executive Government', and said that he hoped some day to see a number of other expert committees, composed along similar lines, working directly under the Prime Minister for the investigation and examination of detailed questions which lay beyond the competence of individual departments. The complex but inter-related issues of social welfare were obvious candidates for this kind of treatment.[1]

The reform of the Defence Committee set a precedent in another respect: the creation of a secretariat in 1904 marked an important stage in the 'professionalization' of government. For so well did this new administrative device prove its worth, that in December 1916 Lloyd George transferred the Defence Committee's secretariat to his small, stream-lined War Cabinet. However, what has since become accepted as an integral and necessary agency of government owed its existence in the first place to the statesmanlike prescience of Balfour and Esher in the winter of 1903–1904.

THE POOR LAW MINORITY REPORT OF 1909

When Sir John Gorst sought in February 1905 to persuade the Commons that the public authorities should be empowered to provide necessitous children with free or subsidized school meals, he quoted from the Report of the Physical Deterioration Committee to show the extent of malnutrition among the poorest classes. He then asked M.P.s: 'How could they carry on this great Empire, if they allowed causes of this kind which affected the physical condition of the people to continue to operate, and thus prevent their having soldiers and sailors fit to serve for the protection of the Empire?'[2]

Caution must be exercised in drawing deductions from such statements as these. One can also find Keir Hardie, hardly, one would have thought, an enthusiast for Empire and military efficiency, discreetly alluding to this consideration in a Commons

[1] Hansard, 4th Series, Vol. 146, cols. 121–2: 11.5.05.
[2] ibid., Vol. 141, col. 145: 14.2.05.

debate.[1] The fact that certain M.P.s were prepared to advocate social reform on hard-headed, 'practical' grounds does not mean that they were not also moved by humanitarian concern. On the other hand, even Keir Hardie's 'tongue in cheek' observations are revealing, since they suggest that he, for one, assumed that many members of his Parliamentary audience would find it difficult to oppose a 'socialistic' measure of reform, once it was based on national efficiency arguments.

It is in this sense that the Boer War panic about 'physical deterioration' made a contribution to the programme of social legislation carried by the Liberal government of 1905–1914. Investigations, such as those pursued by the Physical Deterioration Committee, made social reform 'respectable' in the eyes of men whose political instinct was to resist it. In certain instances, a more direct link exists between the Boer War and the reforms of the Campbell-Bannerman and Asquith Administrations. The School Medical Service, for example, can be seen, with only a little exaggeration, as an institutionalized legacy of the anxieties felt in the Boer War period. The provision of subsidized school meals to poor children occupies a similar status.[2]

Yet other influences were obviously at work in shaping the Liberal Government's social legislation. Most of the measures implemented in these years, old age pensions, health and unemployment insurance and the like, owed less to national efficiency factors than to humanitarian impulse, to calculations of electoral advantage and to the ambition of particular ministers. Moreover, these reforms were improvised in a somewhat hand-to-mouth fashion. There existed no comprehensive plan of action, into which individual measures could be fitted; and this incoherence was reflected in the bewildering variety of expedients adopted by the Government in administering their new welfare schemes. Little wonder, then, that members of the 'efficiency group' could only give, at best, a guarded welcome to the work of the Liberal ministries.

What certain members of the 'efficiency group' hoped to achieve

[1] ibid., Vol. 143, col. 1233: 27.3.05.
[2] There is an excellent discussion of both measures in Bentley B. Gilbert, *The Evolution of National Insurance in Great Britain*, (1966), Ch. 3.

in social welfare, and the reasons for their failure, is illuminated by a study of the fate of the reports produced by the Royal Commission into the Poor Laws (1905–09).[1] This issue has a wider importance still, in that it involves one of the major mysteries of Edwardian political history: the inaction of a Liberal Government, otherwise adventurous and fertile in devising social legislation, in the face of a poor law system, admitted by nearly all reformers, including many Conservatives, to require drastic restructuring.

The failure of the Royal Commission to produce a single agreed report has something to do with the Government's shelving of the whole problem. But there was much more common ground between the Majority and Minority Commissioners than most subsequent commentators have realized; and the Government could, had it chosen, have accomplished a great deal even by confining its attention to those points where both reports were in substantial accord. For example, there was unanimity on the need to abolish the Boards of Guardians; yet these bodies were allowed to survive until as late as 1929, curious relics of a bygone administrative era.

From the moment that the Royal Commission reported in February 1909, a disproportionate share of the public debate centred on the Minority document, written by the Webbs. The principal reason for this is probably that, whereas the Majority Commissioners seemed content to formulate a programme which could, to a large extent, be implemented within the existing structure of local government, an attitude of mind which led them into recommending a needlessly complex machinery of control and enforcement, the Webbs' report had a challenging clarity: the mass of detailed recommendations was logically deduced from a few clear and readily intelligible ideas. Unfortunately for the Webbs, these ideas were not acceptable to the Liberal ministers of the day.

One misconception needs to be cleared up at once. The Minority Report was never thought of by its authors as a socialist manifesto, and, if one reads it dispassionately, one must admit that it bears little trace of socialist thinking. In a private letter to one of her sisters, when she could afford to be frank about her motives,

[1] *Report of the Royal Commission on the Poor Laws and the Relief of Distress* (1909): Cd. 4499.

Beatrice Webb claimed that her intention in framing the report had been to clean up the base of society and establish 'minimum standards': an objective that could be accepted equally by collectivist or individualist, conservative or radical; improving the circumstances of the poorest classes in the community, she added, was necessary, if only to enable Britain to hold her own in competition with such highly regulated races as the Germans or the Japanese.[1] As in so many other respects, Majority and Minority Commissioners here saw eye to eye. The concluding paragraph of the Majority Report asserted that: 'No country, however rich, can permanently hold its own in the race of international competition, if hampered by an increasing load of this dead weight [of destitution]; or can successfully perform the role of sovereignty beyond the seas, if a portion of its own folk at home are sinking below the civilization and aspirations of its subject races abroad.'[2]

Later, when both Front Benches had rejected their proposals, the Webbs tended to attribute their failure to the 'class selfishness' of the two main political parties;[3] indeed, realizing by 1911 that 'permeation' was not getting them anywhere in Poor Law reform, they launched a nation-wide campaign for the 'Break-Up of the Poor Law', which eventually carried them back into the main-stream of the British Labour movement and rekindled their old socialist ardour. Socialist thinking, however, finds no place in the Minority Report itself, unless one believes that the Webbs' schemes for the 'Organization of the Labour Market' qualify as 'Socialism'. The Webbs certainly believed that the able-bodied unemployed, thrown into destitution because of factors quite outside their control, were entitled to receive public assistance which would not carry the stigma of pauperism.[4] On the other hand, far from envisaging an expensive system of social services, financed by a progressive fiscal policy designed to redistribute wealth on a large scale, the Minority Report urged that public assistance should on no account be made either free or unconditional. The Webbs recommended the appointment of a Registrar of Public Assistance,

---

[1] Passfield Papers: II 4 c: B. Webb to M. Playne, 21.8.07: ff. 261–3.
[2] Cd. 4499, p. 644.
[3] See S. and B. Webb, *The Prevention of Destitution* (1911), *passim.*
[4] Cd. 4499: Part II, Ch. V, pp. 1179–1215.

whose task would be to assess the charges incurred by people receiving public aid and to recover whatever portion of that charge a person was considered capable of paying.[1] There was, in short, to be an investigation into the financial circumstances of everyone on public assistance—a means test, it might be called; and no benefit or treatment was to be administered to the necessitous, except on very onerous conditions. Furthermore, the Webbs seem to have been quite sincere in their belief that the economies consequent upon their scheme would actually *reduce*, not increase, the level of public spending on social welfare:[2] a consideration they knew would carry weight with the government and the general public.

What alienated the Majority Commissioners from the Webbs and gave the Minority Report its 'progressive' aura, was the Webbs' refusal to admit that destitution in itself should single out a citizen for distinctive treatment. Along with others of the 'efficiency group', the Webbs believed that community services should be organized around the kind of *service* rendered, not around the type of *person* using that service. This administrative principle underlay the famous Report of the Machinery of Government Committee of 1918, of which Haldane was Chairman and Beatrice Webb and Morant members.[3] Applied to the poor law system, of course, this principle had revolutionary implications. At once the *raison d'etre* of all poor law authorities as such was destroyed. For the Webbs could now argue that all sick citizens, whether destitute or not, should enjoy the same public health service facilities; and similarly that all children, including pauper children, should come under the supervision of the appropriate L.E.A. The Webbs believed that this administrative re-grouping had to be done, if the different social services were to build up a high level of professional expertise.

Now, the sweeping away of the Boards of Guardians which this entailed was recommended by *both* sets of Commissioners. In one sense, such a reform was merely a logical follow-up to the decision which had been made in 1902 to dismantle those other *ad hoc* bodies the School Boards. It was easy to demonstrate that the areas of the Boards of Guardians were too small to permit of efficient manage-

[1] ibid., p. 1019.
[2] ibid., p. 1029.
[3] *Report of the Machinery of Government Committee* (1918): Cd. 9230, pp. 7–8.

ment, and that the 643 separate destitution authorities in England and Wales made administrative uniformity impossible to secure.

Moreover, or so the Webbs maintained, the Boards of Guardians suffered from an additional weakness, which had not afflicted the old School Boards. The provision of elementary education was at least a simple, homogeneous function; but the relief of destitution brought the administrator into touch with a great variety of human needs and of human distress. Indeed, the more enlightened Boards of Guardians, recognizing the complexity of their responsibilities, had already begun to supply a wide range of services for their paupers. Unfortunately, observed the Webbs, no Board of Guardians had the diversified professional staff, the wealth of technical experience or sufficient continuity of work in any one branch to cope successfully with all the many tasks it might choose to perform. In fact, by a grim paradox, it was the conscientious destitution authority which was actually doing the greatest harm, by duplicating some of the work of its neighbouring county and county borough councils. 'Overlapping, confusion and waste', wrote the Webbs, resulted from such competition as that between the poor law medical officers and the Medical Officers of Health, and this, in the long run, demoralized everyone affected by it.[1]

As a solution to this dilemma, the Minority Report advocated that each pauper should be 'scientifically classified' and then handed over to one of the specialized committees of the municipality or county council. In that way, pauper children would come under the control of the new L.E.A.s, lunatics under the local Asylums Committee, the sick under a new public health committee, and so on. Over and above these authorities, the Webbs envisaged the various departments of the national government assisting and stimulating local effort and using their control of grants-in-aid to level up the administration of all the community services to a 'national minimum of efficiency'.[2] They also advocated a re-allocation of responsibilities in Whitehall, to parallel the break-up of the Boards of Guardians, and even recommended the creation of new ministries, such as a Ministry of Labour, for the supervision of services which would otherwise escape adequate central control. This assumed, among other things, a drastic

[1] Cd. 4499, pp. 1007–8.   [2] ibid., p. 1032.

shake-up of the Local Government Board, with its many and heterogeneous duties, and the formation of a new Public Health Department, and, possibly of a new Ministry of Health.

What gave life to these dry matters of administrative reorganization was the burning conviction of the Webbs that the seemingly insoluble problem of destitution could be overcome by a careful examination of its causes. These causes were manifold, but one of the most important was ill-health. It was generally agreed that nearly one third of all classified paupers were suffering from some sort of sickness. By providing a properly organized health service and employing the full resources of preventive medicine, the Webbs believed it possible to cut off much of this existing distress at its source, and, in that way, effect enormous savings in the expenditure of public money. 'It is surely the worst of all forms of national waste,' they wrote in the Minority Report, 'to allow the ravages of preventable sickness to progress unchecked; and this not merely because it kills off thousands of producers prematurely (burdening us, by the way, with the widow and the orphan), but because sickness levies a toll on the living, and leaves even those who survive crippled, debilitated, and *less efficient than they would otherwise have been.*'[1] In support of this conviction, the Webbs pointed to the great achievements of the M.O.H.s in matters of sanitation, the control of infectious diseases and the removal of nuisances. This raised the further question: might not the philosophy and the methods of the M.O.H.s be extended to other social problems, like unemployment? The Webbs, in effect, wished to broaden the conception of what constituted a public nuisance, until it embraced all forms of destitution; then the appropriate preventive action could be taken.

It was at this point that the Webbs parted company with many of their 'progressive' well-wishers. For, true to the whole ethos of the national efficiency ideology, the Minority Report brutally ignored all liberal susceptibilities. If the Webbs had had their way, they would have 'classified' paupers, without any regard to the wishes of individuals. Their scheme vested the various 'expert' public officials with sweeping and compulsory powers of detention over anyone who fell below the minimum of mental and physical fitness

[1] ibid., p. 1030. My italics.

recognized by society.[1] This was justified by the argument that such destitute persons, no matter what the cause of their destitution, were a public danger, against which the community was entitled to protect itself.

Particularly hard would have been the lot of the able-bodied unemployed. The Webbs wanted these men sent to the training establishments which the new Ministry of Labour was to organize. These institutions, to quote the words of the Minority Report, would serve as 'human sorting houses', where the residents could be 'tested' systematically and then put through a course of exercises designed to raise them to the highest state of physical and mental efficiency of which they were capable: an unpleasant, but salutary, experience, likened in the Minority Report to submitting to periodic medical check-ups.[2] There the unskilled and the redundant would be taught new trades. But those whose unemployment was due to mere idleness would have to be given a 'training in character, under the beneficent influence of continuous order and discipline'[3]. The most recalcitrant cases could be committed by order of a magistrate to semi-penal detention colonies.[4] Like the militarists of the National Service League, the Webbs would have had a short way with rebels, 'hooligans', 'loafers' and other social misfits.

Possibly the specific proposals contained in the Minority Report aroused less anxiety than the language in which they were couched. In any case, one can understand the reluctance of any government responsible to an electorate to put these recommendations into practice. The observation of Masterman, that he hoped he would never fall into Mrs. Webbs' hands as a member of the unemployed,[5] represents what must have been a very common reaction—particularly on the Liberal side of the House. The love of bureaucratic regulation which is the other distinguishing feature of the Minority Report also repelled many members of the Government. A revealing episode took place in 1910, when a private member introduced into the Commons a Bill embodying the principal conclusions

---

[1] ibid., p. 889, conclusion 5; p. 1206.
[2] ibid., p. 1206.
[3] ibid., p. 1204.
[4] ibid., pp. 1207–8.
[5] Lord Beveridge, *Power and Influence* (1953), pp. 66–7: letter of 23.3.08.

of the Minority Commissioners. The Conservative leader, Balfour, made a friendly, though non-committal, speech.[1] Asquith, on the other hand, took a similar line to John Burns, the President of the Local Government Board, and, in his anxiety to repudiate the Webbs, seemed to be urging the continued existence of the Boards of Guardians—which *all* the Commissioners had wished to see abolished. Asquith's words were significant: 'I confess, as an old fashioned individual,' he said, 'I note with some amount, I will not say of suspicion, but of doubt and uncertainty, the substitution of a centralized authority with regard to many aspects of the problem of Poor Law administration . . .'.[2] The Webbs, of course, had no intention of compromising their reform plans by meeting 'old fashioned individuals' like Asquith half-way.

Nevertheless, until as late as 1910, the Webbs thought it likely that a large part of their Minority Report would find its way onto the statute book. Much of their optimism stemmed from their knowledge that occupying strategically important positions within the administrative machine they had sympathizers, whose influence would be used on their behalf. Since the Minority Report can be seen as a kind of 'M.O.H.'s Charter', key members of that professional body, including those in government employment, naturally enough were co-operating quite closely with the Webbs. The Chief Medical Officer at the Board of Education, Dr. George Newman, may actually have owed his appointment to an introduction Beatrice Webb had secured for him with the Board's Permanent Secretary, Sir Robert Morant—with whom the Webbs had remained friendly since the time of the Education Act struggles. 'Somehow or other I connect you with this post,' Newman wrote to her in September 1907. 'I have often wondered how much you have had to do with it. I do not forget a pleasant dinner party where I first set eyes on Sir R. Morant. Since then he and I have had something to do with each other and several very plain conversations!'[3] Newman quickly became a great admirer,

---

[1] Hansard, 5th Series (Commons), Vol. 16, cols. 828–36: 8.4.10. The Webbs were grateful that Balfour had not committed his party against the measure: B. Webb, *Our Partnership* (1948), p. 449: 12.4.10.

[2] Hansard, 5th Series (Commons), Vol. 16, col. 838: 8.4.10.

[3] Passfield Papers: II 4 c: Sir George Newman to B. Webb, 19.9.07; ff.277–8.

almost a hero-worshipper of the autocratic Morant, while main-taining close touch with the Webbs: 'I will try to be worthy of you,' he promised Beatrice, 'and I will try to do my duty to the Board and to the great cause of [the] physical and social betterment of the people . . .'[1]

A few months later the Webbs, Morant and Newman joined forces to persuade Burns to appoint as Chief Medical Officer to the L.G.B. Dr. Arthur Newsholme, who was then the M.O.H. for Finsbury. Newsholme was a 'great friend' of Newman,[2] a stout believer in an unified medical service and, as editor of the pro-fessional journal, *Public Health*, an influential publicist for the cause of environmental reform and preventive medicine. Also a protégé of the Webbs was Dr. Mackenzie, Chief Medical Officer at the Scottish Local Government Board. Later, the Webbs were able to make much of the point that the public health section of their Minority Report was based upon the evidence and testimony of the Government's three principal medical functionaries.[3]

Then, too, there was Morant at the Board of Education, aspiring as always to take an active and creative part in the formu-lation, as well as the execution, of policy. Having recently created a School Medical Service 'out of half a dozen lines in a second-class measure', as Newman admiringly put it,[4] Morant was eager to extend the public health services into new areas of social life. He was known to be a warm admirer of the Minority Report, even something of a disciple of the Webbs. William Braithwaite, for one, felt that 'everything that Webb said Morant believed'.[5]

Morant's ambition in 1908 and 1909 was to be transferred to the L.G.B. Like most reformers, he felt that this department was being run on illiberal lines and that, unless it was soon taken in hand, no-one would ever convert it 'into a state of even comparative efficiency'.[6] However, the aged and ineffectual Permanent Secre-tary, Sir Samuel Provis, was shortly due to retire, and until as late

[1] ibid.
[2] Burns Papers, Add. Mss. 46,300: Newman to Burns, 18.1.08: f. 5.
[3] Cd. 4499, p. 888.
[4] Sir George Newman, *The Building of a Nations's Health* (1939), pp. 467–8.
[5] W. J. Braithwaite, *Lloyd George's Ambulance Wagon* (1957), p. 117. Also, Lucy Masterman, *C. F. G. Masterman* (1939), p. 232.
[6] Passfield Papers: II 4 d: Morant to B. Webb, 10.5.08: f. 23.

as the spring of 1908 the Webbs entertained the hope of cajoling Burns into taking on Morant as his successor. They alternated veiled threats with the grossest flattery: 'If you ever think of carrying out any new departure,' wrote Beatrice to Burns in May 1907, 'you will require a really strong subordinate—a man of the type of Morant (who by the way is a great admirer of yours). I do so want your administration to stand out as constructive in the best sense.'[1] Burns' decision to import an able 'outsider' like Newsholme into the department against the advice of his senior officials[2] encouraged the Webbs to increase their pressure.

In May 1908 Burns certainly seemed to be giving serious consideration to Morant's appointment.[3] Masterman, the new Parliamentary Secretary to the L.G.B., also wanted Morant brought in to carry through a thorough reconstitution of the office, where, he believed, 'the position, under present circumstances' was 'an "imposible" one'.[4] Even when it became obvious that Burns and his senior officials had declared all-out war on the Webbs, there was still ground for hope, since Morant believed that Asquith on becoming Prime Minister, had insisted on making the nomination to the Permanent Secretaryship of the L.G.B. *over Burns' head*, when the post next fell vacant.[5] Morant expected that he himself would be the favoured man, and in early 1908 he was actually making plans for carrying out the Webbs' Poor Law Scheme as soon as he took up his new appointment.[6]

In addition, the Webbs had their friends inside the Cabinet. Although no mention of this is to be found in his *Autobiography*, Haldane was giving quite a lot of attention to matters of social reform in 1907 and 1908, and even talking of replacing Burns, once

---

[1] Burns Papers, Add. Mss. 46,287: B. Webb to Burns, 11.5.07: ff. 300–1. Needless to say, Morant never had anything but contempt for Burns; e.g. 'John Burns hates me, I believe; probably on the usual ground that I am a tool of the Bishops or a Jesuit, or some such folly . . .' (Passfield Papers: II 4 c: Burns to B. Webb, 1.5.07: f. 237). The threats took the form of intimating that the Cabinet might take the responsibility of reform out of Burns' hands altogether: see Burns Papers, Add. Mss. 46,287: B. Webb to Burns, 15.1.08: ff.302–3).

[2] Burns Papers, Add. Mss. 46,326: Journals, 13.1.08: f. 3.

[3] B. Webb, op. cit., p. 411: 19.5.08.

[4] L. Masterman, op. cit., p. 105: Masterman to Asquith, 13.4.08.

[5] B. Webb, op. cit., p. 443: 8.1.10.

[6] Passfield Papers, Vol. 26: B. Webb's Journal, 24.3.08: f. 109.

his reorganization of the army had been completed. In late 1907 we find him working out the expenses of old age pensions on the basis of information supplied to him by the Webbs and by his sister, Elizabeth. A month later he embodied his conclusions on this and other related matters in a memorandum, which he submitted to Asquith for consideration by a Cabinet Committee. Breaking the rule of Cabinet secrecy, Haldane showed this memorandum to the Webbs, asking them whether they thought it provided a satisfactory starting-point for discussion. This document was described by Beatrice as 'somewhat "woolly"' but 'all in the right direction'. She had good reason to be satisfied with it, since the memorandum was in effect a general summary of her own Poor Law scheme. The central theme of Haldane's paper was that any old age pension bill should 'involve a comprehensive classification of individuals and of modes of relieving them', and that this would 'ultimately involve a sweeping reform of our Poor Law system'.[1]

The prospects of the Webbs were all the brighter because, after a period of slight estrangement, Haldane and Asquith had come closer together, and it seemed that Haldane might succeed in getting Asquith to take a personal initiative on the Poor Law question, or at least to stir Burns himself into constructive action.[2] In December 1907 Haldane began sending on to Asquith personal letters and papers which he had received from the Webbs.[3] This might, in the long run, have been an unwise move, since it surely confirmed Asquith's prejudice against the Webbs as tiresome intriguers. In the short run, however, Asquith responded to the pressure brought to bear on him. In February 1908 he actually asked Beatrice whether he should adumbrate the 'break-up of the poor law' in the budget speech, when he introduced his old age pensions proposals.[4]

[1] Haldane Papers, Vol. 5907: Haldane to Grey, 6.9.07: ff. 190–1. Passfield Papers: II 4 c: Haldane to B. Webb, 25.9.07: ff. 282–3. ibid.: B. Webb to M. Playne, 27.9.07: f. 284. Cabinet memorandum of 6.9.07: Cab. 37/89/81.

[2] See Haldane Papers, Vol. 5907: Haldane to Grey, 6.9.07: f. 190.

[3] Asquith Papers, Vol. 11: Haldane to Asquith, 17.12.07, enclosing letter from S. Webb to Haldane, 12.12.07 and memorandum by Webb on old age pensions: ff. 131–70.

[4] B. Webb, op. cit., p. 402: 10.2.08. Next month she wrote to Asquith, again

In mid-May 1908 Haldane was saying that in eighteen months' time he would have finished his work at the War Office and would then be prepared to take on the L.G.B. A fortnight later, however, he learnt that Asquith, who was now Prime Minister, had other ideas of his own. After taking Grey along with him to see Asquith about the Poor Law question, Haldane wrote back to the Webbs in much more guarded tones: 'What we want may be difficult—possibly cannot be done'.[1]

The testing point of Asquith's and Haldane's sincerity came in June 1908 when the Old Age Pension Bill was debated in the Commons. In the event, Asquith made no attempt to anticipate the findings of the Poor Law Commissioners, nor did Lloyd George who had taken over responsibility for the Pensions Bill. Many Unionist M.P.s, it is true, argued that the pensions scheme should have been deferred until the Commission had reported: an obvious debating line for an opposition party to have taken. However, the only government spokesman who attempted to defend the measure as a contribution to a broader policy of social reform was Haldane, who, drawing upon his memorandum, entertained the House to a highly academic discourse on the problems of a 'scientific classification' of the welfare services. In so doing, Haldane at times contradicted Lloyd George's most important argumentative points. The *tone* of his speech was in even greater contrast to that of other Ministers. While, for example, Lloyd George struck a note of humanitarian concern, Haldane went stolidly on with his explanation of how the provision of public relief had fallen into confusion, for want of a clear 'principle' to regulate the distribution of work between the various bodies concerned. He made particular play with the unfortunate 'overlapping' between the rival medical authorities. However, he observed, the Poor Law Commission would soon be submitting its report: and he then proceeded to speculate about the Commission's likely recommendations.[2] The

---

pressing him to make this commitment: Asquith Papers, Vol. 11: B. Webb to Asquith, 2.3.08: ff.3–4.
    [1] B. Webb: op. cit., p. 411: 19.5.08. Passfield Papers: II 4 d: Haldane to B. Webb, 30.5.08: f. 44.
    [2] Hansard, 4th Series, Vol. 190; cols. 664–71: 15.6.08.
    R

Webbs could not have received better advance publicity for their Poor Law scheme.

Moreover, by the middle of 1908 the Webbs had acquired another ally inside the Cabinet: Winston Churchill. Before that year, it is true, Churchill had shown little sympathy with their point of view. In June 1904 Beatrice could dismiss his political ideas as 'a quaint jumble of old-fashioned Radicalism and mere Toryism'. 'I tried the "National Minimum" on him,' she added, 'but he was evidently unaware of the most elementary objections to unrestricted competition and was still in the stage of "infant school economics" . . .'[1]

Churchill's conversion to the 'national minimum' seems to have occurred in late 1907. He returned from a visit to East Africa full of the importance of the social question and ready to campaign under the slogans of ' "Social Bulwarks", "Security", "Standardization".'[2] In February 1908 Churchill began to cultivate the Webbs. In March he was brought into contact for the first time, over dinner at the Webbs' house, with a young journalist, William Beveridge; as a result, Beveridge was put in charge of the Labour Exchange scheme later in the year, after Churchill had become President of the Board of Trade.[3] The friendliness between Churchill and the Webbs persisted for several months. 'You will always find the door of my room open whenever you care to come,' he told Sidney in July, 'and I hope you will feed me generously from your store of information and ideas.'[4]

What Churchill imbibed from the Webbs was not so much practical policies and proposals as a style of rhetoric and a vocabulary with which to handle social problems. In recommending his Trade Boards Bill to M.P.s, for example, Churchill spoke of 'sick and diseased industries', which needed to be dealt with in the same spirit as one would deal with sick people.[5] Particularly interesting is the long letter he wrote to Asquith in December 1908, outlining the case for a national minimum. 'There is a tremendous policy in

---

[1] Passfield Papers, Vol. 24: B. Webb's Journals, 10.6.04: f. 87.

[2] Wilson Harris, *J. A. Spender* (1946), pp. 80–1: Churchill to Spender, 22.12.07.

[3] Lord Beveridge, op. cit., pp. 66–8.

[4] Passfield Papers: II 4 d: Churchill to S. Webb, 6.7.08: ff. 249–50.

[5] W. S. Churchill, *Liberalism and the Social Problem* (1909), p. 243.

Social Organisation,' he wrote. 'The need is urgent and the moment ripe. Germany with a harder climate and far less accumulated wealth has managed to establish basic conditions for her people. She is organized not only for war, but for peace. We are organized for nothing except party politics.' This complaint lay at the heart of all the arguments about national efficiency. Churchill concluded: 'Thrust a big slice of Bismarckianism over the whole underside of our industrial system and await the consequences whatever they may be with a good conscience.'[1] This letter reads like a cross between the propaganda of the Webbs and of the Milner circle.

In short, Churchill affected the demeanour of the sober, constructive 'elder statesman', tackling the social question along 'national' lines in a systematic and comprehensive fashion. This style of political activity marked him off from Lloyd George, closely though the two men worked in these years. Lloyd George did, indeed, pick up some of the ideas and attitudes held by the national efficiency group (the influence is most noticeable in the latter half of 1910); but in other respects he was all that these people disliked. Lloyd George's policies were eclectic: clever improvisations designed to meet specific problems and grievances, often presented in the violent language of class warfare. In 1908 and 1909 Lloyd George seemed the very model of the irresponsible demagogue.

Beatrice Webb may have had her doubts as to how long Churchill would stick to his role of social reformer, but she thought that for the moment he was playing it very well. Lloyd George she judged to be inferior by comparison: 'more of the preacher, less of the statesman'.[2] Haldane, who shared the Webbs' intellectualized approach to politics, despised Lloyd George, dismissing him as 'an illiterate with an untrained mind'.[3] On the other hand, Haldane viewed Churchill with mixed feelings, compounded of admiration, irritation and jealousy. He sensed that the younger man was

---

[1] Asquith Papers, Vol. 11: Churchill to Asquith, 29.12.08: ff. 250–3: partly reproduced in R. Jenkins, op. cit., p. 193.   [2] B. Webb, op. cit., p. 417: 16.10.08.

[3] Haldane Papers, Vol. 5923: Notes on Letters Contained in My Boxes (written in Autumn 1926): f. 17. There is every evidence that this was Haldane's opinion of Lloyd George when they were colleagues in the pre-war Liberal Governments.

replacing him in the eyes of his friends, even in the estimation of the Webbs.[1]

In 1908 Churchill was making speeches about the importance of classifying the body of paupers and transferring them to 'authorities specially concerned in their management and care'.[2] From the Webbs' point of view this was most encouraging. Indeed, as late as December 1909 Beatrice thought that Churchill intended to go to the L.G.B., once the general election was over, taking Morant with him to implement the Minority Report. Haldane, too, wanted Churchill to be moved to that department.[3] By late 1909, however, both Churchill and Haldane seem to have settled in their minds for the more modest goal of a 'classified Poor Law', with which the Webbs would not now have been satisfied.[4] In the event, Churchill was sent in 1910 to the Home Office, where he set about 'classifying' the prison system instead.[5] Soon he began to lose interest in *all* matters of social legislation. The Webbs' moment of opportunity has passed.

Why was it, though, that the Liberal ministers, who were tumbling over one another to be 'coached' by the Webbs at the beginning of 1908, should have turned a deaf ear to their proposals when the Royal Commission reported in February 1909. Partly, the Webbs had themselves to blame. Previously their strength had lain in the moderateness of their demands and in their willingness to make the best of modest reforms sponsored by politicians with different philosophies and objectives. By 1909, however, they had become so emotionally involved in the Poor Law question, that nothing short of the full programme outlined in the Minority Report would satisfy them. Hence, they violently attacked the Majority proposals, which went a long way towards meeting their own demands.[6] The consequence was that they left themselves

---

[1] See B. Webb, op. cit., p. 380: 3. 5.07.

[2] W. S. Churchill, *The People's Rights* (1910), p. 117.

[3] B. Webb, op. cit., p. 437: 1.12.09. R. Churchill, *Winston Churchill: Young Statesman, 1901–1914* (1967), p. 362.

[4] Asquith Papers, Vol. 11: Churchill to Asquith, 29.12.08: f. 252. B. Webb, op. cit., p. 430: 22.6.09.

[5] Asquith Papers, Vol. 12: Churchill to Asquith, 27.9.10: ff. 179–80.

[6] e.g. *Contemporary Review*, April 1909, Vol. XCV, pp. 401–13: S. A. Barnett, 'The Poor Law Report'. *Westminster Gazette*, 18.2.09.

open to a sharp counter-attack. The squabble which then developed merely played into the hands of those who wanted no radical reform of the poor law system at all: a number in which Burns himself must certainly be included.[1] A second explanation lies in the unfortunate timing of the publication of the Poor Law Reports. Scarcely had the two bulky volumes come out, than Lloyd George introduced his 'People's Budget'. 'I am stirring about the Poor Law,' Haldane reassured his sister in October 1909, 'but the public mind is, and will for some time remain, full of other things.'[2]

The Webbs ultimately failed, however, because their conception of social reform was disliked, though for different reasons, by both Asquith and Lloyd George, the two main figures in the Cabinet. Probably Asquith had always nourished a suspicion of the Webbs' ideas, as his speech on the 'Prevention of Destitution' Bill indicated. In any case, it was Asquith who was largely responsible for thwarting their plans for poor law reform. Characteristically, he achieved this by the simple expedient of doing nothing—that is to say, by leaving Burns undisturbed at the L.G.B., though few ministers had a good word to say on the latter's behalf. Nor, when it came to it, did Asquith even stand firm on his earlier declared intention of imposing an 'outsider' as Permanent Secretary of the department, on Provis' retirement. Perhaps the Webbs' gossiping and intrigues had had something to do with his change of attitude. In February 1909 Asquith admitted the need for a shake-up at the L.G.B., but Masterman noted how he 'really boiled over at the way the Webbs [had], by "running" Morant as their Candidate, ruined his chances of getting the post.'[3] Yet there is some evidence to suggest that as late as December 1909 the Prime Minister still intended to appoint Morant. But the following month he weakly gave way to Burns (perhaps to avoid an unpleasant scene?), and allowed the Assistant Secretary of the Board, Sir Horace Monro, to be promoted to Provis' place.[4] From the point of view of

[1] B. Webb, op. cit., p. 440.
[2] Haldane Papers, Vol. 6011: Haldane to Elizabeth Haldane, 7.10.09: f. 90.
[3] L. Masterman, op. cit., p. 123: Journal entry, 10.2.09.
[4] 'Went to No. 10 to see P.M. . . . told him I wanted to appoint Munro before we went to the Polls. He seemed to have someone else in mind. I pressed the necessity of an experienced man and a firm one. He said it was rather sudden . . .

Morant and the Webbs, this turn of events was a disaster.[1]

Whether intentionally or unintentionally, Asquith thus blocked the path of the 'environmental' reformers. Meanwhile, Lloyd George was outflanking them by adopting an alternative strategy of reform, which seemed to render the break-up of the Poor Law unnecessary. Lloyd George did not, as Burns gleefully put it, deliberately 'dish the Webbs' when he began work on health insurance.[2] He had committed himself to this measure before the Webbs' scheme had taken final shape; and, judging by his vague and confused references to the Poor Law subject in subsequent years, he probably never bothered to master the contents of either the Majority or the Minority Report.[3] The fact remains, however, that the most powerful member of the social reform group inside the Cabinet was approaching his work from a diametrically opposed vantage point to the Webbs.

The Minority Report concentrated on those environmental factors which produced destitution. Admittedly, the Webbs also believed, in their own fashion, in 'improving character', since they wished to subject the destitute to an expert bureaucracy responsible for seeing that these people did not, through ignorance or misconduct, again become a burden on the efficient members of the community. But the Webbs were avowedly concerned with *causes*. For pragmatic and political reasons alike, Lloyd George preferred to deal with the *consequences* of destitution. His National Health scheme, for example, was never intended, as originally conceived, to be a measure of public health as such: its major purpose was to replace lost income, to rescue the family of a bread-winner stricken by ill health from the degrading clutches of the Poor Law. The fundamental difference between these competing social philosophies has been neatly summarized by Professor Bentley Gilbert: 'Whereas for Lloyd George poverty was the evil

---

I left him feeling convinced that something would happen to me, that much had happened to him . . . I had expected warmer treatment than I received . . .' (Burns Papers, Add. Mss. 46,332: Journals, 4.1.10: f. 27). 'Jerred called with P.M.'s letter of assent to Munro' (Ibid., Add. Mss.46,332: Journals, 4.1.10: f. 27).

[1] B. Webb, op. cit., p. 443: 8.1.10.
[2] ibid., p. 475: 26.5.11.
[3] See Bentley B. Gilbert, op. cit., p. 292, note 3.

that sickness caused, [for the Webbs and their M.O.H. friends] sickness was the evil that poverty caused.'[1]

The logic of Lloyd George's social philosophy led him to espouse insurance, and this in turn provided the Liberal Government with a reform policy free of the authoritarianism that permeated the Minority Report—and the Majority Report, too, to a lesser degree. Lloyd George well knew that few people's private lives would bear the close scrutiny to which the Webbs would have wished to subject them. Churchill seems to have been even more aware of what was at stake, when he 'deserted' the Webbs in late 1908 and began framing a measure of Unemployment Insurance, to complement Lloyd George's scheme. In a memorandum, dated June 1909, he delivered himself of the significant pronouncement that he did not like mixing up moralities and mathematics. Some admixture of personal considerations was, he said, inevitable in the working of any such scheme, but safety lay in the discovery of clear, ruthless, mathematical rules, to which the self-interest of individuals prompted them to conform, and failure to conform to which automatically relieved the funds.[2] Thus did Churchill call actuarial science into service, to ward off the supervision of Beatrice Webb's 'expert bureaucrats'.

Nor was Churchill, as the Webbs were inclined to suppose, simply shrinking from an unpleasant duty when he made this stand. By 1909 he had become familiar with the recent researches of William Beveridge, which, by casting doubt on the existence of a class of 'unemployables', destroyed the case for labour colonies and other paternalistic features of the Minority Report.[3] In many respects, the Webb's analysis of the unemployment problem looked back to an earlier tradition of thinking about the subject, which more exact knowledge had shown to be erroneous.

Unemployment insurance, however, was peripheral to the central struggle fought out between the 'environmental' social

[1] ibid., p. 315.

[2] Beveridge Papers, Bundle 2, Book C: Note by Churchill on Malingering, 6.6.09.

[3] See John Brown: 'Charles Booth and Labour Colonies, 1889–1905' (*Economic History Review*, Aug. 1968, 2d Series, Vol. XXI, no. 2, pp. 349–60) for the importance attached to labour colonies at the end of the 19th and start of the 20th centuries.

reformers and the 'insurers' in 1909 and 1910. It was Lloyd George's measure of *health* insurance that drew the fiercest attacks from the Webb group. These people thought health insurance pernicious because it failed to satisfy the criterion that cash benefits should only be disbursed if they either altered the environment in a beneficial way or 'improved' the character of the recipients. Moreover, Lloyd George had caused additional offence by entrusting the administration of his scheme to a new *ad hoc* organization, a National Health Insurance Commission, which functioned independently of the other public medical services: something that was deplored by the Webbs on political grounds and by Dr. Newsholme because of its implications for public health work.[1]

In 1911 Morant, of all men, was chosen by the Government to be the first chairman of the National Health Insurance Commission. Predictably, he soon formed a very poor opinion of the machine he had to supervise, and did his best to incorporate the county councils in its work.[2] But Lloyd George's political lieutenant, Masterman, remained adamant that the county councils should have nothing whatever to do with health insurance. Not only did Masterman fear that Burns at the unreformed L.G.B. could not be relied upon to operate insurance efficiently; he also distrusted the county councils, which, being controlled as many of them were by Conservative groups, would, he thought, stultify the scheme from party political motives.[3] In many ways, it was the 1902 Education Act dispute being fought out all over again.

However, one must add that in their natural disappointment at the shelving of the Poor Law Minority Report, the Webbs were inclined to exaggerate their differences with Lloyd George. In retrospect, Beveridge could claim that his own great social insurance proposals of 1942 stemmed from what everyone had imbibed from the Webbs and was an application of the doctrine of a national minimum for all.[4] Even at the time, Haldane, stoically

[1] Sir A. Newsholme, *The Last Thirty Years in Public Health* (1936), pp. 105.

[2] L. Masterman, op. cit., p. 220. Morant complained to Sir Almeric Fitzroy in 1913 that the administration of the Insurance Act under Lloyd George and Masterman had 'sunk absolutely to the level of a political machine . . .' (A. Fitzroy, op. cit., Vol. II, pp. 527–8: 25.11.13).

[3] L. Masterman, op. cit., p. 217.

[4] Lord Beveridge, op. cit., p. 86.

accepting that the Cabinet would not follow the Webbs' recommendations, had acted as the 'peacemaker' in the dispute, by suggesting that 'insurance had to be part of a big scheme with conditional relief for those at the bottom, and insurance for those struggling up'.[1] When he took charge of the National Insurance Bill in the House of Lords in 1911, Haldane laid especially heavy emphasis on those aspects of Lloyd George's measure which turned on prevention and supervision, relating health insurance to the other public health services proper.[2] Later, behind the scenes, during the 'revolt of the G.P.s', he pressed hard for the establishment of a National Medical Service, and hoped that at least the principle of this would be kept alive.[3]

As an attempt to conciliate the Webbs, Morant and Newsholme, Haldane's efforts failed. Nevertheless, he was quite right to point out that a National Health scheme, though mainly designed to provide *relief* for the sick and disabled, did also help locate the sources of disease and thus prepared the way for the work of prevention. In fact, in 1914 Lloyd George followed up his insurance measure by making exchequer grants available to enable local authorities to establish a nursing and clinical service.[4] Then, too, Morant's chairmanship of the Insurance Commission ensured that everything possible was done, under the terms of the 1911 Act, to promote the work of preventive medicine. For example, a levy of 1d on each insured person had provided the Commission with a fund of £60,000 a year; and from this fund Morant far-sightedly built up the organization later known as the Medical Research Council. He also developed a free, public service for all tubercular patients out of the sanatorium benefit provided for in the National Insurance Act. These reforms at least were warmly appreciated by the Webbs and their friends.

It remains true, nevertheless, that the Webbs and their allies had failed to convince the Liberal Government of the correctness of their particular 'environmental' analysis of the social problems

---

[1] B. Webb, op. cit., p. 417: 16.10.08.

[2] Hansard, 5th Series (Lords), Vol. 10, cols. 739, 764–5: 11.12.11.

[3] Haldane Papers, Vol. 6011: Haldane to Elizabeth Haldane, 22.10.12: ff. 211–12.

[4] Hansard, 5th Series (Commons), Vol. 62, cols. 78–81: 4.5.14.

S

This failure reflects the incompatability between the national efficiency school of thought and the liberal values which informed the policies of the Asquith Administration. Haldane certainly shared the Webbs' schematized, bureaucratic approach to welfare problems; but Haldane was a very odd and untypical Liberal. The vision of a more 'scientifically-ordered' government also proved attractive for a while to Churchill.

But most ministers shared a total lack of concern for that 'administrative symmetry and logical completeness' so dear to the Webbs. If they had attempted to rationalize their position, they would probably have claimed in justification of their own handiwork that, although untidy, it had the untidiness of life itself, whereas the Minority Report, for all its rigid perfection, bore the marks of death. 'The heart of Liberalism,' wrote L. T. Hobhouse in 1911, 'is the understanding that progress is not a matter of mechanical contrivance, but of the liberation of living spiritual energy. Good mechanism is that which provides the channels wherein such energy can flow unimpeded, unobstructed by its own exuberance of output, vivifying the social structure, expanding and ennobling the life of mind.'[1] To Hobhouse the values of liberalism at once suggested this kind of organic imagery, to be opposed to the mechanistic imagery which he associated with 'illiberal' creeds. In practice, however, the quest for 'national efficiency' often turned on precisely such matters of 'mechanical contrivance'. Traditional Liberals therefore shrank from programmes of action, like the Minority Report, though without always realizing, perhaps, what it was that repelled them.

[1] L. T. Hobhouse, *Liberalism* (1911, Galaxy Book, New York, 1964), p. 73.

POSTSCRIPT

THE BRITISH PEOPLE had yet to learn, in the agony of the world's first total war, how ill-prepared they were for such a struggle. It is true that many of the deficiencies spotlighted by the war had been recognized before 1914; but only under the shadow of military defeat was their gravity sufficiently appreciated. For example, throughout the Edwardian decade it had become a commonplace to complain of Britain's backwardness in technological invention and scientific research. Now the practical consequences of this neglect at last forced the Government into action. Private manufacturers and government departments, cut off from German sources of supply, were crying out for chemicals, drugs, precision instruments and optical glass, which Britain could not make for herself in sufficient quantity. In July 1915 Christopher Addison, the Parliamentary Secretary to the Board of Education, responded to the emergency by setting up the Committee of Scientific and Industrial Research (later the D.S.I.R.): a decision, incidentally, which owed much to the influence and encouragement of Lloyd George and Haldane.[1] The Medical Research Council, too, began to operate on a large scale during the war years, dealing with questions submitted to it by the service departments and the Ministry of Munitions.

This valuable, though belated, state assistance to scientific research shows that the war not only drew attention to the need for particular reforms, but also created the conditions in which a strong government, armed with emergency powers, could force through many of the proposals of the 'efficiency group' which had been politically impossible in times of peace. In fact, as the energies of

[1] Christopher Addison, *Politics From Within, 1911–1918* (1924), Vol. I, pp. 47–54. Christopher Addison, *Four and a Half Years* (1934), Vol I, Chs. III–IV.

the community were focused on the quest for military victory, Parliament went into decline, party exigencies became less pressing and Treasury control of public expenditure was greatly diminished. These developments were accelerated after Lloyd George had replaced Asquith as Prime Minister in December 1916.

It was perhaps Lloyd George's greatest administrative achievement to have been able to reduce the size of the Cabinet, while at the same time bringing the productive resources of the country under tighter government control. Indeed, Lloyd George's reconstituted War Cabinet was precisely the sort of executive council that had all along been envisaged by many members of the 'efficiency group'. It consisted at first of only five ministers, met nearly every day and was the final source of executive authority. Since its members were freed from departmental duties, they could concentrate their minds on the broad strategy of national policy and co-ordinate the activities of the various government departments to that end. The effectiveness of this body was increased when Lloyd George transferred to it the secretariat which Balfour had earlier fashioned for the C.I.D.

Since these changes in the machinery of government largely met the demands of national efficiency, it was fitting that Curzon and Milner should have been put into the new War Cabinet. In fact, Milner's sudden promotion in December 1916 from back-bench critic of the Government to Lloyd George's intimate colleague and adviser is in itself dramatic evidence of how irrelevant pre-war party animosities and considerations had become.

Lloyd George was also anxious to make his government a 'businessman's government'. The Prime Minister carried on the practice he had first adopted at the Ministry of Munitions of employing industrialists and business managers to organize new policy ventures. Some of these business men, like Eric Geddes, served an apprenticeship in subordinate posts in the administration and, having made a success there, were later promoted to ministerial rank; others came straight into positions of ministerial authority, like Sir Joseph Maclay, the shipowner. This invasion of the public service by businessmen may not altogether have pleased the Webbs,[1] who always based their plans for the collectivist

[1] See M. Cole (ed.), *Beatrice Webb's Diaries, 1912–1924* (1952), p. 83: 22.2.17.

society of the future more on the expert bureaucrat than on the business entrepreneur. But with many hitherto unregulated areas of economic activity having to be brought under central control, the government had no real alternative but to secure the co-operation of representatives of the various interests concerned.

The logic of the war situation also forced the Lloyd George Government to take an increasing interest in 'reconstruction'. This word had been frequently used before 1914 to denote the reorganization that was necessary, if Britain were to stand up on her own in a world of highly efficient rivals and prepare herself for the possibility of war. Once this possibility had become an actuality, 'reconstruction' came to mean the measures that would have to be taken to repair the ravages of war, so that out of devastation a more efficient, just, and harmonious society could be achieved. With this end in view, a Reconstruction Committee was formed—it later became an autonomous ministry under Addison—and under its supervision numerous investigations for the future guidance of ministers were set on foot.

For example, there was the small sub-committee, of which Beatrice Webb was a member, which reported in favour of a unified Ministry of Health to take over the responsibilities of the various government departments. In 1919 a Ministry of Health at long last came into being. (Appropriately enough, Morant was its first Permanent Secretary, with Sir George Newman as his Chief Medical Officer). But the recommendations of the Minority Report had not yet been fully implemented, because the L.G.B., supported by Walter Long, succeeded in preserving intact the piece-meal responsibilities of the local authorities. It is doubtful whether even this modest measure would have been carried, but for the shocking discovery that about one-third of all army recruits were medically unfit;[1] the Government knew that the nation's precious manpower must never again be squandered in this way.

This was not the only occasion when the Government was driven by the problems of planning for the post-war world into enlisting the services of the 'efficiency group'. Beatrice Webb and Morant found themselves sitting together on the Machinery of Government Committee, under the chairmanship of Haldane. Not surprisingly,

[1] See Arthur Marwick, *The Deluge* (1956), p. 242.

the report issued by this committee urged the importance 'in the sphere of civil government . . . of investigation and thought, as preliminary to action': the words must surely have been penned by Haldane himself. Considering the committee's membership, it is also interesting to observe that a somewhat disparaging tone is adopted towards political activity in general and towards political parties in particular. As in most pre-war efficiency propaganda, the emphasis in the report falls on the need to secure forceful executive action. It is recommended that the Cabinet remain 'small in number—preferably ten, or, at most twelve', even after the end of the war.[1]

Of course, nothing of the kind occurred. Once the peace settlement had been signed and a single unifying national objective had disappeared, the political forces which the war had held in check were once more liberated. The Cabinet quickly grew to its pre-war size. And back, too, came many other features of the national life which the 'efficiency group' had striven to eradicate. Here, of course, was the principal weakness or limitation of their political stance: it only became vitally relevant and practicable in times of national crisis.

Up to a point, the Thirties formed another such period of national crisis. Accordingly, many Englishmen, convinced that the British political system was unable to cope with the economic recession, turned once more to a version of the national efficiency ideology: a modern version that embodied a strongly 'technocratic' approach to government. The essence of 'technocracy' is that it celebrates science as a kind of self-sustaining force which provides objectively valid solutions to social and political problems, quite independently of the wishes and beliefs of the majority—hence, the authoritarianism, even totalitarianism, towards which most 'technocratic' theories of politics incline. Social salvation, it is alleged, will come about through the activities of the practioners of science, or at least of an intellectual élite whose modes of thought and behaviour conform to scientific criteria. The connection between this style of

[1] *Report of the Machinery of Government Committee* (1918): Cd. 9230: pp. 5–6.

political analysis and certain aspects of the cult of national efficiency hardly needs emphasizing.

It is interesting, therefore, to find a few surviving members of the pre-war 'efficiency group' actively propagating these 'technocratic' views during the inter-war years. In practice this led to their aligning themselves with either the extreme Left or the extreme Right. Shaw's flirtation with Fascist Italy in 1927 is notorious. Soviet Russia, though, was the country most frequently held up as a model. In 1932 the Webbs visited Russia for the first time. They were, of course, powerfully impressed by what they saw. True, the Webbs had always had a considerable contempt for Marxism as an intellectual system, and their 'conversion' of 1932 made no difference to them in this respect. In their book, *Soviet Communism*, they simply treat Marxism as the creed or myth that gives the state cohesion and supplies the dynamic of social change. What they really admired about Russia was the élitist role of the Communist Party—they noted that it had something of the character of the 'Samurai', the self-recruiting aristocracy of service portrayed by Wells in his *Modern Utopia* of 1905. They also praised the way in which science was being utilized, not just to provide material benefits for the community, but also to create new men and women through a transformation of their environment. Nor did the Webbs have much sympathy for the objection that these achievements necessitated a vast and irksome bureaucracy; such carping criticisms, they sharply observe, are 'no more than the average sensual man's impatience with the unavoidable apparatus of any highly developed industrial community'. The Webbs also approved of the stern discipline, the predominantly puritanical ethic and the sense of social solidarity; but, above all, it was as the country with 'an elaborately planned network of more than a thousand research laboratories', that they presented Stalin's Russia.[1]

By contrast, H. G. Wells, the 'technocratic' theorist *par excellence*, preserved a much more sceptical attitude towards the Soviet system. This was partly because he could not shrug to one side the question of the intellectual validity of Marxism quite as readily as the Webbs had done. He knew that his belief in science as an

[1] S. & B. Webb, *Soviet Communism* (1935: Left Book Club edition of 1937), esp. pp. 1131, 805, 1212, 956.

autonomous force, standing outside and beyond any particular society, waiting to be harnessed to beneficent social purposes, was a damnable heresy from the Marxist standpoint. That indeed, was why throughout his life Wells had attracted such bitter criticism and ridicule from Marxist writers.

Nevertheless, socialists, in Britain and elsewhere, managed to reconcile their Marxist commitments with a belief in 'technocracy'. They did so, by arguing that the human energies which were devoted in the capitalist world to the class struggle, would be channelled in a socialist state into the struggle of mankind against its natural environment. As tangible proof of this, they could point to Russia's thousand research laboratories.

This kind of argument was sufficiently plausible in the circumstances of the Thirties to convince many scientists of the merits of Communism as an ideology and as a political cause. Bernal, Blackett and J. B. Haldane were perhaps the most eminent of those British scientists who joined in the cult of Soviet Russia while at the same time making sweeping claims for science as a solvent of contemporary economic and political difficulties. In this they could make common cause with Sir Richard Gregory, the life-long friend of Wells, who had been Sir Norman Lockyer's pupil and had succeeded to the editorship of *Nature* in 1919. Such men as Gregory provide a personal link between the quest for national efficiency in the late nineteenth and twentieth centuries and the 'technocratic' propaganda of the 1930s.[1]

One obviously *new* factor in the situation was the leading part played by scientists themselves. The ideology of national efficiency had itself involved a somewhat half-hearted attempt to convince scientists that they had a special claim to the attention of governments. But few scientists in the past had risen to the bait, perhaps because as a professional group they had not yet acquired sufficient numerical strength or self-consciousness. But by the 1930s the mood and circumstances of one sector, at least, of the British scientific community had undergone a profound transformation.

*

[1] See Neal Wood, *Communism and British Intellectuals* (1959). Ch. V. W. H. G. Armytage, *Sir Richard Gregory* (1957).

The extravagance with which this group of men praised Soviet Russia was in time to prove their undoing and to involve in their discredit the whole approach to politics that they had adopted. How remote and irrelevant most of the 'technocratic' writing of the Thirties now seems. Can the same thing be said of the literature of national efficiency itself? What has dated most heavily is probably the verbal violence, those indiscriminate assaults on all liberal principles and precepts into which certain members of the 'efficiency group' were betrayed.

But although an hysterical element was never far from the surface of this kind of political polemic, to dwell too insistently upon it would give a misleading impression. As expounded by a sophisticated and level-headed politician like Haldane, the creed of national efficiency certainly has a bearing upon our own current preoccupations. True, there have been improvements in the machinery of government and the apparatus of the state over the last thirty years or so, and these have partly set at rest the old fear that Parliamentary Government and the party system put insuperable obstacles in the way of an efficient ordering of the nation's material and manpower resources. A *modus vivendi* of sorts has been established between the liberal state and the imperatives of efficiency, even though at the cost of far-reaching changes in the practice of British parliamentary government. Yet at each successive economic crisis, the mood of national introspection returns, and so too do many of the complaints that were being made at the very start of the century. After all, several of the problems to which the 'efficiency group' first drew attention have never been systematically tackled, and there is a continuing sense of a Britain lagging behind her foreign rivals. The very jargon used to describe politics today is often reminiscent of the Boer War period. Did Lord Robens, when he expounded his managerial conception of government to a television audience and spoke of the Prime Minister as the managing director of a company called 'Great Britain Limited' realize that Lord Rosebery had made almost the identical remark 68 years before?

GLOSSARY OF NAMES

AMERY, Leopold Stennett (1873–1955): Friend and disciple of Lord Milner. *The Times*'s military correspondent during South African War and editor of *The Times History of the War*. After 1903 a forceful advocate of Tariff Reform. Elected Conservative M.P. for S. Birmingham in 1911. Colonial Secretary, 1922–1924. Indian Secretary, 1940–5.

ASHLEY, William James (1860–1927): Economic historian. After holding chairs at Toronto and Harvard Universities, became Professor of the newly established Faculty of Commerce at Birmingham University in 1901. A persuasive advocate of Tariff Reform, who also took a deep interest in matters of social reform.

BIRCHENOUGH, Sir Henry (1853–1937): Old friend of Lord Milner's. President of the British South African Company. Member of the Tariff Commission and of several government committees and commissions.

CURZON, George Nathaniel (1859–1925): Conservative M.P., 1886–98. Having held office as Under-Secretary at India Office and then at Foreign Office in Lord Salisbury's Administrations, went to India as Viceroy, 1899–1905. Member of Lloyd George's small War Cabinet in December 1916. Foreign Secretary, 1919–1924.

DAWKINS, Sir Clinton (1859–1905): Civil servant at India Office. Served as administrator in Egypt under Lord Cromer. Financial Member of the Council of the Governor-General of India under Curzon, 1899–1900. After retirement from public service, became principal London partner in the American financial house of Pierpont Morgan. Chairman of Committee into War Office Organization, 1901. Founder member of the National Service League.

ESHER, Viscount (1852–1930): Liberal M.P., 1880–5 and Private Secretary to Lord Hartington. Secretary to Office of Works, 1895–1902, and friend and confidential adviser of Edward VII. Member of Royal Commission into South African War, 1903, and Chairman of War Office (Reconstruction) Committee, 1904. In late 1905 made a permanent member of the Committee of Imperial Defence.

GARVIN, James Louis (1868–1947): Conservative journalist. Writer of numerous articles on national defence and tariff reform. Author of surveys of current affairs in *Fortnightly Review* under pseudonym of 'Calchas'. Editor of *Observer*, 1908–42. Official biographer of Joseph Chamberlain.

GELL, Philip Lyttelton (1852–1926): Director and later President, of the British South Africa Company. Friend of Milner's.

HALDANE, Richard Burdon (1856–1928): Studied philosophy at Edinburgh and Gottingen Universities. Became successful lawyer. Entered Commons in 1886 as Liberal M.P. for Haddington, holding the seat until 1911, when he became a peer. A tireless worker for an improved and extended system of higher education. Friend of Asquith, Grey and Rosebery, and the 'schemer' of the Liberal Imperialist group of M.P.s War Secretary, 1905–12, and Lord Chancellor, 1912–15. Driven from office in 1915 because of his alleged 'pro-German' sympathies. Left the Liberal Party and served a second term as Lord Chancellor in Ramsay Macdonald's Labour Administration of 1924.

HEWINS, Professor William (1865–1931): Economist. Lecturer in Universities Extension Movement. First Director of London School of Economics, 1895–1903, leaving this post to become Secretary to the Tariff Commission. Unsuccessfully contested the two 1910 elections, but entered Commons as Conservative M.P. at by-election in 1912. Under-Secretary of State for Colonies, 1917–19.

MACKINDER, Sir Halford (1861–1947): Geographer. Reader at Oxford University, 1887–1905; Reader and subsequently Professor of Geography at London University, 1900–25. Succeeded Hewins as Director of London School of Economics, 1903, giving up this post in 1908 to devote himself full-time to the cause of tariff reform. Elected as Unionist M.P. in January 1910, holding his seat until 1922. Chairman of Imperial Shipping Committee, 1920–45.

MILNER, Alfred Viscount (1854–1925): Abandoned the liberalism of his youth at the time of Gladstone's conversion to Home Rule, when he became Private Secretary to Goschen, the Liberal Unionist. Under-Secretary for Finance in Egypt under Cromer, 1889–92, and then Chairman of Board of Inland Revenue, 1892–7. British High Commissioner in South Africa, 1897–1905, and effective architect of the Second Boer War. Active in the National Service League and a supporter of Tariff Reform. Member of Lloyd George's small War Cabinet, from December 1916. War Secretary, 1918–19, Colonial Secretary, 1919–21.

MORANT, Robert (1862–1920): Tutor to the Crown Prince of Siam, before taking position in the Department of Special Inquiries at the Board of Education, 1895. In 1902 became Private Secretary to Duke of Devonshire. The civil servant chiefly responsible for the Education Act of 1902. Permanent Secretary of Board of Education, 1903–11. Chairman of National Health Insurance Commission, 1911–19. Permanent Secretary to the newly created Ministry of Health, 1919–20.

ROSEBERY, Earl of (1847–1929): Wealthy Whig Peer, who came to prominence as 'manager' of Gladstone's Midlothian Campaign. Foreign Secretary, 1886 and 1892–4. In 1894 succeeded Gladstone as P.M. and leader of the Liberal Party. A year after the Liberal defeat of 1895, suddenly resigned the party leadership and retired from active politics. During the Boer War re-emerged on the political scene and was widely regarded as the leader of the 'Liberal Imperialist' M.P.s in their struggle with Campbell-Bannerman and the Radicals. President of the Liberal League, 1902. Not offered a post when the Liberals returned to power in 1905. Subsequently adopted a 'cross-bench' role in the Lords, but soon lost all influence and power.

SHAW, George Bernard (1859–1950): Playwright and early member of the Fabian Society. Edited *Fabian Essays*, 1889. Friend and associate of the Webbs.

WEBB, Sidney (1859–1947): Civil servant of lower middle class background. Early member of the Fabian Society. After marriage to Beatrice Potter in 1892, became a full-time social investigator and propagandist for socialism. A 'Progressive' councillor on the L.C.C. and influential member of its Technical Education Board. Co-author of works on trade unionism, the history of local government and professional associations. After his disappointment at the refusal of the Liberal Government to act on the recommendations of the Minority Report of the Royal Commission on the Poor Laws (of which his wife was a member), became drawn more closely into the work of the Labour Party. Returned to Parliament as Labour M.P. in 1922. Served as President of the Board of Trade, 1924, and as Colonial Secretary, 1929–31. Created Lord Passfield in 1929.

WEBB, Beatrice, née Potter (1858–1943): Daughter of prosperous railway magnate. Abandoned 'society' for the work of a social investigator. Served as rent collector in East London, worked on Charles Booth's survey into the 'Life and Labour' of London. Her first book was a study of the Co-operative Movement. After her marriage to Sidney Webb, her work was mainly done in association with her husband. Member of the Royal Commission on the Poor Laws, 1905–09, and an impassioned crusader for the 'break up of the Poor Law'.

WELLS, H. G. (1866–1946): Novelist and public prophet. Befriended by the Webbs, but after 1906 quarrelled with them on both personal and political grounds. His most influential contributions to the literature of 'national efficiency' are *Anticipations* (1901), *Mankind in the Making* (1903), *A Modern Utopia* (1905) and the semi-autobiographical novel, *The New Machiavelli* (1911)

WHITE, Arnold (1848–1925): Author and journalist. Contested Parliamentary elections on four occasions without any success. Regular contributor to the journal, *The Referee*. Author of *Efficiency and Empire* (1901) and *Views of Vanoc* (1910), among other works. His interest in gunnery and a big navy won him the friendship and confidence of Admiral Fisher.

BIBLIOGRAPHY

PRIVATE MANUSCRIPTS

Arnold-Forster Papers (British Museum).
Asquith Papers (Bodleian Library).
Balfour Papers (British Museum).
Beveridge Papers (British Library of Political and Economic Science).
Bonar Law Papers (Beaverbrook Library).
Bryce Papers (Bodleian Library).
Burns Papers (British Museum).
Campbell-Bannerman Papers (British Museum).
Austen Chamberlain Papers (Birmingham University Library).
Joseph Chamberlain Papers (Birmingham University Library).
Curzon Papers (India Office Library).
Papers of the Eighth Duke of Devonshire (Chatsworth).
Elibank Papers (National Library of Scotland).
Lyttelton Gell Papers (Hopton Hall, Wirksworth).
Herbert Gladstone Papers (British Museum).
Haldane Papers (National Library of Scotland).
Edward Hamilton Papers (British Museum).
Lloyd George Papers (Beaverbrook Library).
Milner Papers (Bodleian Library).
Passfield Papers (British Library of Political and Economic Science).
Ripon Papers (British Museum).
Rosebery Papers (National Library of Scotland).
C. P. Scott Papers (British Museum).
G. B. Shaw Papers (British Museum).
Spender Papers (British Museum).
Graham Wallas Papers (British Library of Political and Economic Science).

NEWSPAPERS AND PERIODICALS

Daily Chronicle	*Morning Post*
Daily Mail	*Observer*
Daily News	*The Times*
Daily Telegraph	*Westminster Gazette*
Manchester Guardian	

Nation	*Speaker*
Nature	*Spectator*
Contemporary Review	*New Liberal Review*
Economic Journal	*Nineteenth Century and After*
Fabian News	*Public Health*
Fortnightly Review	*Review of Reviews*
Independent Review	*Round Table*
Liberal Magazine	*Sociological Review*
Monthly Review	*The World's Work*
National Review	
Quarterly Review	*Annual Register*

Full references to all the Parliamentary Papers, published works and learned articles, upon which I have drawn in this book or to which I have alluded, are contained in the footnotes to the text.

In the references given in the footnotes, it is to be assumed that the place of publication is London, unless it is stated otherwise.

INDEX

T

E6